Selected Topics in Bond Portfolio Management

Edited by

Frank J. Fabozzi, CFA
Adjunct Professor of Finance
School of Management
Yale University

T0339423

Published by Frank J. Fabozzi Associates

© 1997 By Frank J. Fabozzi Associates
New Hope, Pennsylvania

This publication is designed to provide accurate and authoritative information in regard to the subject matter covered. It is sold with the understanding that the publisher is not engaged in rendering legal, accounting, or other professional services.

ISBN: 1-883249-28-7

Table of Contents

Contributing Authors

Joseph Balestrino, CFA	Federated Investors
Robert I. Gerber, Ph.D.	Sanford C. Bernstein & Co., Inc.
Benjamin J. Gord	Miller Anderson & Sherrerd, LLP
Kevin Edward Grant, CFA	Fidelity Management and Research
Frank J. Jones, Ph.D.	Guardian Life Insurance
William R. Leach, CFA	Boston Partners Asset Management, L.P.
J. Hank Lynch, CFA	Scudder, Stevens and Clark
J. Thomas Madden, CFA	Federated Investors
Jack Malvey, CFA	Lehman Brothers
Leonard J. Peltzman	Guardian Life Insurance
Scott F. Richard, DBA	Miller Anderson & Sherrerd, LLP
Ronald J. Ryan, CFA	Ryan Labs, Inc.
Jeffrey D. Slater, CFA	General Reinsurance Corporation
Christopher B. Steward, CFA	Scudder, Stevens and Clark
Francis H. Trainer Jr., CFA	Sanford C. Bernstein & Co., Inc.
Kenneth E. Volpert, CFA	The Vanguard Group, Inc.

Preface

The objective of *Selected Topics in Bond Portfolio Management* is to present the insights of leading bond portfolio managers. The book assumes the reader has a fundamental understanding of the features of fixed income securities and the various products. At the end of the book there are questions for each chapter.

With one exception, all of the contributors are portfolio managers. That is, they work on the "buy side" of the investment management business. One contributor, Jack Malvey, is the Chief Global Fixed Income Strategist at Lehman Brothers — an organization that is on the "sell side" of the investment management business. Of the 16 contributors, 11 have earned the prestigious designation of Chartered Financial Analyst.

In Chapter 1, Scott F. Richard and Benjamin Gord of Miller, Anderson & Sherrerd explain how their firm measures and then manages the interest rate risk of their clients' portfolios. They demonstrate the limitations of duration as a measure of interest rate risk for a bond portfolio and the importance of recognizing how changes in the shape of the yield curve affect interest rate risk. Richard and Gord introduce a measure used by their firm which more accurately captures the interest rate risk of a bond portfolio.

Francis H. Trainer Jr. of Sanford C. Bernstein & Co. explains in Chapter 2 the expected return methodology employed by his firm to assess the potential performance of Treasury securities, mortgage-backed securities, corporate bonds, and foreign bonds. In addition, Trainer explains the portfolio construction process that his firm follows to integrate the expected return measures of individual securities and the market environment. The end result is a single measure that can be applied consistently across market sectors that does not rely excessively on the firm's economic outlook.

In Chapter 3, Kenneth E. Volpert of The Vanguard Group describes the process of indexing a bond portfolio and the motivation for adopting such a strategy. Pure bond indexing and enhanced indexing are explained. The risks associated with constructing an indexed portfolio are illustrated. Volpert concludes the chapter with a discussion of how to measure whether the portfolio manager has added any value and, if so, why.

The methodologies that portfolio managers employ to assess corporate bonds is the subject of Chapter 4 contributed by Jack Malvey of Lehman Brothers. He explains that to obtain the best risk-adjusted return it is necessary to combine the qualitative tools of equity analysis with the quantitative insights of fixed income analysis.

The management of a municipal bond portfolio is covered in Chapter 5. The author, Jeffrey D. Slater of General Reinsurance Corporation, provides an overview of the municipal bond market and the types of security structures. He explains why pension funds and nontraditional investors in this market sector sometimes participate. Slater then goes on to describe the unique challenges associated with municipal bond portfolio management.

Bonds that are rated less than triple-B are referred to as "high-yield bonds." In Chapter 6, J. Thomas Madden and Joseph Balestrino discuss some of the practical aspects of high-yield bond management in a diversified portfolio and the various high-yield investment strategies. Since most investors in this market sector eventually face the problem of deteriorating credit quality of issues held in a high-yield portfolio, the authors present their strategy for dealing with this problem.

In Chapter 7, Christopher B. Steward and J. Hank Lynch of Scudder, Stevens and Clark describe the challenges of managing an international bond portfolio and a disciplined approach to meeting those challenges. The authors discuss the components of return and the mechanics of currency hedging. Steward and Lynch describe the process their firm uses for monitoring the international bond portfolios they manage.

A convertible bond is a bond that can be converted into the issuer's common stock. The conversion option is granted to the investor. Convertible bonds therefore have the characteristics of both a bond and common stock. "Busted convertibles" are convertible bonds that trade with very little sensitivity relative to the underlying common stock price and have relatively high yields. In Chapter 8, William R. Leach of Boston Partners Asset Management explains why busted convertibles offer bond portfolio managers the potential to enhance performance relative to a bond market index.

The benchmark for a portfolio manager can be either a market index (such as the Lehman Brothers Aggregate Index, the Salomon Brothers Broad Investment-Grade Bond Index, or the Merrill Lynch Domestic Market Index) or liabilities. In Chapter 9, Ronald J. Ryan of Ryan Labs explains how a portfolio manager should manage funds when the benchmark is a liability stream. He describes how liabilities should be measured and how performance can be evaluated by creating a liability index. Ryan then argues that Treasury STRIPS should be the vehicle of choice when managing funds where the benchmark is a liability stream.

A key step in the investment management process is the assessment of the performance of the portfolio manager. This step can be divided into two areas. The first is the measurement of portfolio performance. The second is the decomposition of the realized return to explain how the manager achieved that return (i.e., where the manager placed bets and how those bets paid off). This is called return attribution analysis. In Chapter 10, Frank J. Jones and Leonard J. Peltzman of The Guardian Life Insurance Company explain how to measure performance and describe return attribution analysis. The latter is illustrated using a commercially available model. The appendix to the chapter describes the standards for calculating performance as set forth by the Association for Investment Management and Research.

Portfolio managers focus on the interest rate sensitivity of a portfolio as measured by duration. Duration is only a first approximation of how the value of a portfolio will change when interest rates shift in a parallel manner. The duration approximation can be improved by considering the convexity of a portfolio. In Chapter 11, Kevin Edward Grant explains how to evaluate the convexity of a portfolio and how to manage convexity as the portfolio and market dynamically change over time.

In Chapter 12, Robert I. Gerber of Sanford C. Bernstein & Co. provides a guide to bond trading for the portfolio manager. Often market participants talk about the "liquidity" of a security. Generally, a security's liquidity is measured by the spread between the bid price and the ask price. Gerber explains why the exact meaning of the bid-ask spread is subject to interpretation. He carefully discusses the complexities of buy-side trading. The issues he addresses are (1) the relative advantages of an instantaneous auction, a bid list, and a sale order, (2) whether market liquidity or volatility matter, (3) what buy-side traders should expect from sell-side traders, and (4) what an optimal trading strategy is.

Frank J. Fabozzi

About the Authors

Scott F. Richard, DBA

Scott F. Richard is a Portfolio Manager at Miller, Anderson & Sherrerd, LLP and a Managing Director of Morgan Stanley Asset Management, specializing in mortgage securities. Prior to joining MAS, Dr. Richard was co-head of the Fixed Income Research and Model Development Group and head of Mortgage Research at Goldman Sachs & Co. Before that time, he was Professor of Financial Economics at the Graduate School of Industrial Administration, Carnegie-Mellon University; during the 1985-86 academic year, he was Visiting Professor of Finance at the Massachusetts Institute of Technology. His published research includes papers on the term structure of interest rates, equilibrium pricing of financial assets, and the valuation of futures and forward contracts. He is an associate editor of *The Journal of Fixed Income* and *The Journal of Portfolio Management*. He holds a B.S. degree from the Massachusetts Institute of Technology and a Doctor of Business Administration degree from Harvard University.

Benjamin J. Gord

Benjamin J. Gord is a Senior Fixed Income Research Analyst at Miller, Anderson & Sherrerd, LLP and a Vice President of Morgan Stanley Asset Management. In addition to being a member of the Mortgage Team, his responsibilities include research and proprietary modeling. Prior to joining the firm, Mr. Gord was an analyst in Mortgage-Backed Securities Research at Smith Barney. Before that he worked at Alphametrics Corporation. He earned a B.A. in Economics from New York University and spent four years in the Ph.D. program in Economics at the University of Pennsylvania.

Chapter 1

Measuring and Managing Interest-Rate Risk

Scott F. Richard, DBA
Partner
Miller Anderson & Sherrerd, LLP

Benjamin J. Gord
Vice President
Miller Anderson & Sherrerd, LLP

INTRODUCTION

How do we predict what will happen to the value of a client's fixed-income portfolio when interest rates change? This is one of the most important questions we have to answer in managing fixed-income assets. In this chapter we report on our research aimed at answering this question and explain how we use the results of this research in portfolio management.

If a client's portfolio contained only one bond, then the answer would be given, to a good approximation, by the bond's (modified) duration. The duration of the bond measures its percentage price change for a small change in the bond's yield. Suppose a portfolio contained only a 10-year-maturity Treasury note with a 6.5% coupon selling at par. Standard calculations indicate a duration of 7.3 years for this bond. Hence, if the 10-year note's yield rises 10 basis points, the bond's value, and the portfolio's value, will fall by approximately 73 basis points; conversely, if the 10-year note's yield declines 10 basis points, the value of the bond and the portfolio will rise by about 73 basis points.

In reality, portfolios are never so simple that they contain only one bond. The highly diversified portfolios that we manage typically contain more than 100 securities with a wide variety of maturities. Is duration a good measure of the relative interest-rate sensitivity of different portfolios? Consider another portfolio composed of 44.6% in cash, with a duration of zero years, and 55.4% in a 30-year Treasury bond with a 6.5% coupon, selling at par with a duration of 13.1 years. Standard calculations show that the portfolio has a duration of 7.3 years, which is the weighted average of zero years and 13.1 years. Usually portfolio managers

1

who use duration as a measure of interest-rate risk think of this barbell as having about the same interest-rate risk as the 10-year bullet we just discussed. But what does this duration figure mean? Presumably, it means that if yields rise by 10 basis points, the portfolio will decline in value by about 73 basis points. We must be more precise, however, about exactly what we mean by "if yields rise by 10 basis points" in order for 73 basis points to be the realized loss. In fact, both the 30-year and 10-year yields must change in the same direction and in the same amount for the price change of the bullet to equal the price change of the barbell. If both yields do not typically change in the same direction or by the same amount, then the change in the portfolio's value will be different, and duration will mismeasure the interest-rate risk of the portfolio.

Now let's extrapolate our reasoning to a portfolio containing many bonds with all maturities between cash and 30 years (or longer). Separating these bonds into their coupon and principal payments, we see that such portfolios commonly have cash flows at all points on the yield curve. Will the average duration[1] of all the bonds be an accurate measure of the portfolio's interest-rate risk? Extending our reasoning from the two bond portfolios, *we see that duration is an accurate measure of interest-rate risk for a portfolio only if all yields typically change in the same direction and by the same amount (i.e., if a typical yield-curve change is a parallel shift).*

We have now deduced that duration is an adequate measure of interest-rate risk only if parallel shifts typify changes in the yield curve. Luckily, this is an empirical issue that we test by examining yield-curve data.[2] If it is true, then we are done; if not, we must create a new measure of interest-rate risk that is consistent with the way yield curves actually reshape.

HOW DO YIELD CURVES CHANGE?

To answer this question, we examined yield data for zero-coupon Treasury bonds. We used zero-coupon bonds for two reasons. First, zero-coupon bonds are the building blocks for all coupon bonds, which can be separated into portfolios of zero-coupon bonds. Second, zero-coupon bonds give us a much richer set of bond durations to examine. The maturity of a zero-coupon bond is nearly equal to its duration, so that the duration range for zero-coupon bonds is one to 30 years. In contrast, coupon bonds have a duration range of about one to 13 years, the duration of a 30-year Treasury security.

---

[1] Actual Portfolios contain callable bonds such as mortgages and corporates. For callable bonds, when we refer to "duration," we mean the option-adjusted duration.

[2] There are solid theoretical foundations for thinking that parallel shifts are not likely. For example, if interest rates mean-revert, even very weakly, then long yields must be less volatile than short yields, which rules out a parallel shift. There is an increasing volume of empirical evidence from term-structure modeling and option pricing showing that interest rates mean-revert very slowly.

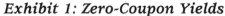

Exhibit 1: Zero-Coupon Yields

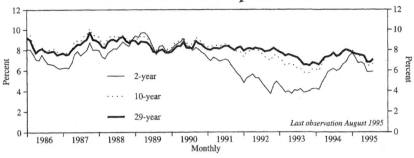

Sources: Goldman Sachs and EJV Partners LP.

Exhibit 1 shows monthly yield data for the 2-year, 10-year, and 29-year zero-coupon Treasury bond since 1986.[3] It appears that yields tend to change in the same direction across the yield curve, but not by the same amount. Just by looking at the data, it is difficult to identify a typical yield-curve shift, but it appears that short-term interest rates are more volatile than long-term interest rates (i.e., short-term yields have tended both to fall more and to rise more than long-term yields). In other words, the yield curve has tended to steepen during a rally and to flatten during a sell off.

Although Exhibit 1 is sufficient to confirm this general observation, we need to use statistical techniques to estimate typical yield-curve movements more precisely. In making this analysis, we examined beginning-of-month yields from October 1986 through August 1995 on zero-coupon bonds of constant maturities one through 29 years. Although these data represented 29 different yield series, the results — not surprisingly — did not suggest that there are 29 independent sources of change in the yield curve. Indeed, using principal-components analysis (discussed in the Appendix) we found that two types of systematic yield-curve reshapings explained almost 97% of the variation in interest rates. Remaining changes in yields at different maturities appear random.

We call the first type of systematic change a "yield-curve shift." This shift describes the movement in the yield curve that typically accompanies a general upward or downward movement of interest rates. Exhibits 2a and 2b show shifts for the yield curve of August 1, 1995. The yield-curve shift shown in Exhibit 2a corresponds to a bond-market decline and causes all yields to rise, but not by equal amounts; typically, short yields rise twice as much as very long yields. Exhibit 2b shows the yield-curve shift for the corresponding bond-market-rally scenario; again all yields fall, but not by equal amounts. Yield-curve shifts account for about 90% of the systematic variation in monthly yields over our sample. Each month the yield-curve shift will be slightly different because it depends on the level of yields and the shape of the yield curve.

---

[3] Our data for zero-coupon Treasury bonds begin in 1986 because that is when a 29-year-maturity noncallable zero-coupon bond was first available. We have replicated our study using coupon-bond data from 1952 through 1995 and have found nearly identical results.

Exhibit 2: Yield-Curve Shift
(a): Yield Curve Shift Up

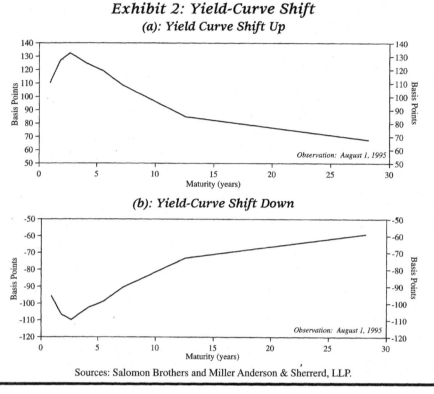

(b): Yield-Curve Shift Down

Sources: Salomon Brothers and Miller Anderson & Sherrerd, LLP.

Yield-curve shifts are not the whole story, though. There is a second systematic change, called a "yield-curve twist," as shown in Exhibits 3a and 3b for the yield curve of August 1, 1995. The yield-curve twist shown in Exhibit 3a causes yields under five years to rise and those over five years to fall. The opposite twist, shown in Exhibit 3b, causes short yields to fall and long yields to rise. Yield-curve twists account for approximately another 7% of the systematic variation in monthly yields. Yield-curve shifts and yield-curve twists are independent reshapings of the yield curve: knowledge of the direction and magnitude of a yield-curve shift is not helpful in predicting either the direction or magnitude of any simultaneous yield-curve twist.

Although yield-curve twists explain a smaller amount of systematic variation than yield-curve shifts, they are nevertheless quite important. The actual change in the yield curve during 1994 and the changes predicted by a yield-curve shift are shown in Exhibit 4. The predicted yield-curve shift shown in Exhibit 4 is calculated by observing the actual change in the yield of the 5-year zero-coupon bond and then using the statistical model to predict the change in the rest of the yield curve.[4] That is why the actual and the predicted changes exactly agree for a 5-year bond. The yield-curve shift captures most of what happened in 1994.

---

[4] Exhibit 4 shows the concentration of monthly changes for 1994.

Exhibit 3: Yield-Curve Twist
(a): Flattening Yield Curve

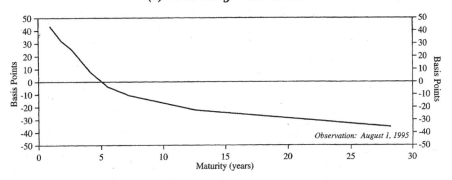

Observation: August 1, 1995

(b): Steepening Yield-Curve Twist

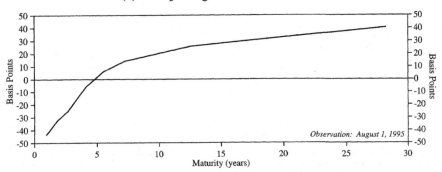

Observation: August 1, 1995

Sources: Salomon Brothers and Miller Anderson & Sherrerd, LLP.

Exhibit 4: Yield-Curve Shift in 1994

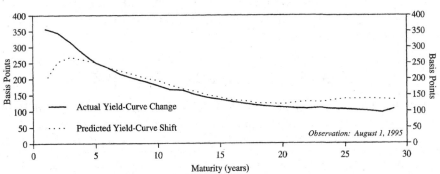

Actual Yield-Curve Change
···· Predicted Yield-Curve Shift

Observation: August 1, 1995

Sources: EJV Partners LP and Miller Anderson & Sherrerd, LLP.

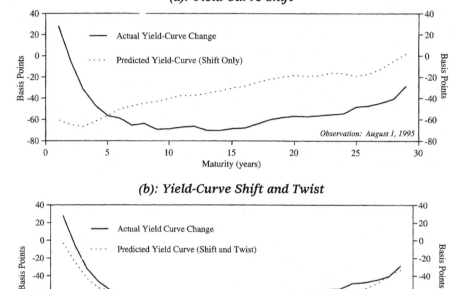

Exhibit 5: Yield Curve Changes in 1995
(a): Yield-Curve Shift

(b): Yield-Curve Shift and Twist

Sources: EJV Partners LP and Miller Anderson & Sherrerd, LLP.

For 1995, however, the yield-curve twist is vital in explaining changes in yields. Exhibit 5a shows the changes in actual yields from year-end 1994 to August 1, 1995, and the effect of a yield-curve shift. We can see that something besides a yield-curve shift has been important in 1995. In Exhibit 5b we added the appropriate yield-curve twist for 1995 to show that together the shift and twist capture the dynamics for the year.[5]

MANAGING INTEREST-RATE RISK

Recall that duration is a good measure of interest-rate risk only if a parallel shift is the predominant form of yield-curve change. Examining Exhibits 2a and 2b, we see that we can rule out a parallel shift as the usual yield-curve change. Rather,

---

[5] To calculate the effect of a yield-curve twist, we first observe the actual change in the yield of 5-year zero-coupon bonds and use the statistical model to predict a yield-curve shift. Next, we observe the part of the change in the yield of a 20-year zero-coupon bond that is not explained by the yield-curve shift and use the statistical model to predict the yield-curve twist. This is why the actual and the predicted changes exactly agree for both a 5-year bond and a 20-year bond.

we see that short yields usually move more than long yields; duration is therefore not an accurate measure of interest-rate risk for a diversified portfolio.

We have replaced duration with *interest-rate sensitivity* (IRS) as our standard measure of portfolio interest-rate risk. Duration measures a portfolio's percentage price change in response to a parallel shift in the yield curve. IRS measures a portfolio's percentage price change in response to a yield-curve shift. The unit of both measures is years. Exhibit 6 shows the relationship between duration and IRS as of August 1, 1995. IRS is measured relative to the yield change in a benchmark zero-coupon bond. We typically choose the 5-year zero-coupon bond as the benchmark because its interest-rate risk is closest to the interest-rate risk in the broad market indices, such as the Lehman Brothers Aggregate Index and the Salomon Brothers Broad Index. In constructing Exhibit 6, we used the 5-year zero-coupon bond as our benchmark security, so its duration and IRS are equal. The IRS of a lower-duration bond (e.g., the 2-year zero-coupon bond) is usually slightly higher than its duration, while a large-duration bond (e.g., the 25-year zero-coupon bond) has an IRS substantially lower than its duration.

The importance of using IRS instead of duration can be demonstrated by running an experiment that compares the performance of two portfolios, one managed with duration and one with IRS. Suppose a portfolio manager thought, in September 1992, that long yields were too high and likely to decline and that the yield curve was too steep and likely to flatten.[6] Hence, the manager thought that the rewards for bearing interest-rate risk and yield-curve risk were unusually high. To profit from the view that the bond market would rally, the manager wanted a portfolio with longer duration than the index's, and to profit from the view that the yield curve would flatten, he wanted a barbell portfolio. The manager recommended a portfolio composed of cash and long-maturity zero-coupon Treasury bonds with 50% more interest-rate risk than that of the broad market index. The question he had to answer was how many long zero-coupon bonds to buy. The table below shows the calculations for constructing the portfolio using duration and IRS.

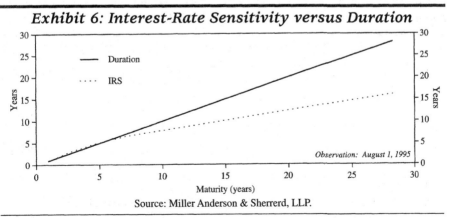

Exhibit 6: Interest-Rate Sensitivity versus Duration

Source: Miller Anderson & Sherrerd, LLP.

---

[6] This is an unusual situation. Typically a downward yield-curve shift produces a steepening yield curve (i.e., yield curves typically steepen in a rally.)

	Duration Management	IRS Management
Index	4.5 years	4.6 years
Target	6.75 years	6.9 years
30-Year Zero-Coupon Treasury Bond	29.0 years	17.8 years
Fraction of Portfolio in Zero Coupons	23.3%	38.8%
Fraction of Portfolio in Cash	76.7%	61.2%

The subsequent bond-market rally would have resulted in some disappointment for an investor using duration, but not for someone using IRS. From September 30, 1992, to September 30, 1993, the yield curve rallied strongly and flattened as shown in Exhibit 7. Over this 12-month period, cash (1-month CDs) returned 3.3%, and 30-year zero-coupon Treasury bonds returned 56.0%. The portfolio constructed using duration returned 15.6%, which is only 30 basis points better than the 15.3% return on the equal-duration bullet portfolio composed of the 7-year zero-coupon Treasury bond. There was very little extra return from the equal-duration barbell portfolio over that of the bullet portfolio, despite a substantial flattening of the yield curve. In contrast, the portfolio constructed with use of IRS has a return of 23.7%, which is 840 basis points above that of the equivalent-IRS 7-year zero-coupon Treasury bond.

Since 1993, we have used IRS rather than duration as our primary measure of interest-rate risk. Over this period, the risk of our core portfolios relative to a broad market index differs significantly when calculated using the two risk measures. In Exhibit 8, we show the duration of our core fixed-income portfolios in comparison with that of the Salomon Brothers Broad Index.

If duration is used as a measure of interest-rate risk, it appears that we were longer than the index until March 1995, significantly so throughout most of 1993. However, in 1993, our portfolios were barbelled, using long-maturity zero-coupon Treasury bonds as part of the barbell, and the distinction between IRS and duration was vital, as can be seen in Exhibit 9. This exhibit compares the IRS of our core fixed-income portfolios with the IRS of the Salomon Brothers Broad Index.

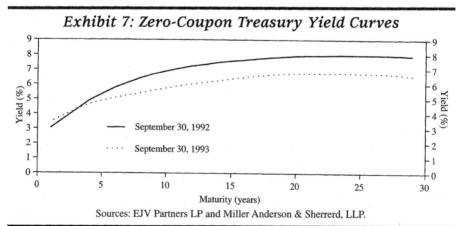

Exhibit 7: Zero-Coupon Treasury Yield Curves

——— September 30, 1992

· · · · September 30, 1993

Maturity (years)

Sources: EJV Partners LP and Miller Anderson & Sherrerd, LLP.

Exhibit 8: MAS Core Fixed-Income Duration

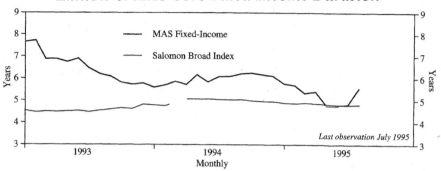

Sources: Salomon Brothers and Miller Anderson & Sherrerd, LLP.

Exhibit 9: MAS Core Fixed-Income Interest-Rate Sensitivity

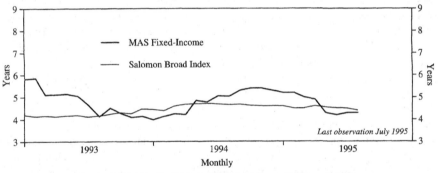

Sources: Salomon Brothers and Miller Anderson & Sherrerd, LLP.

In our core portfolios, interest-rate risk as measured by IRS has varied much less than interest-rate risk as measured by duration. In fact, for 1993, 1994, and 1995, we have been alternately longer or shorter than the index rather than uniformly longer. The distinction between the two measures is important — not only as an internal tool for better managing assets, but also as a means of communicating our decisions to our clients. Solely on the basis of the duration of our core fixed-income portfolios, one would probably conclude that we have been bullish since the middle of 1993; on the basis of IRS, one can see that we have been alternately slightly bullish and slightly bearish.

Although IRS is a useful tool for portfolio management, its successful use requires a mixture of technical skill and judgment. Technically, using IRS requires a daily updating of our proprietary empirical model because IRS measures are sensitive to both the level of yields and the shape of the yield curve. Furthermore, the internal analytical models we use to evaluate callable securities, such as mortgages, are consistent with IRS in that the typical changes in the yield curve are very similar to empirical yield-curve shifts and yield-curve twists. This internal consistency is very important in managing a highly diversified portfolio of mortgage, corporate, and Treasury securities.

IRS is not a substitute for the critical judgments of our interest-rate team, which seeks to add value by deciding how much interest-rate risk and yield-curve risk we should bear. Our interest-rate team still must form a judgment about the likely direction of a yield-curve change. The team's view is then implemented with our IRS model rather than duration to ensure that our portfolios have the proper amount of interest-rate and yield-curve risk relative to their benchmark indices.

APPENDIX

In this appendix, we give a brief description of the statistical analysis through which we found the systematic yield-curve changes. The first step in our analysis is to adjust the data so that percent yield changes are of similar volatility over time.[7] This adjustment is required so that the data from periods of predictably high volatility do not swamp the statistical analysis. In Exhibit A-1, we have plotted the volatility of percent yield changes for 2-year, 10-year and 29-year zero-coupon bonds. We see that yield volatility generally declines with maturity. In other words, the volatility of zero-coupon yields typically falls as maturity lengthens.

We can also see from Exhibit A-1 that there is reason to believe that yield volatility is not constant over time. A comparison of Exhibit 1 and Exhibit A-1 suggests that yield volatility is related to yield levels. For example, for short-maturity zero-coupon bonds volatility tends to be high when rates are low and vice versa. Conversely, at long maturities we find the opposite effect: Volatility tends to be high when rates are high. The adjustment we make uses the beginning-of-month yield to help explain subsequent volatility. This adjustment is most important for shorter-maturity yields, especially those under five years. For example, Exhibit A-2 shows the effect of this adjustment on 2-year zero-coupon yield volatility. Having adjusted the data for changing volatility over time, we are now ready to perform our statistical analysis.

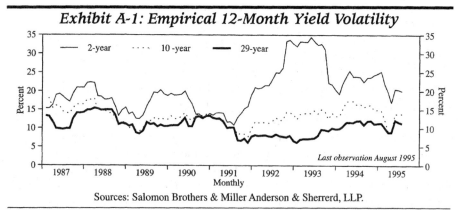

Exhibit A-1: Empirical 12-Month Yield Volatility

Sources: Salomon Brothers & Miller Anderson & Sherrerd, LLP.

---

[7] Technically, we use the changes in the natural logarithms of the yields.

Exhibit A-2: Two-Year Yield Volatility

Sources: Salomon Brothers & Miller Anderson & Sherrerd, LLP.

The question we want to answer is how the yield curve is ordinarily reshaped. We answer this question by using a statistical technique called principal-components analysis. Principal-components analysis allows us to identify and to simplify the joint movement (or covariation) of many data series. Our complete data series are the beginning-of-month yields from October 1986 through August 1995 on zero-coupon bonds of constant maturities one through 29 years. We performed principal-components analysis on the correlation matrix of the volatility-adjusted series of monthly yield-curve changes. As we reported in the text, we found two statistically significant principal components, which taken together explain 97% of the correlation in our monthly yield series. We also analyzed the covariance matrix of the volatility-adjusted series of monthly yield-curve changes, with very similar results.[8]

---

[8] The original study of systematic risks in the yield curve is Robert Litterman and José Scheinkman, "Common Factors Affecting Bond Returns," *Journal of Fixed Income* (June 1991). Our findings differ in two ways. First, they report that there are three systematic risks affecting yield-curve changes, while we found only two that are statistically significant. More important, their yield-curve shift is nearly a parallel shift. There are two reasons our results differ from theirs. First, we adjusted our data for the change in yield volatility associated with changes in yield levels. Second, we used more data from a longer time period. When we restrict our study to their time period (1984-1989) and do not adjust for yield levels, we closely replicate their results. As we mention in footnote 2, we have replicated our study using coupon-bond data from 1952 through 1995 with results nearly identical to our original ones. We conclude that the parallel yield shift found in data from 1984 through 1989 was an anomaly.

About the Author

Francis H. Trainer Jr., CFA

Frank H. Trainer Jr. is Director of Fixed Income and a member of the Board of Directors at Sanford C. Bernstein, Inc. He is chairman of the Fixed-Income Investment Policy Group and a member of the Global Investment Policy Group, and also serves as a Senior Vice President of the Sanford C. Bernstein Fund, Inc. He joined the firm in 1980 as a manager of Fixed-Income Investments. Prior to that he was a senior portfolio manager at Monumental Capital Management, Inc. and a fixed-income portfolio manager at United States Fidelity & Guaranty Co. He is the author of "The Uses of Treasury Bond Futures in Fixed-Income Portfolio Management," published in *Financial Analysts Journal,* and "Controlling Derivative (and Other) Risk" and "Holding Period is the Key to Risk Thresholds," published in *The Journal of Portfolio Management.* Mr. Trainer is a co-author of "A Systematic Approach to Bond Management in Pension Funds," also in *The Journal of Portfolio Management,* and "Active Bond Portfolio Management" in *The Financial Analysts Handbook.* A Chartered Financial Analyst, Mr. Trainer earned a B.S. in 1968 from St. Joseph's University and an M.B.A. in 1972 from Temple University.

Chapter 2

Active Bond Portfolio Management: An Expected Return Approach

Francis H. Trainer Jr., CFA
Director — Fixed Income Investments
Sanford C. Bernstein & Co., Inc.

INTRODUCTION

Many years ago, we were struck by the notion that if we preferred one bond over another, we ought to be able to quantify this preference; what exactly was it that we liked about this bond, and how much was this characteristic worth? We quickly discovered that what we sought was a quantification of *expected return*, taking into account our best judgment about each characteristic of the bond. At the time, the most popular way of evaluating a bond's attractiveness was through a forecast of the direction of the economy. From such a forecast a coherent and consistent framework could be developed to evaluate individual bonds, as well as to determine larger themes for the portfolio, such as duration strategy, sector weightings and maturity distribution. While this was (and still is) a logical way to evaluate bonds, it had two problems. First, since the investment decisions are all based upon a common forecast, there is a good chance that they will succeed or fail at the same time. If the manager's economic outlook is correct, the chances for superior performance are quite good. However, the sword cuts both ways; an incorrect forecast in a volatile year can lead to disappointing returns. Hence, a "top-down" investment approach tends to be accompanied by high relative-performance volatility, or tracking error.

A second potential limitation of the top-down approach is that, while it points the manager in the general direction of the action to be taken, it does not permit direct comparison between securities or strategies. For example, a manager's economic forecast might indicate that he should both barbell the portfolio (avoid intermediate-term securities) as a yield curve strategy, *and* purchase mort-

The author wishes to recognize the substantial contribution of the fixed income policy committee who are responsible for the ideas presented in this chapter. Sloane Lamb's role in the preparation of the chapter was invaluable.

gage passthrough securities, which have intermediate-term durations, as a sector strategy. Top-down portfolio management does not easily reconcile this conflict and, thus, was not the solution that we sought.

Our challenge, therefore, was to develop a single measure of a bond's attractiveness that incorporated all of the important price effects we could anticipate — a measure that could be used for directly comparing securities and strategies, and that did not rely excessively on our economic outlook. Our solution was a process that allows us to calculate expected returns on a wide range of bonds — a methodology which we believe resolves these problems.

Yet our approach is not without elements of controversy. In calculating expected returns, some of the inputs, such as yield, are straightforward. For others, such as the value of embedded options, the differences between alternative approaches are technical in nature and not usually substantive. But, many of the most significant elements of calculating expected return have to do with predicting a bond's future behavior, and the relevance of historical data in this estimation process is the subject of considerable debate. In the introduction to *Against the Gods: The Remarkable Story of Risk*, Peter Bernstein summarizes the issue nicely: "The story that I have to tell is marked all the way through by a persistent tension between those who assert that the best decisions are based on quantification and numbers, determined by the patterns of the past, and those who base their decisions on more subjective degrees of belief about the uncertain future. This is a controversy that has never been resolved."[1]

Fortunately, this is not an either/or choice and there is value in both approaches depending upon the circumstances. However, we tend to lean towards the quantification of past relationships in our estimation of expected returns. In relying heavily on historical data, our goal is *not* to supplant judgment, but to bring our best judgment to bear on all aspects of the investment management process. This manifests itself in the historical periods that we choose, the relative weightings that we apply to those periods, the modifications made to empirical results, and countless other decisions. In the final analysis, the framework that we have evolved can only be valuable if the judgments that underlie it are valuable as well.

The expected return methodology we follow, as well as the portfolio construction process that ties all of this together, is detailed below. The more technical aspects of this methodology are discussed in the appendix.

CALCULATING EXPECTED RETURNS

Treasuries

Since we want to limit the influence of our interest-rate forecast, we set the duration of the portfolio and then independently calculate expected return with the

---

[1] Peter L. Bernstein, *Against the Gods: The Remarkable Story of Risk* (New York, NY: John Wiley & Sons, Inc., 1996), p. 6.

basic assumption that interest rates, *on average*, will be at the same level in the future as they are today. If we make this assumption, what is the expected return on a Treasury security? Our first approximation of expected return is the bond's yield. To this we add expected price changes due to "roll," convexity, and the reshaping of the yield curve.

As time passes and a bond approaches maturity, it typically decreases in yield — and increases in price — as it "rolls" down the yield curve. We refer to this change in price associated with the passage of time as the value of "roll." In addition, although we assume that, overall, the interest-rate level will not change over the measurement period (we use six months), we do allow for interest-rate volatility. Volatility has a positive price effect on non-callable bonds called convexity.[2]

The final and most significant component is the price gain/loss due to the reshaping of the yield curve. Normally, the yield curve is upward sloping, more so at first, then leveling off. At any particular point in time, however, the yield curve can look considerably different. The principal cause for variations in the shape of the yield curve is market participants' expectations for future interest rates — in particular, their expectations for Federal Reserve action. One school of thought suggests that, since the distortions in the yield curve are due to economic forecasts, yield curve strategies should likewise be based on an economic forecast.[3]

We believe that one need not rely on an economic forecast to predict future yield curve shapes. If the yield curve is distorted because market participants are anticipating changes in the federal funds rate, this distortion will tend to dissipate over time, either because the expected change occurs and no further shifts are expected, or because it does not occur and the forecast is abandoned. Either way, the yield curve should eventually revert towards a more normal shape.[4] We calculate the price change associated with reversion to a normal shape using a reversion rate that is consistent with historical experience.[5]

In Exhibit 1, we have plotted the Treasury yield curve as of December 31, 1995, beside our conception of a normally shaped curve.[6] Note the striking flatness at the short end of the actual curve. This reflected the widespread expectation at that time of a weak economy and continued easing by the Federal Reserve.

---

[2] Non-callable bonds have positive convexity, which reflects the beneficial shifts in duration as interest rates change, as well as the non-linear effects of compounding on bond prices.

[3] Frank J. Fabozzi, *Bond Portfolio Management* (New Hope, PA: Frank J. Fabozzi Associates, 1996), p. 326.

[4] We have found that the slope at the very short end of the curve — i.e., out to one year — accurately predicts the changes in short rates over the subsequent three months 57% of the time. However, when the market's forecast is wrong, the change in interest rates in the opposite direction is larger than when rates move in the predicted direction, offsetting the value of the market's accuracy.

[5] Since we do not know the shape of the normal yield curve with complete certainty, small deviations from our conception of normal are not considered deviations and we make no assumption of reversion. However, as the yield curve becomes more significantly distorted, the chances improve that it will revert towards normal in the future.

[6] We believe that the slope of the yield curve from three months to 30 years will normally be in the range of 175 basis points, and that most of this rise will take place in the first few years. A more complete explanation of this assumption can be found in the appendix.

Exhibit 1: Actual versus Normal Treasury Yield Curves: December 31, 1995

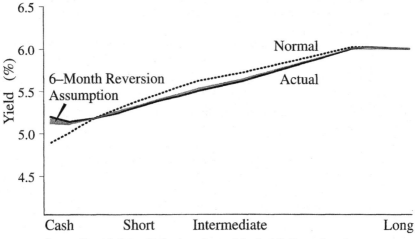

Source: Street Software Technology, Inc. and Sanford C. Bernstein estimates

Exhibit 2: Calculating Expected Return
Treasury 5.875% due 11/15/05 priced as of December 31, 1995

Yield	5.58%
+/– Expected Price Changes from:	
Roll	0.19
Convexity	0.24
Yield Curve Shift	(0.36)
Expected Return	5.65%

Given our assumption that, over the following six months, the curve will revert back towards normal (denoted by the shaded area in Exhibit 1), we calculate the corresponding price change.[7] We can thus determine the expected return for any specific Treasury (Exhibit 2).

We apply this analysis to the entire yield curve to arrive at a Treasury expected return curve (Exhibit 3). Note that the expected return curve looks very different from the yield curve of the same date; the expected return line is relatively flat in the short to intermediate maturity range, then rises rapidly.

For a Treasury portfolio with an intermediate-duration benchmark, a barbell maturity structure (short and long maturities as indicated by the shaded areas) had a higher expected return than either a laddered (evenly distributed maturities) or a concentrated portfolio. These price effects from expected changes in the

---

[7] While this analysis assumes a rotation of the yield curve back towards normal at the longest maturity, the location of the rotation point is not critical to the results.

shape of the yield curve are used to help determine the maturity distribution of the portfolio as we include other sectors of the bond market.

Corporates

When we move from Treasury to corporate analysis, the process becomes more complicated. Corporate expected returns include the values of embedded options (which depend largely on estimates of volatility), default and event (e.g., takeover or restructuring) risks, estimates of rating changes, and spread reversion, in addition to price changes attributable to roll, convexity, and changes in the shape of the yield curve.

An enormous amount of work has gone into the valuation of the embedded options in corporate bonds, and the estimation process is not very controversial.[8] However, the value of the option depends heavily on the assumed level of volatility and, in this respect, there is little agreement. Using the past 12 years of yield changes and weighting the most recent data more heavily, the proportional volatility of yields on 5- to 10-year bonds has been roughly 16%.[9] Some Wall Street strategists use a volatility estimate of only 8% for callable bonds — considerably below ours.[10] The effect of this difference on the value of a call option is significant. In Exhibit 4, we have calculated the option-adjusted spread (OAS) on a hypothetical corporate bond, using the different volatility estimates. The 8% volatility assumption causes the OAS to increase significantly.

Exhibit 3: Treasury Expected Return Curve: December 31, 1995

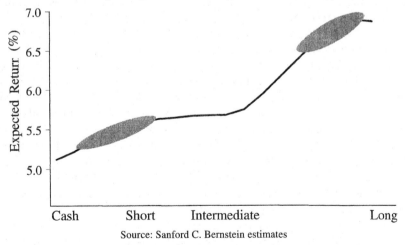

Source: Sanford C. Bernstein estimates

[8] For a very intuitive discussion of the issues involved, refer to Fabozzi, *Bond Portfolio Management*, pp. 157–190.
[9] If interest rates were at 10%, this would translate into a yield volatility — i.e., a one standard deviation change in rates over a 1-year period — of 160 basis points.
[10] While a different measurement period will produce an estimate other than 16%, there has never been an extended period during which volatility was as low as 8%.

Exhibit 4: The Effect of Volatility on Option-Adjusted Spreads
10-Year Maturity; Callable in 5 years; Price: $100

Coupon	Volatility	OAS
7.5%	16%	37 b.p.
7.5%	8%	65 b.p.

Exhibit 5: Adjustments to Corporate Expected Return for Default and Event Risk

Maturity	AAA	AA	A	BBB
1 year	2 b.p.	4 b.p.	7 b.p.	19 b.p.
5 years	8	13	23	55
10 years	12	18	32	76
30 years	17	27	46	110

Although it is important to model option risk, many corporates are not callable. However, one risk shared by every corporate bond is credit risk. Such risk can be realized through company-specific difficulties, overall deterioration in the economy, or an external event such as a takeover. Moody's Investors Services has done a comprehensive study of default experience over the past 25 years; translating default rates into expected return penalties is a relatively straightforward task.[11, 12]

To model event risk, we have tracked the effect of corporate restructuring on ratings since the mid-1980s. Though it is much lower now than a decade ago, it can still be an important effect. For example, in early 1996, Lockheed Martin leveraged its balanced sheet to purchase Loral, causing Lockheed Martin's debt to be downgraded from A+ to BBB+. More recently, Reebok repurchased 23% of its common stock, triggering a downgrade from A− to BBB. These "events" caused the yields on their bonds to rise relative to comparable Treasuries, and their prices to fall correspondingly. Our combined estimates of default and event risk are shown in Exhibit 5.

By working with our company analysts, we assign an appropriate rating to a bond and then incorporate the appropriate costs into our analysis by subtracting them from the bond's yield. This produces an estimate of the return we can expect on a corporate security, assuming that spreads don't change.[13] However, spreads do fluctuate, and we need to incorporate the corresponding expected price changes into our estimates of potential return.

---

[11] Moody's Investors Service, "Corporate Bond Defaults and Default Rates: 1938–1995," *Moody's Special Report* (January 1996).

[12] Thomas L. Bennett, Stephen F. Esser and Christian G. Roth, "Corporate Credit Risk and Reward," *Journal of Portfolio Management* (Spring 1994), pp. 45–46.

[13] The OAS calculation assumes that spreads are constant across a range of interest rates. We have not found evidence of any correlation between the level of corporate spreads and the level of interest rates (discussed further in the appendix). However, the volatility of corporate spreads is positively related to the level of interest rates.

Exhibit 6: Historical Spreads
Five-Year Industrial Corporates; through December 31, 1995

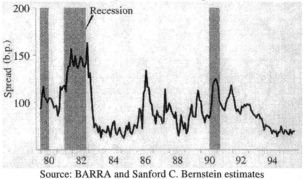

Source: BARRA and Sanford C. Bernstein estimates

Since spreads are compensation for risk, changes in market participants' perception of risk causes spreads to change and, evidently, these perceptions change quite a bit. Exhibit 6 shows that the incremental yields over Treasuries of intermediate-term, A-rated corporate bonds have been quite variable over time, though over the past few years they have been low and stable.[14]

As discussed earlier, there is a philosophical division among investment professionals as to the relevance of historical data. There are some managers who believe that the best predictor of spreads in the future is the current level of spreads — essentially an efficient market hypothesis. The fact that they might be historically wide or narrow is irrelevant.

Given the volatility of spreads, and the potential effect that spread changes can have on performance, we have devoted considerable resources towards forecasting spread changes. Inasmuch as spreads are fundamentally a risk premium, it is logical to assume that some econometric measures of economic health and the direction of the economy would be valuable in predicting spread changes. However, our results to date are limited. There is historical evidence that an improving economy is associated with narrowing spreads, and recessionary periods are associated with wide spreads. However, beyond these relationships, which are not especially strong, we have been unable to find reliable explanations. What we have concluded is that spreads are subject to a plethora of forces, and that the best way to predict spreads is to assume that they will revert toward their long-term average, influenced somewhat by the current state of the economy. Exhibit 7 shows actual spreads and our predicted spreads over the past five years.[15]

---

[14] The spreads in this exhibit are calculated on an absolute rather than a proportional basis. Therefore, when Treasury yields are at 5% and a comparable corporate is at 6%, we call that a spread of 100 basis points, rather than 20%.

[15] Note that we are using the average spread over the period to predict spread changes in the same period — a potentially fatal flaw in modeling. However, when we performed simple out-of-sample testing, using the first half to predict the second, and vice versa, the quality of the fit was not meaningfully lower. Furthermore, the economic data that we use for this purpose was not our forecast, but data that have already been released. Finally, the fit in Exhibit 7 may appear to be particularly good, yet we said that the relationship was weak. This illusion is the result of plotting spread levels rather than changes in spreads.

Exhibit 7: Actual and Predicted Spreads
Five-Year Industrial Corporates; through December 31, 1995

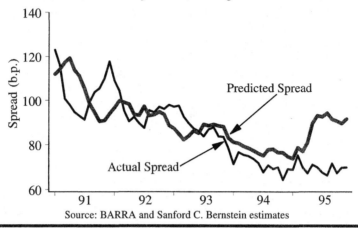

Source: BARRA and Sanford C. Bernstein estimates

When actual spreads deviate from our prediction, we assume that they will revert at a rate that is roughly one-third of what we have observed historically.[16] This reversion in spreads translates into an expected price change, which we combine with the yield (now adjusted for options, and default and event risks) to arrive at an estimate of expected return. In Exhibit 8, we calculate the expected return of a specific corporate, as well as the return on a comparable Treasury, in order to highlight the adjustments that we make.

The Quaker Oats bonds were rated "A" by both Moody's and Standard & Poor's on December 31, 1995. Their yield on that date was 75 basis points higher than a comparable Treasury, but we assessed 32 basis points for default and event risk (Exhibit 5). The roll, convexity, and yield curve shift effects were identical for each bond. Based on our analysis of the credit, we expected Quaker Oats to be downgraded, which we estimated would reduce the price by 0.25 percentage points. However, the bonds were already selling on the cheap side (for their rating), so some of the downgrade was already in the price (specific security misvaluation). The really significant negative to this bond (and all corporates on that date) was the expected deterioration in price from a general widening in corporate spreads — (0.68) percentage points — reflecting the historical narrowness of spreads. Finally, the bid/asked spread on corporates is wider than on comparable Treasuries. If we buy a bond with the intention of selling it in the future, we will incur this cost. Hence, we reduce the corporate's expected return for the incremental trading costs (i.e., a liquidity penalty).

---

[16] The "haircut" in the reversion rate is an attempt to recognize that the forces that shaped spreads in the past may change in the future. The average spread could change because of developments in other sectors — for example, the asset-backed market — could affect spreads. Furthermore, regression estimates tend to overstate reversion rates.

Exhibit 8: Expected Return for Quaker Oats MTNs 7.51 % due 5/02/05

	Quaker Oats	Comparable Treasury	Difference
Yield	6.33%	5.58%	0.75%
(adjustment for default costs and event risk)	(0.32)	0.00	(0.32)
+/– Expected Price Changes from:			
Roll	0.19	0.19	0.00
Convexity	0.24	0.24	0.00
Yield Curve Shift	(0.36)	(0.36)	0.00
Ratings Changes	(0.25)	0.00	(0.25)
Specific Security Misvaluation	0.06	0.00	0.06
Sector Spread Changes	(0.68)	0.00	(0.68)
Liquidity Penalty	(0.06)	0.00	(0.06)
Expected Return	5.15%	5.65%	(0.50)%

Exhibit 9: Corporate Expected Returns: December 31, 1995

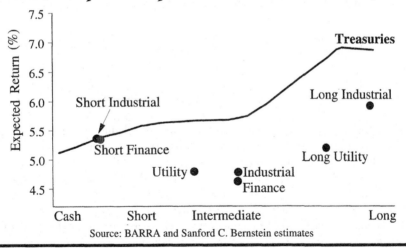

Source: BARRA and Sanford C. Bernstein estimates

When all of the adjustments are complete, the spread of 75 basis points turns into an expected return *deficit* of 50 basis points. This represents our best judgment about how this bond will perform. We first do this analysis for a broad range of generic corporate sectors, and then try to isolate specific areas of the market that warrant further study. Exhibit 9 reflects this analysis as of December 31, 1995.

With the exception of certain very short-term corporates, we expected corporates to universally underperform Treasury securities. Thus, most of the corporate market was not very interesting on that date, and we limited our in-depth investigation at that time to short-term corporates.

Mortgages

The basic framework for estimating a mortgage expected return is similar to that for a corporate: we calculate an option-adjusted yield and combine it with the price effect of likely spread changes, changes in the shape of the yield curve, credit risk, and so on. However, these steps are considerably more complicated for mortgage-backed securities.

When the first mortgage securities were issued in the late 1960s, the state of mortgage analysis was pretty crude. Over the years, the technology required to analyze mortgages has been developed by investment banking firms, independent analytical consultants, and money management companies. The major challenge continues to be the principal source of risk in mortgage-backed securities — the right of homeowners to prepay at any time.

In the corporate arena, options are exercised fairly efficiently, and their valuation is, therefore, principally a mathematical exercise. However, individuals don't necessarily act as predictably as corporations in exercising their prepayment option. Not only do they not have the wherewithal to evaluate their option, but their prepayment decision is complicated by a host of non-financial factors — relocation, job uncertainty, or other personal disruptions.[17] Drawing upon our prepayment model and given an estimate of volatility, we can calculate the option-adjusted spread of a mortgage.

In order to translate option-adjusted spreads into expected returns, we need to subject the bond to a scenario analysis. There are two reasons for this. First, OAS analysis assumes that a bond's spread relative to Treasuries does not change with movements in interest rates. But this is not the case with mortgages. In fact, the spreads on discount, par, and premium mortgages are nearly always different. Second, based upon our analysis, market participants price mortgage bonds consistent with an 11% volatility, but we believe that a more appropriate volatility is in the mid-teens. To reconcile this difference, we calculate the value of the option using 11%, but then evaluate the expected returns using scenarios consistent with our higher volatility.

To model a passthroughs' likely spread change, we have measured the option-adjusted spreads on a variety of mortgage relative coupons (discount/par/premium), mortgage issuers (GNMA/FNMA/ FHLMC), and ages (seasoned vs. newly issued), since 1983.[18] In an attempt to compensate for the "learning curve" regarding market understanding of mortgage behavior, we weight recent spreads more heavily when averaging historical spreads. We then calculate the change in price, assuming that the OAS will revert toward this average.

---

[17] For a comprehensive review of a mortgage prepayment model, see Gregg N. Patruno, *Mortgage Prepayments: A New Model for a New Era* (New York, NY: Goldman Sachs, 1994).

[18] A potential pitfall here is that we are using our current prepayment model in combination with historical pricing to calculate option-adjusted spreads. Our model incorporates years of incremental improvements in our understanding of the prepayment process — an understanding that did not exist a decade ago. Therefore, the prices and the associated spreads may not accurately reflect what market participants thought they were getting in these past periods. We attempt to offset this effect by weighting recent spreads more heavily in our averaging process.

Exhibit 10: Calculating Expected Returns for Mortgage Passthroughs

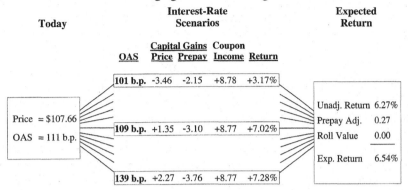

Exhibit 11: Mortgage Expected Returns: December 31, 1995

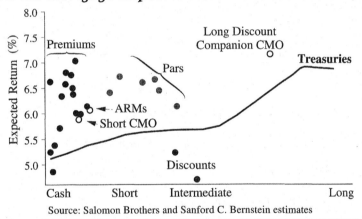

Source: Salomon Brothers and Sanford C. Bernstein estimates

Therefore, we specify a variety of interest-rate environments and the expected option-adjusted spread in each. We also specify a short-term rate of interest and our yield curve reversion assumption (discussed above). To calculate the expected return of a mortgage under each scenario, we calculate the change in price given the expected OAS (adjusted for reversion to the expected OAS it will have in each interest-rate environment) and combine it with income (adjusted for cash flows from prepayments) to produce the scenario return.

We subject the bonds to 13 such scenarios: six up, six down and one unchanged. The average of the returns in each scenario is our expected return (Exhibit 10).[19] As of December 31, 1995, par and premium coupon mortgages were attractive relative to Treasuries, while discounts were relatively unattractive (Exhibit 11).

---

[19] The scenarios are spread out so that a simple average of the outcomes is statistically appropriate.

We analyze CMOs using a method similar to the one described above for mortgage passthroughs. While standard PAC and sequential deals are relatively easy to analyze, as we move away from the simpler structures, the potential error of our expected return and risk estimates grows materially. In these cases, we typically limit the exposure we are willing to take.

Foreign Bonds

As we extend our investment universe beyond the United States, we use a similar analytical approach. The opportunity set is, in some respects, much greater, since each country has its unique yield curve, economic dynamics, and associated currency decision. However, the corporate and mortgage markets are fairly undeveloped abroad, making credit and cash flow structure analyses less valuable. Accordingly, there are two principal components of the decision to invest in foreign markets — (1) how attractive is the country and (2) should the position be hedged?

As with domestic bonds, yield is a good starting point. When we examine a foreign bond on a hedged basis, its hedged yield is equal to its quoted yield plus the effect of hedging. For example, if 1-year Italian interest rates were 12% while U.S. interest rates were 8%, the effect of hedging the Italian lira would be to lock in a 4% loss. This must be true, because otherwise you could purchase Italian bonds at the 12% yield, hedge out the currency risk, and be left with a 12% riskless return.[20] So, the gain (loss) of hedging for a 1-year horizon is:

$$\text{Hedging Effect} = \text{U.S. 1-Year Yield} - \text{Foreign 1-Year Yield} \qquad (1)$$

If we buy a 5-year bond and hedge it for one year, the yield is:

$$\text{Hedged 5-Year Yield} = \text{Foreign 5-Year Yield} + \text{Hedging Effect} \qquad (2)$$

Combining equations (1) and (2) and rearranging, we get:

$$\text{Foreign 5-Year Hedged Yield} = \text{Foreign 5-Year Yield} - \text{Foreign 1-Year Yield} \\ + \text{U.S. 1-Year Yield} \qquad (3)$$

We can see that the hedged yield depends on how *steep* the foreign yield curve is — i.e., what the yield *difference* between intermediate and short bonds is, not the absolute level of those yields.

When a foreign yield curve is steep, an investor can pick up a lot of yield for taking interest-rate risk in that country. But will that yield pick-up translate into return? A simple version of efficient markets suggests that it should not. The steep curve reflects investor expectations of rising rates which, if the expectations

---

[20] U.S. investors will force the locked-in loss to be at least 4%. Italian investors could exploit the spread if it were greater than 4%, so in practice it will be within 4% (plus or minus transactions costs, which are quite small).

are met, will create capital losses offsetting the extra yield. However, our research suggests that these expectations, on average, are not met. This means that the yield pick-up translates into excess expected return.

We have also observed that foreign interest rates are autocorrelated. [21] This means that if they have fallen recently they will more than likely fall in the next month. We attribute this to two factors. First, central banks move in a very autocorrelated manner. While the market recognizes this, it does not adjust for it completely. Second, the market seems to underreact to economic news, so if interest rates rise in reaction to strong economic news, there is a better than even chance that they will continue to rise in the near future. This autocorrelation effect is translated into a price expectation for the specific bond.

Finally, we need to decide whether or not to hedge. For clients with U.S. benchmarks, our neutral position is to take no currency risk. However, there are times where we believe we can add return by accepting a limited amount of currency exposure. We have developed a currency model that assesses the attractiveness of each currency based upon four measures: current account, interest-rate differentials, purchasing power, and currency trends. Because of the possibility of Economic and Monetary Union (EMU) within Europe, we have modified the model for those countries likely to be part of the unified currency.

Exhibit 12 shows our estimates of international expected returns as of December 31, 1995.

Exhibit 12: International Expected Returns: December 31, 1995

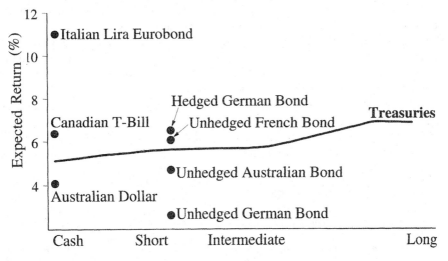

Source: Bloomberg L.P., *Financial Times,* and Sanford C. Bernstein estimates

---

[21] U.S. interest rates are too, as we will discuss below.

Financial Futures

In most cases, interest-rate futures are a low-transactions-cost replication of the class of securities on which they are based. Therefore, in the case of Treasury futures, the analysis can be reduced to determining which Treasury security the future's price is likely to track. Because the future obligation must be satisfied by delivery of an actual security (unless it is closed out prior to the contract's expiration), it is safe to assume that the deliverer will choose a bond that will maximize his profit — i.e., the bond that is *cheapest to deliver*. We should therefore determine which deliverable bond is likely to be chosen.[22] The future's expected return, then, is the expected return on the deliverable bond, less the cost of financing.[23]

Since futures are simply an alternative method of purchasing or selling a Treasury security, they can be quite useful (and cost effective) for altering the duration and/or the duration distribution of a portfolio.

DURATION SHIFTS

We target the duration of the portfolio to within one year on either side of the benchmark,[24] making adjustments in response to and in anticipation of various economic and financial market events. We place the greatest emphasis on the recent and anticipated rate of growth in the economy, our view of the latter being governed primarily by the relationship between sales and inventories. These factors seem to have the greatest influence on the Federal Reserve, which determines the direction of short-term interest rates, which in turn influence the direction of long-term ones.

While acting upon already-released economic data runs contrary to the concept of market efficiency, it seems to work because either (1) bond market participants fail to completely respond to such information, or (2) economic data tend to be autocorrelated — that is, strong data tend to be followed by strong data. Regardless of the cause, there is value to be realized from reacting to publicly available data.

Furthermore, the Federal Reserve has adopted a counter-cyclical strategy that has typically resulted in a series of small interest-rate changes during each phase of the interest rate cycle, in lieu of a single, larger change. Thus, their moves tend to be highly autocorrelated. We have incorporated this autocorrelation into our duration strategy.

---

[22] Generally, when yields are below 8%, the shortest deliverable bonds are most likely to be chosen; above 8%, the longest bonds are the most likely. When yields are around 8%, the duration of the futures tends to be quite unstable and the future's price is negatively convex (its duration will shorten if rates fall and lengthen if rates rise).

[23] While it is probable that there will be a single security that is most likely to be delivered, there will typically be several others that will become deliverable if interest rates change by a meaningful amount. The calculation of the expected return on the future must include the option value of this possibility.

[24] This is the duration band for our service that is benchmarked to the broad market index. For shorter duration benchmarks, where the client presumably desires less risk, we use a tighter band.

PORTFOLIO CONSTRUCTION

The analysis described above produces a set of expected returns for all of the major components of the bond market (except for the duration target). We can now directly compare securities; absent risk considerations, if two bonds have the same duration, we will prefer the one with the higher expected return. Furthermore, since we have incorporated all of the price changes that we anticipate, the problem of conflicting strategies is eliminated — we can purchase an attractive mortgage even if we dislike intermediate securities, because the effect has already been incorporated into the mortgage's expected return.

However, return is only half of the equation; we also need to measure the risk of each of these bonds. This raises the obvious question: What is risk? Since, typically, the mandate of an active manager is to outperform an index, then the portfolio must differ from the index — and it is precisely this difference that generates portfolio risk. The calculation of risk begins at the individual security level. For each bond, we need to estimate its exposure to changes in the level of interest rates, to changes in yield spreads versus Treasuries, to changes in the shape of the yield curve, and, for foreign bonds, to changes in foreign interest rates and currencies.[25]

To calculate the variability of a portfolio's return relative to its index — i.e., its tracking error — we compare the relative exposure of the portfolio versus the index to the individual sources of risk. The total tracking error can then be calculated by summing up the differences, taking into account the correlation of the sources of risk.

Once we have a complete specification of the expected returns and risks on the sample of bonds that we have analyzed, we are in a position to optimize the portfolio. To this end, we evaluate the expected returns of various portfolio constructions relative to the amount of tracking error (performance risk) each entails. For each level of risk, there is a portfolio that maximizes expected return. Exhibit 13 shows this "efficient frontier" as of December 31, 1995, plotting the incremental returns as we move out from the minimum risk portfolio. The more risk we are willing to incur, the more return we can expect to pick up. The selection of an actual portfolio along this curve depends on our estimate of our client's appetite for trading off risk and return.[26]

At any point in time we can characterize a market environment by the degree of incremental return offered in exchange for incremental risk. When there is not much return to be picked up for taking risk, the efficient frontier is fairly shallow. Conversely, when the market is rich with opportunities, the frontier is steep — a good time to make significant bets.

---

[25] For a more complete discussion of these risks, see Francis H. Trainer, Jr., "Controlling Derivative (and Other) Risk," *Journal of Portfolio Management* (Spring 1996), pp. 77–87.

[26] Refer to the appendix for a discussion of the mathematics involved in this process.

Exhibit 13: Efficient Frontier on December 31, 1995

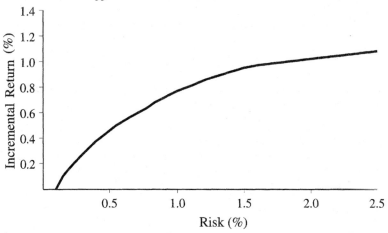

Exhibit 14: Efficient Frontiers on December 31, 1990, and December 31, 1995

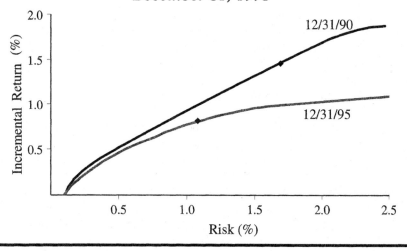

To illustrate this point, we have added a second efficient frontier for December 31, 1990. As of December 31, 1995, the optimal portfolio for our typical client, marked by a diamond, was at 110 basis points of risk. At year-end 1990, when the frontier was considerably steeper, the optimal portfolio was at a higher level of risk (170 basis points). As may be seen in Exhibits 15 and 16, the optimal portfolios on these two dates were considerably different. Although conventional sector and duration distributions are helpful in highlighting those differences, we believe that the performance risk profile (or tracking error) shown in Exhibit 17 provides the most meaningful description.

Exhibit 15: Historical Sector Distributions

	12/31/90	12/31/95
Treasuries	34%	49%
Mortgages	19	35
Corporates	46	5
Foreign	11	16

Exhibit 16: Historical Duration Distributions

	12/31/90	12/31/95
Short (0-2)	15%	25%
Intermediate (2-7)	58	54
Long (7+)	27	21

Exhibit 17: Portfolio Performance Risk

	12/31/90	12/31/95
Security and Sector	135 b.p.	40 b.p.
Yield Curve	20	25
Duration	50	35
Foreign	35	50
Total	170	110

As may be seen in Exhibit 17, most of the risk at the end of 1990 came from the heavy corporate weighting, which reflected the wide spreads at that time and the associated heightened expected returns. At the end of 1995, corporate spreads were at very narrow levels and we *under*weighted the portfolios — also leading to tracking error, albeit considerably less.

WHY SHOULD THIS METHODOLOGY WORK?

Implicit in most of this analysis is the assumption that the bond market is *ineffi*cient. We have assumed that we can use widely available public information to outperform the market as a whole. We believe that opportunities are the result of a number of factors — biased decision-making rules, technical factors such as temporary changes in the supply of, or demand for, a bond, incremental central bank policies, complexity, etc.[27] We are reasonably confident that biased decision making will continue, and technical factors are likely to have irregular effects on the market. Complexity is potentially more problematic, given the increased availability of advanced analytical tools, but if financial engineering continues at its recent rapid pace, complexity will continue to be a source of misvaluation.

SUMMARY

The investment management process described above comprises the calculation of expected return on a broad range of bonds, and the optimal combination of these bonds given (1) the scope of opportunities at any point in time and (2) our risk preferences. The expected return measure enables us to integrate all of our judgments about an individual bond and about the market environment into a single measure that we can apply consistently across time and market sectors, without excessively relying upon our economic outlook. As a result, there are rarely just one or two themes in the portfolio at any point; more often, there is a multitude of strategies, whose successes or failures are largely independent of one another. Thus, we believe that this approach not only achieves superior returns, but does so with relatively low risk.

APPENDIX

Volatility

An essential component of the analyses described above is our estimate of interest-rate volatility. We use this volatility estimate to build the interest-rate trees in our option analysis, to determine the value of convexity, to construct our mortgage scenario analysis, to analyze the delivery option in futures, and so forth.

The interest-rate volatility that we expect over the next six months is based on our volatility assumption, which is drawn from both very recent and longer-term volatility levels. We have found that recent volatility levels are as valuable in predicting future volatility as is the longer-term history; consequently, we use both.

Exhibit 18 shows our current volatility assumptions, which combine both the overall experience from 1984–1995 with the volatility for the six months ending December 31, 1995.

Exhibit 18: Yield Volatility Assumptions as of December 31, 1995

Maturity	Proportional Volatility
1	16.7%
3	17.8
5	16.6
10	14.6
30	12.5

[27] The arguments for biased decision-making rules are thoroughly reviewed in: Daniel Kahneman, Paul Slovic, and Amos Tversky, *Judgment under Uncertainty: Heuristics and Biases* (Cambridge, England: Cambridge University Press, 1982); and, Richard H. Thaler, *The Winner's Curse: the Paradoxes and Anomalies of Economic Life* (Princeton, NJ: Princeton University Press, 1992). For a summary of these arguments, see Bernstein, *Against the Gods*, pp. 269-303.

As shown here, short-term interest rates tend to be more variable than long ones. This is consistent with our belief that, when the Federal Reserve moves short rates, longer rates do not change as much, since investors expect an eventual reversal of short rates. Additionally, given that the yield curve is normally upward-sloping, a *level* shift in interest rates across maturities would result in a larger percentage change in short rates than in long.

Yield Curve Analysis

Judging from some of the Street strategy reports that we have reviewed, there seems to be some controversy about the interpretation of the shape of the yield curve. For example, the federal funds futures and Eurodollar futures curves, both of which are consistent with the forward rates derived from the yield curve, are often cited as a reflection of market expectations; specifically, if they are upward sloping, they are interpreted as a forecast of rising rates. In order to believe this interpretation, one would have to accept the "pure expectations" hypothesis, which states that, after adjusting for the effects of convexity, any slope in the yield curve is a predictor of interest-rate shifts.

This theory directly contradicts the persistent upward slope of the yield curve historically. For most of the period between 1950 and the late 1970s, the slope of the curve averaged 100 basis points;[28] from 1983 until mid-1996, it averaged 240 basis points.[29] Since it seems implausible that investors have been perpetually pessimistic, we subscribe to the theory that there is a risk or liquidity premium in the yield curve, and that the *normal* yield curve is upward sloping, more so at first, then flattening off, and perhaps turning back down at the long end to reflect the value of convexity.

Rather than postulating an exact mathematical description of a normal yield curve, we picture a broad band, within which any shape can be considered normal. When the actual yield curve is inside of this band, we do not anticipate reversion. However, when the yield curve is severely distorted — as it was in 1992, when its slope approached 500 basis points — it is clearly not sustainable, and we consider reversion likely.

Another important issue in our yield curve analysis is the assumed speed of reversion, which determines the expected change in yield. Because change in price is a function of a bond's duration and the expected change in yield, price changes for long-term bonds are quite sensitive to the reversion rate that we have assumed. Because regression-based reversion rates tend to overstate the underlying reversion process and because we don't know exactly the slope or curvature of a normal yield curve, we reduce the actual reversion speed that we observed between 1983 and 1995.

---

[28] Salomon Brothers, Inc., *Analytical Record of Yields and Yield Spreads* (New York, NY: Salomon Brothers, Inc., 1945–95).

[29] Federal Reserve Board, *Selected Interest Rates*, Statistical Release, no. G.13 (1983–96). In virtually all of our analyses, we ignore the October 1979–October 1982 period. During this time, the Federal Reserve changed its operating procedures, causing interest rates to be substantially more volatile than they had been at any time before or since.

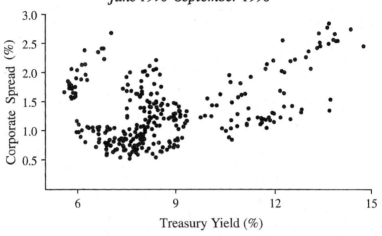

Exhibit 19: Raw Long Corporate Spreads versus Long Treasury Yields
June 1970–September 1996

Corporates

An enduring debate among fixed-income researchers is whether spreads should be calculated as a percentage of the yield level or as an absolute number. For instance, if Treasury yields were at 5%, and corporate yields at 6%, this could be interpreted as a 20% spread or a 100 basis point spread. If Treasury yields were to fall to 4%, and corporate yields to 5%, the 100 basis point difference would now be a 25% spread. If spreads were relative, we would see wider spreads in conjunction with higher interest rates when we plot corporates spreads against Treasury yield levels. Exhibit 19 shows long-term corporate spreads plotted against long Treasury yields for the 26-year period covering June 1970 to September 1996 and, although some parts seem consistent with an upward-sloping distribution from lower left to upper right, generally there is not a clear relationship.

When we studied this data sequentially, we found distinct periods where spreads clustered together, and examining these clusters of data led to a clearer understanding of this issue. From June 1970 to December 1972 (Exhibit 20) and from October 1979 to October 1982 (Exhibit 22), we see a pretty strong tendency for spreads to increase with interest rates. However, Exhibits 24 and 25 provide a stark challenge to this theory; there is no clear relationship between spreads and the level of interest rates from 1985 to 1996. Therefore, we use the absolute value of spreads in our analysis.

Duration

Because of the prepayment option, the calculation of a mortgage duration is complicated. We calculate two mortgage durations — yield duration and prepayment duration. Yield duration is approximately equal to the modified duration of a non-callable bond. It is calculated as the percentage change in the price of a mortgage if we change the Treasury tree by a small amount, but leave the option-adjusted spread and mortgage cash flows at their previous levels. The prepayment duration quantifies the sensitivity of the mortgage price to a small change in refinancing incentives measured separately from a change in interest rates. The sum of the two durations is called the total, or option-adjusted, duration.

Exhibit 20: Raw Long Corporate Spreads versus Long Treasury Yields — June 1970–December 1972

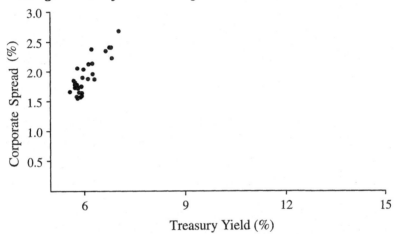

Exhibit 21: Raw Long Corporate Spreads versus Long Treasury Yields — January 1973–September 1979

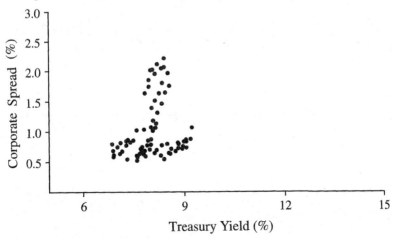

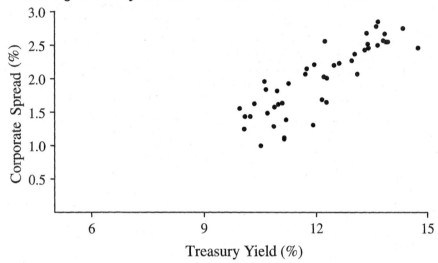

Exhibit 22: Raw Long Corporate Spreads versus
Long Treasury Yields — October 1979–October 1982

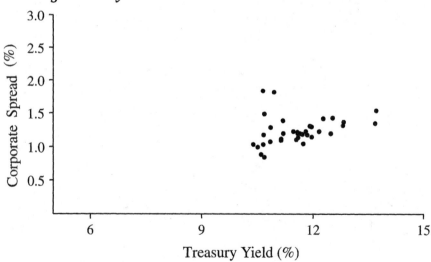

Exhibit 23: Raw Long Corporate Spreads versus
Long Treasury Yields — November 1982–October 1985

Exhibit 24: Raw Long Corporate Spreads versus Long Treasury Yields — November 1985–September 1991

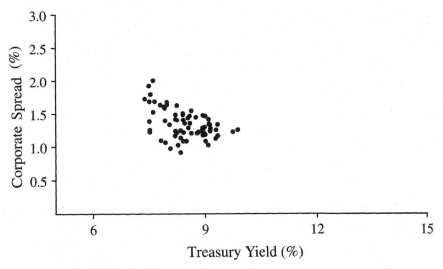

Exhibit 25: Raw Long Corporate Spreads versus Long Treasury Yields — October 1991–September 1996

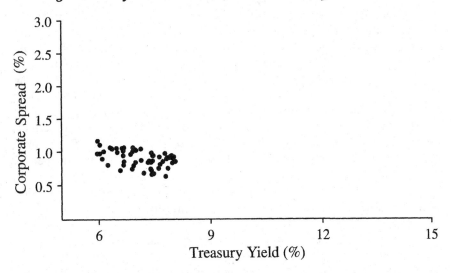

The total duration measures the sensitivity of the mortgage price to changes in interest rates, taking into account the relationship between interest rates and the incentive to refinance. Although we use total duration as a measure of overall interest-rate exposure, it is important to identify its constituent durations, because they allow us to quantify the impact of several different factors — such as the shape of the yield curve — on mortgage performance.

When we incorporate foreign bonds into U.S. portfolios, we need to assess the durations of these bonds from a U.S. perspective. This is a more subtle process than it might at first appear. By duration, we mean the expected price change resulting from a change in *U.S.* interest rates. First, consider cash holdings in British pounds. A British investor will, correctly, consider it to have a duration of zero. However, currencies, such as the pound, are somewhat correlated with interest rates. When U.S. interest rates rise 100 basis points, the value of the pound (in U.S. dollars) declines on average by 1.3 percentage points. So, the *U.S.* duration of the British pound is 1.3 years.

Similarly, the duration of a British bond to a U.S. investor is not the same as it is to a British investor. When U.S. interest rates move 100 basis points, British interest rates on average move roughly half as much because they are not perfectly correlated. Thus, the duration of a hedged British bond would be half of its British duration. An unhedged British bond is influenced by both British interest rates and currency changes; its duration is equal to the hedged bond's duration plus the duration of the British pound.

Optimization

At any point in time, we can identify the various portfolios that offer the highest expected returns for a given level of risk (defined as tracking error); the curve describing these portfolios is typically referred to as the efficient frontier. In Exhibit 14 (above), we showed our estimates of the frontiers in the domestic bond markets for two dates — December 31, 1990 and December 31, 1995. The important feature to note is that the slope of the frontier in 1990 was steeper than the slope at the end of 1995 — i.e., the environment at the end of 1990 was pretty exciting, and there were meaningful rewards for taking risk. The rewards to be had in December 1995 were much shallower. Not surprisingly, therefore, the optimal portfolio for 1995 — indicated by the diamond — had less risk than the portfolio we would have picked in 1990.

This is because the portfolio that maximizes our "utility" in 1990 has a different risk level than the one in 1995. We define utility as:

$$\text{Utility} = \text{Expected Return} - \text{Constant} \times \text{Tracking Error}^2 \qquad (4)$$

At any point in time, there is a portfolio that maximizes utility. For example, when we calculate utility as of December 31, 1995, based on equation (4), we get the curve pictured in Exhibit 26.

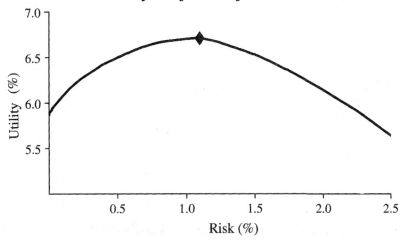

Exhibit 26: Utility Profile as of December 31, 1995

The portfolio with the maximum utility is the optimal portfolio on that date. It is important to note that this utility calculation is dependent upon the constant in equation (4), which is effectively a risk-aversion parameter. The higher the constant, the more risk we will incur for a given pick-up in return. The risk aversion we use varies across the different services. For shorter duration portfolios, we are more risk averse and therefore use a lower constant.

About the Author

Kenneth E. Volpert, CFA

Kenneth E. Volpert is Principal and Senior Portfolio Manager at The Vanguard Group. He currently manages over $6.5 billion in mutual fund assets in the four Vanguard Bond Index Fund Portfolios and two other bond index portfolios. Mr. Volpert has over 15 years fixed income management experience (over 10 years bond indexing experience), is a Chartered Financial Analyst, and holds a B.S. in Finance from the University of Illinois-Urbana and an M.B.A. from the University of Chicago.

Chapter 3

Managing Indexed and Enhanced Indexed Bond Portfolios

Kenneth E. Volpert, CFA
Principal and Senior Portfolio Manager
The Vanguard Group, Inc.

OVERVIEW OF DOMESTIC BOND MANAGEMENT

Domestic bond management can be likened to a sailing regatta. The index is the lead boat, since it does not have expenses and transaction costs to contend with, and all managers (including index fund managers) are the other boats, trying to make up the distance and pass the index boat. Strategies that may be used to make up the difference and pass the lead boat comprise a wide spectrum of styles and approaches. Exhibit 1 displays the major elements of these approaches.

Pure Bond Index Matching

Pure bond indexing is the lowest risk (and lowest expected return) approach to bond management versus a specific benchmark. This approach essentially guarantees that returns will lag behind the index boat by the cost difference (expenses plus transaction costs). Pure bond index matching attempts to fully replicate the index by owning all the bonds in the index in the same percentage as the index. Hence, this approach is also called the *full replication approach*. In the bond market, however, such an approach is very difficult to accomplish and very costly to implement. Many bonds in the index were issued years ago, and are consequently illiquid. Many bonds were also issued when interest rates were significantly different from current rates. Today's holders may be unwilling to incur a gain or loss by selling their bonds to an index fund.

The author wishes to acknowledge the professional and personal contribution of Irwin E. Jones, who retired from the business in 1996. Irwin introduced the author to the bond indexing business in 1986. Irwin's highest integrity, his inquisitive nature, his professional mentoring role, and his personal friendship have deeply affected the author. Thank you Irwin!

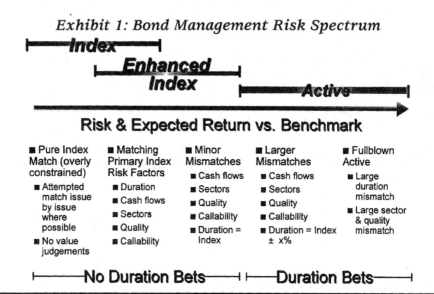

Exhibit 1: Bond Management Risk Spectrum

On September 30, 1996, the Lehman Brothers Aggregate Bond Index contained 169 Treasury issues, 1,144 federal agency issues, 3,507 corporate issues, 106 asset-backed issues, and 611 broadly categorized mortgage issues (essentially hundreds of thousands of mortgage pools). Full replication is feasible (although not desirable for reasons to be mentioned later) in the Treasury market, but cannot be reasonably implemented in the agency, mortgage or corporate markets. Thousands of the agency and corporate issues are locked away in long-term bond portfolios and could only be purchased from these investors by paying extremely high prices. For this reason, full replication of a broad bond index (including corporates and mortgages) is very inefficient, if not impossible.

Enhanced Indexing/Matching Primary Risk Factors

The *enhanced bond indexing/matching primary risk factors approach* involves investing in a large sample of bonds such that the portfolio risk factors match the index risk factors. The result is a portfolio that, when fully implemented, will have higher average monthly tracking differences (standard deviation of tracking differences) than the full replication (i.e., pure index matching) approach, but it can be implemented and maintained at much lower cost resulting in net investment performance that is much closer to the index. Returning to the regatta analogy, the portfolio boat stays on the same "tack" as the index boat, but "trims its sails" to run a little more efficiently. Staying on the same "tack" means that the sails are set to take the portfolio boat in the same direction as the index boat, thereby being exposed to the same winds and elements. "Trimming the sails" means that the little details of the sail position and sail shape are performed better and executed more efficiently than on the index boat. The risk factors that need to be matched are duration, cash flow distribution, sector, quality, and call exposure (more on this later). This approach is considered a form of enhanced indexing because the return is enhanced (more on this later) relative to the full replication indexing approach.

Enhanced Indexing/Minor Risk Factor Mismatches

The *enhanced bond indexing/minor risk factor mismatches approach* allows for minor mismatches in the risk factors (except duration) to tilt the portfolio in favor of particular areas of relative value (sector, quality, term structure, call risk, etc.). Because the mismatches (and impact on tracking) are very small, this is still considered enhanced indexing. These additional enhancements are essentially "sail trimming" strategies designed to make up additional distance versus the index boat, while staying on the same tack, and being exposed to the same elements.

Active Management/Larger Risk Factor Mismatches

The active management/larger risk factor mismatches approach is a conservative approach to active management. The manager will make larger mismatches in the risk factors to attempt to add greater value. This approach may also make small duration bets. In most cases, the management fee and transaction costs are significantly higher than for pure or enhanced indexing, yet the net investment return is usually lower. The addition of these additional costs is the reason why a typical index portfolio often outperforms the average active manager in performance universes. Since this strategy has higher costs (higher expenses and transaction costs), the manager will moderately "change tack" to seek greater winds elsewhere, resulting in increased manager risk (i.e., greater risk of deviating from the "market" return and structure).

Active Management/Full-Blown Active

The *active management/full-blown active approach* is an aggressive active style where large duration and sector bets are made, and where significant value-added (or lost) relative to an index can be experienced. Above-average performance consistency is difficult to find in this group of managers, so investors who choose this management style need to look deeper than just at recent performance to discern the good from the bad. This approach may significantly change the "course" relative to the index boat and may risk significant tracking and portfolio structure variations from the index boat in the hope of adding much greater return.

WHY INDEX BOND PORTFOLIOS?

There are several reasons for indexing: broad diversification, competitive performance, low cost, consistent relative performance, market performance predictability, time-tested, and redirection of focus on asset allocation. Each reason is discussed below.

Broad Diversification

Broad bond index portfolios provide excellent diversification. The Lehman Brothers Aggregate Bond Index, which is designed to capture the entire U.S. investment-grade bond market, has over 5,500 issues and more than $4.5 trillion in market value as of September 30, 1996. A large bond index portfolio designed to replicate this Index may have 500 or more issues, resulting in significant issuer diversification benefits. Most active portfolios have much heavier specific issuer concentrations, resulting in significant exposure to issuer event (credit) risk.

In addition, an index portfolio designed to match the Lehman Brothers Aggregate Bond Index will have exposure to not only Treasury and agency sectors, but also to mortgages, industrials, electric and telephone utilities, finance, dollar-denominated foreign, and asset-backed sectors. Such a portfolio will also have broad exposure to the yield curve with holdings from one year to over 30 years to maturity. These sources of diversification result in a portfolio with lower risk for a given level of return than is available from less diversified portfolios.

Competitive Performance

Since index portfolios have lower management fees and lower transaction costs (resulting from significantly lower portfolio turnover), it is not surprising that they usually outperform the average active portfolio in most universes. After all, a broad index is by design a representation of the whole pie of investment alternatives. Therefore, the sum of all active managers should equal the index in composition. Also, the sum of the investment performance of all active managers (grossed up for the higher management fees and transaction costs) should also equal the index in performance. In the mutual fund market, where the bond index expense ratio advantage is about 0.8% per year, the largest bond index portfolio (managed against the Lehman Brothers Aggregate Bond Index) outperformed over 85% of its Lipper Group over 1, 3, and 5 years ending 12/31/95. In the large institutional market, where the expense advantage of indexing is lower, index portfolios outperformed 60% to 75% of actively managed portfolios over the same period (depending on the universe chosen).

Low Cost

The primary reason for competitive performance of index funds is lower cost. This lower cost takes two forms: (1) lower management fees and (2) lower transaction costs associated with lower portfolio turnover rates. This lower cost advantage is durable and predictable — year after year. Don Phillips, President of Morningstar, summarizes the impact of higher costs: "if you pay the executive at Sara Lee more, it doesn't make the cheesecake less good. But with mutual funds (investment management), it comes directly out of the batter." Indeed it does!

Consistent Relative Performance

Exhibit 2 shows the performance for the largest bond index mutual fund against its Lipper universe (Intermediate Government) for calendar years starting in 1989.

In fairness, this portfolio has approximately 30% in corporates (the other 70% is U.S. Treasury and agency securities, and agency mortgage-backed securities), so a comparison against a government universe is not entirely appropriate. The only year where the portfolio outperformed less than 50% of the universe was 1990 (42%). For all the other years the portfolio outperformed between 65% to 88% of the competition in its maturity and quality category. The primary reason for this consistent outperformance is the significantly lower expenses and transaction costs incurred by the portfolio.

Market Performance Predictability

A properly managed broad bond index portfolio can be assured of performing in line with the market as a whole. Therefore, regardless of the direction the market takes, the investor can be assured of the performance of a diversified broad index (the "market").

Time Tested

Bond index portfolios have been successfully managed since the early 1980s — through rising and falling interest rate cycles as well as through increasing and declining credit spread cycles. Through all these market changes, bond indexing has proven to provide a more than competitive return with low to moderate risk.

Redirects Focus to Most Important Decision — Asset Allocation

Perhaps the most significant reason to index bonds is that it enables investors to concentrate on the more important asset allocation decision. Very often, limited decision-making time and effort is wasted on the hope of adding 20-40 basis points on the bond portion of a portfolio, when existing misallocation of assets to stocks or international investments are resulting in hundreds of basis points of underperformance for the entire portfolio. Indexing helps facilitate more effective use of limited decision-making resources available to most investors.

Exhibit 2: Annual Performance Consistency Analysis
Index Portfolio versus Lipper Intermediate Government

	Index Portfolio Return (%)	Lipper Rank	Total in Lipper Group	Percent Outperformed (%)
1989	13.65	4	25	84
1990	8.65	15	26	42
1991	15.25	5	24	79
1992	7.14	4	32	88
1993	9.68	12	50	76
1994	-2.66	27	77	65
1995	18.18	13	98	87
1996 (Oct.)	2.67	37	124	71

Exhibit 3: Lehman Brothers Aggregate Bond Index Composition (As of 9/30/96)

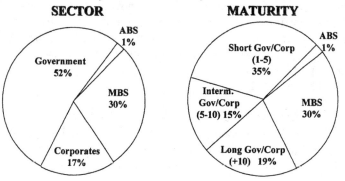

SECTOR

Government 52%
ABS 1%
MBS 30%
Corporates 17%

MATURITY

Short Gov/Corp (1-5) 35%
ABS 1%
Interm. Gov/Corp (5-10) 15%
MBS 30%
Long Gov/Corp (+10) 19%

WHICH INDEX SHOULD BE USED?

A bond index is defined by a set of rules (characteristics) that are then applied to all issues in the marketplace. The rules include maturity, size, sector, and quality characteristics. The issues that fit the rules are then combined, as if in a portfolio, with each issue's weight determined by its relative market value outstanding.

For indexing, the broader the Index (for a given level of risk) the better the benchmark. The broadest U.S. bond index is the Lehman Brothers Aggregate Bond Index (essentially identical to the Salomon Broad Investment Grade Index and the Merrill Lynch Domestic Master Index). At September 30, 1996, the Lehman Brothers Aggregate Bond Index had more than 5,500 issues representing a market value of over $4.5 trillion. Exhibit 3 shows that the composition of the Aggregate Bond Index as of September 30, 1996 was 45% Treasury bonds, 7% agency bonds, 19% corporate and asset-backed bonds, and 29% mortgage-backed securities. The option-adjusted duration (a duration number that reflects the possibility of bonds being called by the issuer) was 4.7 years, with an average maturity of 8.7 years, making it the broadest domestic intermediate index available. Sub-indices of the Lehman Brothers Aggregate Bond Index can be created that result in different risk/return profiles. For example, a corporate-only index can be replicated for those who do not want as much quality as exists in the Lehman Brothers Aggregate Bond Index; or a 1-5 year government/corporate Index can be created, for those who would rather have a short duration portfolio.

Market Value Risk

Generally, the longer the maturity of the bond portfolio, the higher its yield, assuming a "normally" sloped yield curve. The total return on a bond is made up of the coupon (or income) component and the principal (or price change) component. Since the yield curve (which impacts the principal component of total return) is highly unlikely to remain unchanged, the longer bond portfolio will not necessarily have a higher total return. Exhibit 4 shows the 1-year total return of different maturity securities (short: 3 years; intermediate: 7 years; and, long: 20 years) in both high-rate and low-rate environments, assuming yields rise or fall 1%. Clearly, as the maturity or duration of the portfolio lengthens, the greater the market value risk. In addition, the lower the yield environment, the greater the market value risk, especially for the intermediate-term and long-term portfolios. This is the result of the portfolio having a longer duration (greater duration risk) in the low-rate environment, in which the portfolio's lower yield provides less of a cushion to offset principal losses. Therefore, for investors who are risk averse in terms of their principal, the short-term or intermediate-term index as a benchmark may be more appropriate than the long index.

Income Risk

Many investors invest for income, spending only the income distributed by an investment without dipping into principal. Foundations and retirees invest for a stable and hopefully growing income stream that they can depend on for current and future consumption. Exhibit 5 shows the income stream (distributed mutual fund income) from a $10,000 investment in a short (3-year), intermediate (7-year), and long (20-year) mutual fund over the last 15 years, assuming equivalent growth rates for the portfolios. It's obvious that if stability and durability of income are the primary concerns, than the long portfolio is the least risky and the short portfolio is the most risky.

Liability Framework Risk

Pension funds and financial institutions invest to finance future liabilities. Long-term liabilities (like active retired lives liabilities) require investments in long-term assets to minimize risk, resulting in both a portfolio and a liability stream that is equally sensitive to interest-rate changes. A portfolio that invests in short bonds may look less risky on an absolute return basis, but it is actually much riskier (because of its mismatch with long liabilities) when the portfolio market value is compared to the present value of the pension liability (the difference is the surplus or deficit). The "surplus" risk will be minimized on a fully funded plan against small changes in market rates when the duration of the portfolio is matched (or immunized) to the duration of the liability.

Exhibit 4: Market Value Risk

High Interest Rate Environment				1 Year Return (Income + Price Return	
Coupon	Maturity	Price	Duration	Rates Rise 1%	Rates Fall 1%
12	3 year	100	2.5	9.6	14.5
12	7 year	100	4.6	7.5	16.8
12	20 year	100	7.5	4.9	20.0

Low Interest Rate Environment				1 Year Return (Income + Price Return)	
Coupon	Maturity	Price	Duration	Rates Rise 1%	Rates Fall 1%
6	3 year	100	2.7	3.3	8.8
6	7 year	100	5.6	0.5	11.8
6	20 year	100	11.6	−4.7	18.6

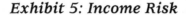

Exhibit 5: Income Risk

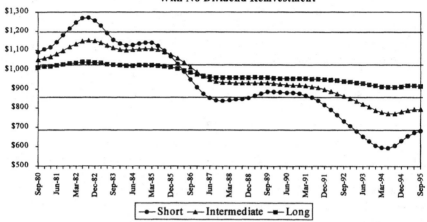

Dividend Volatility Analysis
Assumes Initial $10,000 Investment
With No Dividend Reinvestment

Exhibit 6: Bond Market Risk Summary

NAV Type	Market Value Risk	Income or Liability Risk	Average Maturity	Current Duration	Portfolios
Stable Dollar NAV	Lowest	Highest	30-90 Days	0.1	Money Market Portfolios
Variable NAV	Low	High	2-4 Years	2.5	Short-Term Portfolios
	Medium	Medium	7-10 Years	5.0	Intermediate-Term Portfolios
	High	Low	15-25 Years	10.0	Long-Term Portfolios

Exhibit 6 contains a summary comparison showing that the investment with the lowest market value risk has the highest income or liability risk. Likewise, the investment with the highest market value risk has the lowest income or liability risk. Clearly, the risk framework chosen depends on whether the investment objective is principal preservation or income durability.

PRIMARY BOND INDEXING RISK FACTORS

Effective bond indexing does not require full replication, nor is it desired. What is required is matching the primary risk factors of the benchmark index in a credit diversified portfolio. Exhibit 7 lists the primary risk factors that apply to the government, corporate, and mortgage sectors, accompanied by an explanation of these primary risk factors.

Exhibit 7: Primary Bond Index Matching Factors

	Government	Corporate	MBS
Modified Adjusted Duration	X	X	
Present Value of Cash Flows	X	X	
Percent in Sector and Quality		X	
Duration Contribution of Sector		X	
Duration Contribution of Credit Quality		X	
Sector/Coupon/Maturity Cell Weights		X	X
Issuer Exposure Control		X	

Modified Adjusted Duration

The modified adjusted duration (or option-adjusted modified duration) is a simple single measure of interest rate risk of the portfolio. It's a great place to start, but is entirely too rough of a measure to adequately track an index. The portfolio duration will give the manager a rough approximation of the price change observed if interest rates rise or fall (in a parallel fashion) immediately by 1%. If rates rise by 1%, a 5-year duration portfolio will experience an approximate 5% decline in value ((+1% yield change) × (5-year portfolio duration) × (−1)). If the yield curve does not move in a parallel fashion, then the duration is of limited value. For obvious reasons, it is important to match the duration of the portfolio to the duration of the benchmark index.

Present Value Distribution of Cash Flows

A more accurate way to capture yield curve risk is by matching the cash flow distribution of the index. Yield curve changes are composed of parallel shifts, curve twists (e.g., short rates down, intermediate rates unchanged, long rates up), and curve butterfly (e.g., short and long rates down, intermediate rates up) movements. By decomposing the index (and portfolio) into a stream of future payments and discounting each payment to the present value and summing these values, one calculates the index (and portfolio) market value. By matching the percent of the portfolio's present value that comes due at certain intervals in time (each vertex) with that of the benchmark index, the portfolio will be largely protected from tracking error (versus the benchmark) associated with yield curve changes. Since the portfolio duration is equal to the benchmark index duration (duration is the sum of all vertices (Exhibit 8), of the percent of present value multiplied by the vertex (time)), this method will guard against parallel changes in yield. Since all points in time (vertices) are closely matched in percent, any local term structure movements (non-parallel changes) will not affect tracking (these yield change risks are essentially immunized). For callable securities, the cash flows need to be distributed to the vertices in accordance with the probability of call. A 10-year bond that is highly likely to be called in three years should have cash flows that are primarily allocated to the 3-year vertex.

Exhibit 8: Cash Flow Distribution Analysis

Time	Percent of Value	Duration Contribution	Percent of Duration
0	3.1	0.00	0.0
0.5	6.6	0.03	0.7
1	8.5	0.09	1.8
1.5	10.1	0.15	3.2
2	13.1	0.26	5.6
3	13.1	0.39	8.4
4	10.2	0.41	8.6
5	7.4	0.37	7.9
6	5.2	0.31	6.6
7	4.5	0.32	6.8
8	3.7	0.29	6.2
9	3.4	0.30	6.4
10	2.7	0.27	5.7
12	2.4	0.29	6.1
15	2.2	0.33	7.0
20	2.3	0.45	9.7
25	1.0	0.24	5.1
30	0.6	0.18	3.8
40	0.0	0.01	0.3
Total	100.0	4.70	100.0

Percent in Sector and Quality

The yield of the index is largely replicated by matching the percentage weight in the various sectors and qualities, assuming that all maturity categories are fully accounted for by the replicating portfolio. Exhibit 9 shows the Lehman Brothers Aggregate Bond Index weights in the various sectors and qualities as of 9/30/96.

Duration Contribution of Sector

The best way (without excessively constraining the process) to protect a portfolio from tracking differences associated with changes in sector spreads (industry risk) is to match the amount of the index duration (Exhibit 9) that comes from the various sectors. If this can be accomplished, a given change in sector spreads will have an equal impact on the portfolio and the index.

Duration Contribution of Quality

Similarly, the most effective way to protect a portfolio from tracking differences related to changes in quality spreads (leverage/economic risk) is to match the amount of the index duration that comes from the various quality categories. This is particularly important in the lower-rated categories, which are characterized by larger spread changes.

Exhibit 9: Sector and Quality Distribution Analysis

Sector	Percent of PV	Duration	Duration Contribution	Percent of Duration
Treasury	45.2	4.76	2.15	45.8
Agency	6.5	4.75	0.31	6.6
Industrial	6.1	6.28	0.38	8.2
Telephone	1.1	6.75	0.08	1.6
Electric/Gas	1.9	5.81	0.11	2.3
Finance	4.7	4.56	0.22	4.6
Canadian	1.1	6.55	0.07	1.6
Sovereign	0.9	5.34	0.05	1.0
Foreign Corporate	1.5	6.18	0.09	1.9
Supranational	0.3	6.12	0.02	0.4
GNMA	8.5	4.11	0.35	7.4
FNMA	9.9	3.95	0.39	8.3
FHLMC	1.3	4.02	0.45	9.6
Asset-Backed	1.0	2.90	0.03	0.6
Total	100.0	4.70	4.70	100.0
Quality				
AAA	83.2	4.49	3.73	79.5
AA	3.3	5.42	0.18	3.8
A	9.4	5.81	0.55	11.6
BAA	4.2	5.84	0.24	5.2
Total	100.0	4.70	4.70	100.0

Sector/Coupon/Maturity Cell Weights

The call exposure of an index is a difficult factor to replicate. The convexity value (convexity measures how a bond's duration changes as yield levels change) alone is inadequate since it measures expected changes in duration over a small change in yield levels. In addition, the change in convexity can be very different as yield levels change. Managers who attempt only to match the index convexity value often find themselves having to buy or sell highly illiquid callable securities to stay matched and, in the process, generate excessive transaction costs. A better method of matching the call exposure is to match the sector, coupon, and maturity weights of the callable sectors. By matching these weights, the convexity of the index should be matched. In addition, as rates change, the changes in call exposure (convexity) of the portfolio will be matched to the index, requiring little or no rebalancing.

In the mortgage market, call (prepayment) risk is very significant. The volatility in the option-adjusted duration of the Lehman Brothers Mortgage Index, which measures the extent of the call exposure of the mortgage market, is shown in Exhibit 10. Also shown in the exhibit is the Mortgage Bankers Refinancing Index (inverted), which measures the extent of mortgage refinancing occurring in the market. Clearly, the greater the refinancing activity, the shorter the index duration due to the greater likelihood that the higher coupons (issues priced above par) will be refinanced with lower coupon securities. For this reason, matching the coupon distribution of the mortgage index is critical. The best risk management is accomplished by matching the index weights in a multi-dimensional matrix of the maturity (balloon, 15-year, 30-year), sector (FNMA, FGLMC, GNMA), coupon (50 basis point increments), and seasoning (new, moderate, and seasoned). This level of detail is easily accomplished in a large portfolio (more than $1 billion in assets), but more difficult to accomplish in smaller portfolios.

Issuer Exposure

If the major risk factors described above are matched, but with too few issues, there remains significant risk that can still be diversified away. "Event" risk, a risk widely watched in the late 1980s, when there was significant corporate leveraging taking place (LBOs), is the final primary risk factor that needs to be measured and controlled. Issuer exposure, like sector and quality, needs to be measured in more than percentage terms only, versus the index benchmark. Setting percent of market value limits without regard to issuer duration risk and issuer index weights is not adequate. Immediately after a negative credit event, the spread widens. Therefore, the best measure of the issuer event risk impact on a portfolio is the impact on portfolio market value of that spread widening. This can be measured by calculating how much of the portfolio duration ("duration contribution") comes from the holdings in each issuer. This calculation should also be figured for the index. The basis point impact on tracking of a spread-widening event will be the spread change (of the issuer) multiplied by the difference in duration contribution (portfolio − index) multiplied by (−1).

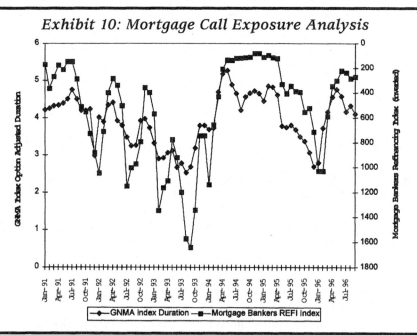

Exhibit 10: Mortgage Call Exposure Analysis

Exhibit 11: Issuer Exposure Comparison — Percent of Market Value versus Duration Contribution

	Portfolio		
	Percent of Market Value	Duration	Duration Contribution
XXX Corp	4	8	0.32
ZZZ Corp	4	4	0.16
XYZ Corp	4	2	0.08

	Index			Portfolio-Index	
	Percent of Market Value	Duration	Duration Contribution	Percent Difference	Contribution Difference
XXX Corp	4	4	0.16	0	0.16
ZZZ Corp	4	4	0.16	0	0.00
XYZ Corp	4	4	0.16	0	−0.08

Exhibit 11 contains an example of this analysis. Issuer XXX Corp has an equal percent weight to the Index, but its duration contribution is 0.16 greater. If an event occurred that would widen XXX Corp spreads by 100 basis points, the portfolio would suffer an unfavorable tracking difference of 16 basis points versus the index (100 basis point spread change × 0.16 duration contribution overweight × −1). If the same 100 basis points widening were to occur to XYZ Corp bonds, the tracking difference would be a favorable 8 basis points (100 basis point spread change × −0.08 duration contribution underweight × −1), even though the percent weight is matched to the index. For effective index fund management, duration contribution exposure limits (versus the index) need to be set at the issuer level.

BOND INDEX ENHANCEMENTS

Details, Details, Details

As in sailing, speed (returns versus the benchmark) comes from paying close attention to the details, not simply from "watching the wind" (interest rates). Portfolio managers can "trim" their portfolio sails to more efficiently compete in the investment management race. The trimming strategies include: (1) lower costs, (2) issue selection, (3) yield curve positioning, (4) sector and quality positioning, and (5) call exposure positioning.

Why Enhancements are Necessary

Since the index does not incur expenses or transaction costs, enhancements are necessary just to provide a net return equal to the index. A primary source of return shortfalls besides expenses is the transaction costs associated with portfolio growth.

Exhibit 12: Why Enhancements are Necessary
Analysis of the Tracking Impact of Growth
Single Contribution versus Multiple Contributions

	Portfolio Market Value	Contributions	Trans. Cost ($ at 18bp)	New Portfolio Value	Tracking Error from Trans Cost (bp)	Cumulative Tracking Error from Trans Cost (bp)
Single Contribution	$ —	$250,000,000	$450,000	$249,550,000	18.0	18.0
Multiple Contributions	$ —	$50,000,000	$90,000	$49,910,000	18.0	18.0
	$49,910,000	$50,000,000	$90,000	$99,820,000	9.0	27.0
	$99,820,000	$50,000,000	$90,000	$149,730,000	6.0	33.1
	$149,730,000	$50,000,000	$90,000	$199,640,000	4.5	37.6
	$199,640,000	$50,000,000	$90,000	$249,550,000	3.6	41.2
		$250,000,000	$450,000			

Exhibit 13: Why Enhancements are Necessary
Return Impact of Transaction Costs Over 1 Year

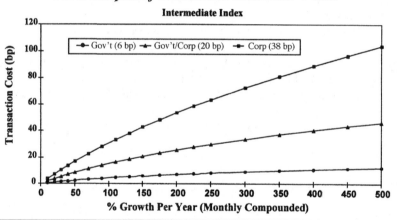

Exhibit 12 shows the transaction costs and resulting tracking error associated with single contribution growth versus multiple contribution growth. In the example, the single contribution portfolio had tracking error of 18 basis points associated with investing net cash flow. In the multiple contribution portfolio the tracking error is a significantly higher 41 basis points, even though the dollar cost of transaction costs is the same ($450,000). Therefore, portfolios with high growth rates will suffer additional negative tracking error, making enhancements necessary simply to stay equal to a no-growth or slow-growth portfolio.

Exhibit 13 shows in graphical form the cumulative adverse tracking impact resulting from portfolio growth for Treasury, government/corporate, and corporate portfolios. The greater the growth rate and/or the less liquid the market, the greater the adverse impact on tracking error.

Lower Cost Enhancements

One of the simplest but most overlooked forms of enhancements is to keep costs down. Costs that impact portfolio performance are expenses/management fees and transaction costs.

Enhanced indexers work hard to add an incremental 10 to 30 basis points per year to portfolio returns, yet in the mutual fund arena, the average bond fund expense ratio is 80 basis points greater than the lowest index portfolio expense ratio. As a result, returns of such funds are significantly lower. Even in the indexing arena, expenses vary by large margins. Simply shopping around for the index fund with the lowest expenses, provided the net return is competitive with other index funds, is a simple way to enhance returns. For a plan sponsor with outside index managers, having the existing manager and one or two other reputable indexers re-bid the business every few years will make sure the expenses are as low as possible.

The other major cost factor is transaction costs. Since bond index funds have low annual turnover (about 40%) versus active portfolios (generally over 100%), transaction costs are significantly lower for index portfolios. In addition, the development of a competitive trading process will further reduce the transaction cost impact. It's obvious when seeking bids to include many brokers in the bidding process. For rapidly growing portfolios, where most of the transactions are offerings, an effective competitive trading process is essential. Since there is no central exchange for corporate bonds, an efficient system of evaluating real-time offerings of target issuers from many different brokers to compare relative value, will yield significant transaction cost savings, hence further enhancing the returns.

Issue Selection Enhancements

For U.S. Treasury securities, the primary tool for selecting cheap bonds is comparing actual bond prices to the theoretical "fitted" price. The theoretical curve is derived that will minimize the pricing errors of all Treasury issues in the market, subject to various curve-smoothing rules. Each actual bond's yield is then compared to the bond's "fitted" yield (calculated using the theoretical curve). Bonds yielding more than the "fitted" yield are cheap, and those yielding less are rich. Another useful supplement is an analysis of the recent history of the bond yield versus the fitted yield. This analysis will indicate whether a cheap bond has been getting cheaper or richer.

Corporate issue selection enhancements come primarily from staying clear of deteriorating credits, and owning (generally overweighted versus the index) improving credits. The greater the quality of the credit opinion (based on the quality and timeliness of the credit analyst), the larger can be the maximum issuer exposure limit. (This is discussed later in this chapter.)

Yield Curve Enhancements

Various maturities along the term structure are consistently overvalued or undervalued. For example, the 30-year Treasury region tends to be consistently overvalued, resulting in an inverted yield curve from 25 to 30 years. Likewise, the high-coupon callable bonds maturing in 2009-2012 tend to be consistently undervalued. Strategies that overweight the undervalued maturities and underweight the overvalued maturities, while keeping the same general term structure exposure, will tend to outperform the index. This analysis is similar to looking for the maturities that have the more favorable "roll down" characteristics — meaning that the near-term passage of time may result in the bond rolling down the yield curve and, therefore, it will trade at a lower yield resulting in potential price appreciation. Cheap parts of the curve tend to have favorable "roll down," while rich parts of the curve (e.g., 30-year area) tend to have little or no "roll down" opportunities.

Sector/Quality Enhancements

Sector and quality enhancements take two primary forms: (1) ongoing yield tilt toward short duration corporates and (2) periodic minor over or underweighting of sectors or qualities.

The ongoing yield tilt enhancement (also called "corporate substitution") strategy recognizes that the best yield spread per unit of duration risk is available in short-term corporates (under 5 years). A strategy that underweights 1-5 year government bonds and overweights 1-5 year corporates will increase the yield of the portfolio with a less than commensurate increase in risk. Exhibit 14 shows the rolling 12-month return differential of the Lehman Brothers 1-5 Year Corporate Index versus the Lehman Brothers 1-5 Year Treasury Index.

Exhibit 14: Lehman 1-5 year Corporate Index versus Lehman 1-5 year Treasury Index

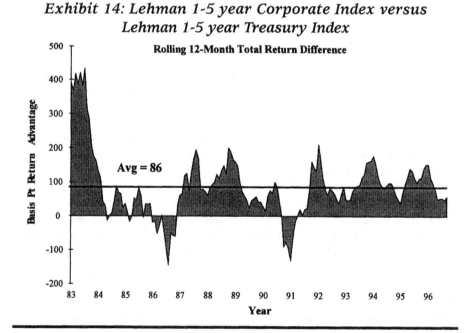

Exhibit 15: Breakeven Spread Widening Analysis — Corporates versus Treasuries

Maturity	Wide Spreads	Breakeven additional Widening	Moderate Spreads	Breakeven additional Widening	Narrow Spreads	Breakeven additional Widening
2 year	60	75	40	53	20	32
3 year	70	48	50	37	30	26
5 year	80	29	60	23	40	17
10 year	100	19	75	14	55	11
30 year	130	12	100	9	75	7

The persistent return enhancement is obvious for all periods except the brief spread widening periods of 1986-87 and 1990-91. The primary reason the strategy is effective is that the yield advantage of short corporates requires a significant corporate spread widening move over a 1-year period for short corporates to perform as poorly as short Treasuries. Exhibit 15 shows the spread increases that would be required to break-even with equal risk Treasury securities over a 1-year holding period for corporates of varying maturities and spreads levels. With the passage of time, the duration of corporate bonds shorten, and the yield spread over comparable Treasury securities generally narrows (positive credit curve spread). These two risk reducing and return enhancing forces, when combined with the yield spread advantage, provide compelling reasons to overweight short corporates. Even at narrow spreads, significant protection is available in maturities under five years. A 2-year corporate with a yield spread of 20 basis points, can widen by 32 basis points versus a comparable Treasury security over the next year before it performs as poorly as the comparable Treasury security. Clearly, as the maturities increase, the spread widening protection decreases.

The risks involved in the strategy are recessionary spread widening risk and issuer default risk. The recessionary spread widening risk tends to be short lived and quickly overcome by the increased yield advantage of the strategy. The issuer default risk can be minimized by broad issuer diversification (50 or more issuers) and by credit analyst oversight.

The periodic over- or underweighting of sectors and qualities is a scaled back version of active "sector rotation." The primary way this can be implemented on a cost effective basis is to allow new cash flow (net new portfolio growth) to facilitate the mismatching. For example, if spreads are narrow going into the fourth quarter and the manager expects some widening, new money may be invested primarily in Treasury securities, resulting in a gradual reduction in the corporate exposure versus the index. Once the corporate spread widening materializes, Treasury securities (with low transaction costs) can be sold and corporates overweighted. Expected first quarter asset growth will eventually bring the corporate weighting back in line with the Index. A strategy of outright selling of corporates to buy Treasury securities is always difficult to justify because of the higher corporate transaction costs involved, in addition to the yield "penalty" associated with Treasury securities.

Call Exposure Enhancements

The option-adjusted duration of a callable bond is the average of what the model duration is, if rates rise and fall marginally. These durations (under rising and falling rates) can be quite different for bonds that are trading at a price where the bond changes from trading to maturity, to trading to call (or visa versa). The result is a situation where the actual performance of a bond could be significantly different than would be expected given its beginning of period option-adjusted duration.

Generally, the greater the expected yield change, the greater the desire to have more call protection. With regard to near-term yield changes: (1) for premium callable bonds (bonds trading to call), the empirical duration (observed price sensitivity) tends to be less than the option-adjusted duration, resulting in underperformance during declining rates and (2) for discount callable bonds (bonds trading to maturity), the empirical duration tends to be greater than the option-adjusted duration, resulting in underperformance in rising rates. Any large deviations from the index exposure to call risk should recognize the potential significant tracking implications and the market directionality of the bet.

MEASURING SUCCESS

Common sense dictates that "you can't manage what you can't measure." Managers know this to be true, yet so often find themselves without the tools necessary to measure the extent of their bets and the value added or lost from those bets. Measuring the extent of the bets was covered earlier in this chapter. This section will discuss how to measure whether any value has been added and from what bets.

Outperform Adjusted Index Returns

Returning to the sailing theme, how is the portfolio sailboat doing versus the index sailboat? Is the portfolio making any ground against the index? To evaluate relative performance, the portfolio returns need to be adjusted for each of the following: (1) pricing, (2) transaction costs of growth and rebalancing, and (3) expenses. Pricing is a critical factor that needs to be considered, especially in enhanced indexing where deviations versus the index are small and pricing errors can hide valuable information. If a Lehman Brothers Index is the benchmark, then the portfolio needs to be re-priced with Lehman Brothers prices. Small differences in either the time of pricing or the pricing matrix, may result in large differences (among pricing services) in periodic returns over short measurement periods. Over longer periods, these pricing differences will average zero, but for value-added measurement purposes, periodic pricing accuracy is critical.

Exhibit 16: Consistent Positive Tracking

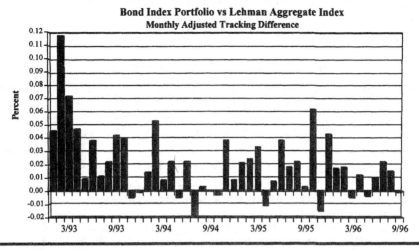

Bond Index Portfolio vs Lehman Aggregate Index
Monthly Adjusted Tracking Difference

Since the index does not have transaction costs associated with asset growth, principal reinvestment, or income reinvestment, accurate adjustments need to be made to portfolio returns to account for these differences. A simple way to account for this is to maintain a trading log with implied transaction costs as a percent of total portfolio assets. The periodic summation of these implied costs will provide a good estimate of tracking error drag associated with growth and income reinvestment.

Finally, an adjustment for expenses is required. As was discussed earlier, keeping low expenses is a simple way to enhance returns. Nevertheless, portfolio returns should be "grossed up" by these expenses to put the portfolio on equal footing with the index for measurement purposes.

Exhibit 16 shows the monthly *adjusted* tracking of the largest bond index (enhanced) mutual fund. This portfolio is managed against the Lehman Brothers Aggregate Bond Index. If the sources of enhancements are multiple and of a controlled nature, it's expected that the average tracking difference would be small and usually positive. As shown, the monthly tracking differences are small (between +12 basis points and -2 basis points) and mostly positive. Exhibit 17 shows a rolling 12-month summation of the monthly *adjusted* tracking differences. An enhanced indexing strategy that has good risk management and diversified enhancements should be able to consistently perform above the index. Falling below the index return over 12 months most likely would be the result of either not matching the index risk properly, or, of the enhancement strategies not be adequately diversified.

Low and Stable Monthly Tracking Differences

The other measure of success, from an indexing standpoint, is how closely the portfolio is exposed to the same risk factors of the index. This can be measured by evaluating the rolling 12-month standard deviation of *adjusted* tracking differences of the portfolio versus the index. Exhibit 18 is an example from the same bond index mutual fund managed against the Lehman Brothers Aggregate Bond Index. If a portfolio is properly exposed to the index risk factors, the standard deviation will be low and stable, as shown.

Detailed Performance Attribution

To accurately measure the success of risk factor management and the enhancement strategies, the manager needs excellent performance attribution tools. The performance attribution analysis should be able to attribute tracking error to term structure factors, sector bets, quality bets, and issue selection across sectors and qualities.

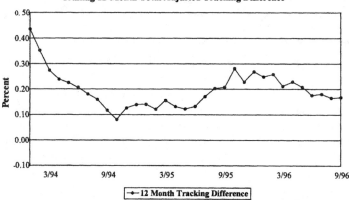

Exhibit 17: Consistent Positive Tracking

Bond Index Portfolio vs Lehman Aggregate Index
Trailing 12-Month Total Adjusted Tracking Difference

Exhibit 18: Consistently Low Tracking Error

Bond Index Portfolio vs Lehman Aggregate Index
Trailing 12-Month Standard Deviation of Adjusted Tracking Difference

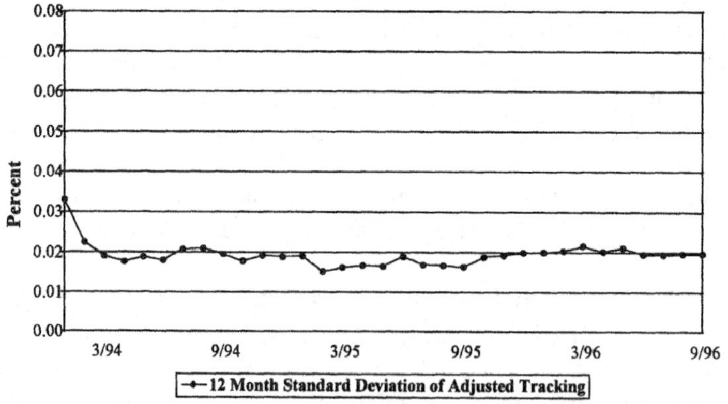

The term structure attribution should be analyzed at the portfolio level versus the index. The sector and quality attribution (allocation and issue selection) should be analyzed at the sector and sub-sector levels (detailed sector and maturity categories) with the ability to drill down to issue level detail. Issue performance should be risk adjusted (versus Treasury equivalent returns) with sub-sector, sector, and portfolio returns rolled up from the security level. This level of attribution will provide the manager with the tools to measure with precision the risk matching and return enhancing strategies, with the result being "winning the race" against the index and against most managers.

About the Author

Jack Malvey, CFA

Jack Malvey is a Managing Director and the Chief Global Fixed Income Strategist at Lehman Brothers. Prior to joining Lehman Brothers in 1992, Mr. Malvey was Director of Corporate Bond Research at Kidder Peabody and an analyst at Moody's Investor Service. A Chartered Financial Analyst, Mr. Malvey is a member of the Financial Management Association, the New York Society of Security Analysts, the Fixed Income Analysts Society, and the Society of Quantitative Analysts. Currently, he is president of the Fixed Income Analysts Society. Mr. Malvey received an A.B. in economics from Georgetown University and did graduate work in economics at the New School for Social Research in New York. Mr. Malvey has lectured at the Georgetown, Wharton, Columbia, Yale, and Polytechnic University graduate business schools. Mr. Malvey serves on the Advisory Council of Polytechnic University's Graduate Program in Financial Engineering. In 1993, 1994, 1995, and 1996, Mr. Malvey was elected to *Institutional Investor's* first team for corporate bond strategy.

Chapter 4

Global Corporate Bond Portfolio Management

Jack Malvey, CFA
Managing Director
Lehman Brothers

INTRODUCTION

The corporate bond market is the most fascinating subset of the global capital markets. Beyond the abstractions of rating symbols, media reports of new issues each day, and portfolio performance measurement, thousands of organizations with different credit "stories" sell debt to finance their expansion. These organizations range from Canadian provinces, development banks such as the Asian Development Bank, sovereigns like Italy, Poland, and Malaysia to corporations in North America, Europe, and Asia; their credit quality spans from impeccable to defaulted. These corporate borrowers use dozens of different types of debt instruments (first mortgage bonds, debentures, equipment trust certificates, subordinated debentures, medium-term notes, floating-rate notes, private placements, preferred stock) in multiple currencies (dollar, yen, Euro's, mark, Swiss franc, pound) at any maturity ranging from one year to a hundred years. Sometimes, these debt structures carry embedded options, which may allow for full or partial redemption prior to maturity at either the option of the corporate borrower or the investor. Sometimes, the coupon payment floats every quarter with short-term interest rates or resets to a higher rate after a fixed interval or a rating change.

Each day, hundreds of corporate bond portfolio managers face thousands of choices in the primary (new issue) and secondary markets. These portfolio managers consist of individuals in the pursuit of high yields, commercial banks arbitraging the difference between the higher yields on floating-rate notes and their lower cost of funding, mutual funds attempting to maximize both yield and total return, insurers and state pension funds seeking to fund their projected long-term liabilities, and "pure" total-return maximizers competing against each other on a monthly, quarterly, and annual basis to please their clients or risk their loss. These investment choices are partially driven by the existing security population of the corporate market (sector, issuer, structure, and currency) and partially by the psychology of the portfolio managers (overall risk tolerance, shortfall risk aversion, and internal politics of the investment-management institution).

61

Borrowers and investors intersect mainly through dealers. Each day, a few dozen corporate bond dealers convey information about secondary positions and new issue offerings from any of the thousands of corporate borrowers to the hundreds of corporate bond portfolio managers. Through their investment banking and syndicate operations, dealers also advise issuers on when and how to sell new debt. Through their fixed-income research, sales, and trading arms, dealers convey investment recommendations to portfolio managers.

The task of global corporate bond portfolio management is to process all of this rapidly-changing information about the corporate bond market (issuers, issues, dealers, and competing managers) and to construct the portfolio with the best risk-adjusted return. This discipline combines the excitement and qualitative tools of equity analysis with the quantitative precision of fixed-income analysis. This chapter provides a guide to methodologies which may help portfolio managers meet this formidable challenge.

CORPORATE RELATIVE-VALUE ANALYSIS

Should U.S. investors add Eurobonds of non-U.S. issuers? Should London portfolio managers buy fixed-rate U.S. industrial paper and swap into floating-rate notes? Should U.S. insurers buy perpetual floaters issued by British banks and swap back into fixed-rate corporates? When should investors fade the corporate sector and increase allocation to governments, pursue the "strategic upgrade trade" (sell Baa/BBBs and add higher-rated A corporate debt), rotate from industrials into Yankees, and deploy a credit derivative (i.e., short the high-yield index) to hedge their portfolios? To respond to such questions, investors need to begin with an analytical framework (relative-value analysis) and to develop a strategic outlook for the global corporate market.

Economists have long debated the concept and measurement of "value." But fixed-income practitioners, perhaps because of the daily pragmatism enforced by the markets, have developed a consensus about the definition of value. In the bond market, "relative value" refers to the ranking of fixed-income investments by sectors, structures, issuers, and issues in terms of their expected performance during some future interval.

For the day trader, relative value may carry a maximum horizon of a few minutes. For a large insurer, relative value may have a multi-year horizon. Accordingly, "relative-value analysis" refers to the methodologies used to generate such rankings of expected returns.

Within the global corporate market, "classic" relative-value analysis is a dialectical process combining the best of top-down and bottom-up approaches. This method picks the sectors with the most potential upside, populates these favored sectors with the best representative issuers, and selects the structures of the designated issuers at the curve points that match the investor's outlook for the benchmark curve.

For many corporate investors, the use of classic relative-value analysis has been sufficient to ensure a measure of portfolio success. Although sector, issuer, and structural analyses remain the core of superior relative-value analysis, the increased availability of information and technology has transformed the analytical process into a complex discipline. To assist their endeavors, corporate portfolio managers in the 1990s have far more data than ever on the total returns of sectors, issuers, and structures, quantity and composition of new-issue flows, distribution of product demand by investor classes, aggregate credit-quality movements, multiple sources of credit analyses on individual issuers, and spreads.

RELATIVE VALUE METHODOLOGIES

In this section, the main methodologies for corporate relative-value maximization are reviewed.

Total Return Analysis

Corporate relative-value analysis begins with a detailed dissection of past returns and a projection of expected returns. Capital markets have regular rhythms. For instance, the economic cycle is the major determinant of overall corporate spreads. During recessions, the escalation of default risk widens spreads (which are risk premiums over underlying, presumably default-free government securities). Conversely, economic prosperity reduces bankruptcies and tightens corporate spreads.

Thanks to the development of corporate indices (effectively databases of prices, spreads, issuer, and structure composition), analysis of monthly, annual, and multi-year total returns has uncovered numerous patterns (i.e., seasonality, election-cycle effects, and auction effects) in the global corporate market. Admittedly, these patterns do not always reoccur. But an awareness and understanding of these total-return patterns are essential to optimizing portfolio performance.

Total return analysis also justifies portfolio objectives and constraints. After years of admonitions by various academics, market analysts, and consultants, total return data have been used to justify the relaxation of credit-quality constraints for many U.S. corporate portfolios during the 1990s.

Primary Market Analysis

Supply is often a misunderstood variable in the tactical relative-value calculus. Prospective new supply induces many traders, analysts, and investors to advocate a defensive stance toward the overall corporate market as well as toward individual sectors and issuers. Yet the premise, "supply will hurt spreads" is more cliche than fact. In the first quarters of 1991, 1992, 1993, and the first two months of 1996, origination surges were associated with market spread contraction and strong relative returns for corporates. In contrast, the sharp supply decline during the first quarter of 1994 was accompanied by spread expansion and a major decline in both relative and absolute returns for corporates.

In the investment-grade corporate market, heavy supply often helps spreads/returns as the new primary valuations validate and enhance secondary valuations. When primary origination declines sharply, secondary traders lose reinforcement from the primary market and tend to raise their bid spreads. Counter to intuition and cliche, relative corporate returns often perform best during periods of heavy supply.

Given their immediate focus on the deals of the day and week, portfolio managers often overlook market-structure dynamics in making portfolio decisions. Because the pace of change in market structure is gradual, market dynamics have less effect on short-term tactical investment decision-making than on long-term strategy.

The composition of the global corporate bond market has shifted markedly during the 1980s and 1990s. Medium-term note (MTN) origination has come to dominate the front end of the corporate curve. Rule 144A bonds (quasi-private placement bonds) have captured a growing share of Yankee, high yield, and emerging-market debt. Structured notes and index swaps have heralded the introduction of derivative instruments into the mainstream of the corporate market. The high-yield corporate sector has become just another asset class after having been stress-tested in 1989-1990. Global origination has become a more popular technique for agencies, supranationals, sovereigns, Canadians, and some large corporate borrowers.

Although the growth of derivatives and high-yield instruments stands out during the past decade, the globalization of the corporate market has been the most profound development. The rapid growth of the Eurobond market since 1975 and the emergence of the Dragon bond market (dollar offerings initially made only in Asia) in the early 1990s have led to the proliferation of truly transnational corporate portfolios. From a broad viewpoint, the rapid development of the emerging-debt market may be seen as a subset of this globalization process.

Partially offsetting this proliferation of issuers, the global corporate market has become structurally more homogeneous during the past decade for three reasons. First, there has been a continued shift away from utility issuers, who had preferred long-dated maturities to fund long-term capital assets. Second, new origination was less costly at the front of very steep yield curves. Third, the emergence and tremendous growth of the swap market made intermediate origination more convenient.

The trend toward bullet securities does not pertain to the high-yield market, where callables remain the structure of choice. With the hope of credit-quality improvement, many issuers expect to refinance prior to maturity at lower rates.

There are three strategic portfolio implications for this structural evolution. First, scarcity value must be considered in corporate relative-value analysis. The dominance of bullet structures translates into scarcity value for structures with embedded call and put features. This aspect is not captured by option-valuation models.

Second, long-dated maturities will decline as a percentage of outstanding corporate debt. This shift will lower the effective duration of all outstanding corporate debt and reduce aggregate sensitivity to interest-rate risk. For asset/liability managers with long horizons, this shift of the maturity distribution suggests a rise in the value of long corporates and helps to explain the warm reception afforded to every new Century offering (100-year maturity).

Third, corporate derivatives are in their adolescence. The maturation of corporate bond derivatives, whether on a stand-alone basis or embedded in structured notes, will give rise to new strategies for investors and issuers.

Liquidity and Trading Analysis

Short-term and long-term liquidity influence portfolio management decisions. Citing lower expected liquidity, some investors are reluctant to purchase equipment trust certificates, Rule 144A's, private placements, MTN's, and non-local corporate issuers. Other investors gladly exchange a potential liquidity disadvantage for incremental yield. For investment-grade issuers, these liquidity concerns often are exaggerated.

During the past decade, secondary trading has boomed from an accumulation of factors: the great refunding blitz of the early 1990s; the resulting multiplier effect of record origination as most new issues were sold partially on swap against existing issues; the market volatility triggered by the 1990-1991 recession; a variety of secular sector swings (such as buying U.S. bank debt in the early 1990s); the effects of the descent of the yield curve as investors sought call protection in bullets, some defense against the yield curve in put structures in 1994, and short-term yield maximization in high-coupon callables in 1992-1993; the cyclical steepening of the yield curve, which facilitated the expansion of dealer inventories to take advantage of the "positive carry trade;" the entrants of new dealers into the corporate bond market, especially from the ranks of commercial banks; the conversion of some total-return managers to an equity-style approach; and the conversion of some insurers to a total-return style approach.

Secondary Trade Rationales

Capital-market and issuer expectations constantly change. Recession may arrive sooner rather than later. The yield curve may have steepened instead of flattened. The auto and paper cycles may be moving down from their peaks. An industrial may have announced a large debt-financed acquisition, earning an immediate ratings rebuke from the agencies. A major bank may plan to repurchase 20% of its outstanding common stock, great for shareholders but leading to higher financial leverage for debtholders. In response to daily information flows, portfolio managers amend their portfolios. To understand trading flows and the real dynamics of the corporate market, investors should consider the most common rationales to trade and to not trade. There are dozens of rationales to execute secondary trades. Several of the most popular are discussed below.

Yield/Spread Pickup Trades

These trades represent the most common secondary transaction across all sectors of the global corporate market. Based on our observation, 60% of all secondary swaps reflect investor intentions to add additional yield within the duration and credit-quality constraints of a portfolio. If 5-year, A3/A– GMAC paper trades at 60 bp, 10 bp behind 5-year, A1/A+ Ford Motor Credit at 50 bp, then some investors will deem the rating differential irrelevant and swap into GMAC for a spread gain of 10 bp per annum. This "yield-first psychology" mirrors the institutional yield needs of long-term asset/liability managers, commercial banks, and mutual funds. Despite the passage of two decades, this investor bias toward yield maximization also may be a methodological relic left over from the era prior to the introduction and market acceptance of total-return indices in the mid-1970s. There is empirical support for the effectiveness "yield-first psychology." Baa corporates (11.01%) outperformed A-rated securities (10.09%) by 92 bp from 1973 through 1995 according to Lehman indices. But this tactic is not without risk. As measured by the standard deviation of total return, Baa returns (11.91%) have been considerably more volatile than A's (10.62%). In general, yield/spread maximization works reasonably during periods of economic growth.

Credit-Upside Trades

Credit-upside trades are closely related to yield/spread maximization transactions. In the illustration of the GMAC and Ford Motor Credit trade described above, some investors may swap based on their view of potential credit-quality improvement for GMAC. Credit-upside trades are particularly popular in the crossover sector (securities with ratings between Ba2/BB to Baa3/BBB- by either rating agency). From the early 1990s through the mid-1990s, such notable issuers as Chrysler, McDonnell Douglas, and Transco Energy regained investment-grade status and produced exceptional relative returns for holders.

Credit-Defense Trades

Credit-defense trades become more popular with the gathering of economic storm clouds. Secular sector transformations often generate uncertainties and induce defensive repositioning by investors. In anticipation of greater competition, some investors have reduced their portfolio exposures in the mid-1990s to sectors like electric utilities and telecommunication firms. Unfortunately because of yield-maximization needs and a general reluctance to realize losses by some institutions (i.e., insurers), many investors tend to react more slowly to credit-defense propositions. Ironically once a credit sours sufficiently to invoke the wrath of the rating agencies, internal portfolio guidelines often dictate security liquidation immediately after the loss of single-A or investment-grade status. This is usually the worst possible time to sell a security and maximizes the harm incurred by the portfolio.

New-Issue Swaps

New-issue swaps contribute to secondary turnover. Because of perceived superior liquidity, many portfolio managers prefer to rotate their portfolios gradually into more current, on-the-run issues. This disposition, reinforced by the usually superior market behavior of newer issues in the U.S. Treasury market, has become a self-fulfilling prophecy for some issues. In addition, some portfolio managers buy certain new issues to generate sufficient commissions to pay vendors through soft dollars. Rarely, an underwriter may insist on cash-only purchases for "hot" transactions. As a result of these practices, investors usually pay for their new-issue purchases through some combination of cash and swap of an existing security in their portfolio.

Sector-Rotation Trades

Sector-rotation trades, within corporates and among fixed-income asset classes, have become more popular during the 1990s but do not rival the activity in the equity market. As soon as the Fed launched its preemptive strike against inflation in February 1994, some investors exchanged fixed-rate corporates for floating-rate corporates. In 1995, the specter of U.S. economic weakness prompted some investors in high-yield corporates to rotate from consumer-cyclical sectors like autos and retailing into consumer non-cyclical sectors like food, beverage, and healthcare.

Curve-Adjustment Trades

Curve-adjustment trades are undertaken to reposition overall portfolio duration. For most corporate investors, their portfolio duration resides within a range from 20% below to 20% above the index duration. If corporate investors could have predicted yield curve movements perfectly in 1994 and 1995, then they would have lowered their portfolio duration at the beginning of 1994 and extended their duration in late 1994. Although most fixed-income investors prefer to reconfigure the duration of their aggregate portfolios in the more-liquid Treasury market, strategic portfolio duration tilts also can be implemented in the corporate market.

Structure Trades

These trade also gain appeal with movements in volatility and the shape of the yield curve. As shown during the second quarter of 1995, the rapid descent of the yield curve contributed to underperformance of callable structures. With curve stabilization during the third quarter of 1995, investors were more willing to trade into an extra 35 bp of spread for high-quality callables compared to bullets of similar quality and less put off by the possible cost of negative convexity.

Cash Flow Reinvestment

Cash flow reinvestment needs force investors into the secondary market on a regular basis. Some cash flows arrive during interludes in the primary market. And sometimes, the composition of recent primary supply may not be compatible with portfolio objectives.

Bias for Activity

Bias for activity affects both passive (indexers) and active managers as well as dealers. Referring to the overall capital markets, the late Fisher Black perfectly characterized some of this activity as "noise trading." Dealers closely monitor the aging of their security inventories. Stale positions, usually on the books for more than 90 days, justifiably are viewed with suspicion by risk managers. Ancient holdings may be worth less than their marks, otherwise they would have been purchased by investors. Accordingly, all corporate traders seek to limit their stale positions. At the same time in their quest for portfolio optimization, indexers are rebalancing their portfolios to conform with the ever shifting composition of indices and active managers are surfing among primary and secondary flows for the slightest glimmer of incremental value. The sum total of dealer activity, indexer realignments to cut tracking error, and active managers searching for valuation nuances breeds a natural bias for activity in the global corporate market.

Trading Constraints

Market analysts should also understand the main rationales for not trading.

Portfolio Constraints

Collectively, these inhibitions are the single biggest contributor to the persistence of market inefficiency across the global corporate market. Many U.S. state pensions cannot purchase corporate securities with ratings below A3/A- and Rule 144A's under administrative and legislative guidelines. Some pension funds also have limitations on MTN's and non-U.S. corporations. Regulators have limited the exposure of U.S. insurers to high-yield corporates. At the same, many European investors are restricted to issues, rated at least single-A and sometimes Aa, manufactured originally in annual-pay Eurobond form. Globally, many commercial banks must operate exclusively in the floating-rate realm; all fixed-rate securities, unless swapped, are out of bounds.

"Story" Disagreement

Traders, salespersons, sell-side analysts and strategists, and buy-side colleagues have dozens of potential trade rationales that will supposedly benefit portfolio performance. The proponents of the secondary trade may have a legitimate point, but the portfolio manager may be unwilling to accept the "shortfall" risk if the investment recommendation does not pan out.

Buy-and-Hold

Although many long-term asset/liability managers claim to have become more total-return focused in the 1990s, accounting constraints (cannot sell positions at a loss compared to book cost or take too extravagant a gain compared to book cost) limit the ability of these investors to transact. Effectively, these investors are traditional "buy-and-hold" investors.

Administrative Burdens

Compliance and accounting demands have soared during the 1990s. Many portfolio managers spend almost 50% of their schedule on these administrative chores. Moreover, some investors are burdened with multiple functions: analysis; portfolio management; and marketing. In particular, portfolio managers with heavy marketing obligations to existing and potential clients may be limited in their capability to react to short-term valuation anomalies in the corporate bond market.

Seasonality

Secondary trading slows at month ends, more so at quarter ends, and the most at the conclusion of calendar years. Dealers often prefer to reduce balance sheets at year-end. And portfolio managers take time to mark their portfolios, prepare reports for their clients, and chart strategy for the next period. During these intervals, some of the most compelling secondary offerings can languish.

Spread Analysis

By custom, some segments of the high yield and Eurobond markets still prefer to measure value by bond price or bond yield rather than spread. But for the rest of the global corporate market, nominal spreads (the yield difference between corporate and government bonds of similar maturities) have become the basic units of both price and relative-value analysis. Eventually, the Eurobond and high-yield markets also will switch to spreads to be consistent with other markets.

Unlike the mortgage-backed securities market, the corporate market has not adopted and is not likely to adopt option-adjusted spreads or zero-volatility spreads as measures of price/value for two reasons. First, almost all Eurobonds and MTN's as well as a growing percentage of public investment-grade corporate debt (87% in 1995) are bullet securities that do not feature embedded options. Second, the standard one-factor binomial models in use today do not take into account credit-spread volatility.

Investors should develop a rigorous understanding of the strengths and weaknesses of spread tools. The most common technique for analyzing spreads among individual securities and across industry sectors is mean-reversion analysis. Buy this *cheap* sector or issuer because the spread used to be much tighter. Sell this *rich* sector or issuer because the spread used to be much wider.

Mean-reversion analysis can be instructive as well as misleading. The mean is highly dependent on the interval selected. And there is no market consensus on the appropriate interval.

Quality-spread analysis examines the spread differentials between low and high-quality credits. "Percent yield spread" analysis (the ratio of corporate yields to government yields for securities of similar duration) is another popular technical tool with some investors. This methodology has serious drawbacks that undermine its usefulness. Percent yield spread is more a derivative than an explanatory or predictive variable.

Structure Analysis

Leaving aside credit, issue structure analysis and structural allocation decisions usually hinge on yield curve and volatility forecasts as well as interpretation of option-valuation model outputs (see the discussion below). In the short run, these factors largely will influence structural performance. But investors should also take into account long-run market dynamics.

Specifically, callable structures have become a rare species in the investment-grade corporate bond market. Thanks to an almost continuous positively-sloped yield curve during the 1990s, the curve's decline to approximately three-decade lows in 1993, the composition of the public U.S. corporate bond market has been converging toward its intermediate-bullet Eurobond cousin. Bullets climbed from 24% of Lehman's investment-grade index at the start of 1990 to 76% at year-end 1995. Over the same interval, callables declined at an astounding rate from 72% to an 18% index share. Sinking-fund structures, once the structural mainstay of natural-gas pipelines and many industrial sectors, are on the "structural endangered species list" with a drop from 32% of the public bond market in 1990 to only 4% in 1995. Despite a flurry of origination in 1994 and early 1995, put market share also has fallen from 5% in 1990 to 3% in 1995. Pure corporate zero's are in danger of extinction with a fall from 4% market share in 1990 to negligible in 1995 (only 12 bonds left).

Bullets

Front-end bullets (1-5 year maturities) have great appeal to the growing cadre of barbellers (use corporates at the front of the curve and Treasuries in longer maturities) and asset swappers (non-U.S. institutions who convert short bullets into floating-rate products). Intermediate corporates (5-12 maturities), especially in the 10-year neighborhood, have become the most popular segment of the U.S. investment-grade and high-yield corporate markets. Fifteen-year maturities are comparatively rare and have been favored by banks who occasionally uncover arbitrages in the asset-swap market. Because 15-year structures take five years to roll down a positively-sloped yield curve, these structures hold less appeal for many investors.

In contrast, 20-year structures are favored by many investors. Spreads for these structures are benched off the 30-year Treasury. With a positively-sloped yield curve, the 20-year structure provides higher yield than a 10-year or 15-year security and less vulnerability (lower duration) than a 30-year security.

The 30-year maturity is the most popular form of long-dated security in the global market. But in 1992, 1993, and late 1995, there was a minor rush to issue 50-year (half-Centuries) and 100-year (Centuries) securities. These longer-dated securities provide investors with extra positive convexity for only a modest increase in modified-adjusted duration.

Callables

Typically after a 5-year or 10-year wait, these structures are callable at the option of the issuer at any time. Call prices usually are set at a premium above par (par +

the initial coupon) and decline linearly on an annual basis to par 5-10 years prior to final scheduled maturity. The ability to refinance debt in a potentially lower-interest rate environment is extremely valuable to issuers. Conversely, the risk of earlier-than-expected retirement of an above-current market coupon is bothersome to investors. To place callables, issuers pay investors an annual spread premium (about 30 bp to 40 bp for high-quality issuers) for being short the call option. This call premium varies through time. During 1993, some high-quality issuers sold new 30-year callable structures at market-clearing spread premiums of only about 20 bp over a bullet to the same maturity. In 1994, callable spread premiums rose with rates. By the second quarter of 1995, callable spread premiums for some high-quality issuers like DuPont, Wal-Mart, and Wisconsin Power & Light had risen to 40 bp to 45 bp over a bullet to the same maturity.

Sinking Funds
This structure allows an issuer to execute a series of partial call (annually or semi-annually) prior to maturity. There is also usually a provision to retire an additional portion of the issue on the sinking fund date, typically ranging from 1 to 2 times the mandatory sinking fund obligation.

Putables
Put structures are simpler than callables. Unlike American-option callables (allow call at any time at the designated call price after expiration of the noncallable/nonredemption period), puts typically feature a single one-time, one-date put option (European option). Less frequently, put bonds offer a second or third put option. With falling rates, issuers have shied away from new put structures during the 1990s. Rather than run the risk of refunding the put bond in 5-years or 10-years at a higher cost, many issuers would prefer to pay an extra 10 bp to 20 bp for the privilege of issuing a longer-term liability. Put structures provide investors with a partial defense against sharp increases in interest rates.

Corporate Curve Analysis
The rapid development of credit derivatives in the mid-1990s has inspired a groundswell of academic interest in the development of more rigorous techniques to analyze the term structure of corporate spread curves. In particular, the corporate market has a fascination with the slope of issuer credit curves between 10-year and 30-year maturities. Like the underlying Treasury benchmark curve, corporate spread curves change shape over the course of economic cycles. Typically, spread curves steepen when the bond market becomes more wary of interest rate and general credit risk.

Credit Analysis: Cornerstone of Corporate Portfolio Analysis
Superior credit analysis has been and will remain the most important determinant of the relative performance of corporate bond portfolios. For too many years, investors and dealers have had to relearn the hard way that credit analysis has no

easy shortcuts or model magic. Specifically, variables like interest-rate volatility and binomial processes imported from option-valuation techniques are not especially helpful in ranking the expected performance of a pool of individual credits like British Gas, Commonwealth Edison, Pohang Iron & Steel, and Tenneco.

Credit analysis is both non-glamorous and arduous for many top-down portfolio managers and strategists, who focus primarily on macro variables. Genuine credit analysis encompasses actually studying issuers' financial statements, interviewing issuers' management, evaluating industry issues, reading indentures and charters, and developing an awareness of (not necessarily concurrence with) the views of the rating agencies about various industries and issuers.

Unfortunately, the advantages of such analytical rigor may clash with the rapid expansion of the universe of global bond credits. At the beginning of 1996, there were 4,000 different credits in the dollar-denominated corporate bond market. With continued privatization of state enterprises, new entrants to the high-yield club, and the rapid growth of the developing markets, the global roster of issuers could reach 5,000 by 2000.

Asset Allocation/Sector Rotation

Sector rotation strategies have long been popular with equity investors. In the corporate bond market, "macro" sector rotation strategies also have a long history. During the past two decades, there have been major shifts in investor sentiment toward the four major sectors: utilities (wariness of nuclear exposure in the early-to-mid 1980s); financial institutions (concern about asset quality in the late 1980s and early 1990s); industrials (event risk in the late 1980s and recession vulnerability during 1990-1992), and Yankees (periodic wariness about the implications of sovereignty for Quebec and political risk for sovereigns).

In contrast, "micro" sector rotation strategies have a briefer history in the corporate bond market. A detailed, unbundling of the four main corporate sectors into their prime subcomponents (i.e., breaking financial institutions down into banks, brokerage, finance companies, insurance, REITs) was not available from the firms providing corporate indices until 1993. During the mid-1990s, "micro" sector rotation strategies have become much more influential as portfolio managers gain a greater understanding of the relationships among intra-corporate sectors.

About the Author

Jeffrey D. Slater, CFA

Jeff Slater is a Vice President at General Reinsurance Corporation where he is currently responsible for the management of the firm's municipal bond portfolio. Mr. Slater began his career at General Reinsurance Corp. as a fixed income credit analyst. Prior to joining the firm, he was an analyst with Municipal Bond Investors Assurance (MBIA). Mr. Slater received a B.S. in Mathematics from Syracuse University and an M.B.A. in finance from the State University of New York at Albany, where he occasionally lectures. A Chartered Financial Analyst, Mr. Slater is a member of the New York Society of Securities Analysts.

Chapter 5

Managing Municipal Bond Portfolios

Jeffrey D. Slater, CFA
Vice President
General Reinsurance Corporation

BACKGROUND

The municipal bond market makes up a minor portion of the total domestic fixed income markets. However, with $1.3 trillion of debt outstanding at year-end 1995, this portion of the market warrants the attention of all fixed income portfolio managers, not just those with a mandate to shelter income. The municipal market encompasses all of the debt issued by state and local governments either directly, or through their issuing authorities. The municipal market is segregated from the Treasury and corporate bond markets due to the preferential income tax treatment that investors receive for holding municipal bonds. Tax preferences include the full exemption of interest on the federal level for those individual investors not subject to the alternative minimum tax, and an almost full exemption for property and casualty insurance companies. State income tax preferences do also exist for certain investors, as some states exempt interest from in-state bonds on their returns. The magnitude of these tax preferences, and how they affect each investor class, are normally the driving force behind security valuation.

The exemption of municipal bond interest on the federal level can be viewed in the context of a government sponsored interest rate subsidy to municipalities. Like all government aid programs, this subsidy may not always exist. The federal government exempts interest on bonds that are issued by a municipality to serve a public purpose (build a school, road, or bridge), or for qualified private purposes. Examples of qualified private purpose bonds include student loan bonds, bonds issued to provide mortgage funds for lower income classes, and bonds issued for airport improvements. The exemption is not universal. The proceeds of tax exempt bonds may not be used for non-qualified private purposes, such as to speculate on the financial markets, or lend money to a private corpora-

I am grateful for the assistance of Brad Smith in the preparation of this analysis and to Ken Kramer for his constructive comments on the text.

tion. When municipalities need to raise cash for a non-public purpose, they occasionally enter the taxable bond market. However, the level of outstanding taxable municipal debt is insignificant. The federal government is continually revising their guidelines with regard to the issuance of tax-exempt debt. The bias has been on becoming more stringent on what is defined as being for the public benefit and what is not.

The individual investor is by far and away the dominant force in the municipal marketplace. Either directly, through mutual funds, or individual trusts, the individual investor holds 72% of the total debt outstanding as of December 31, 1995. The next largest investor class is property and casualty insurance companies (13%), followed by commercial banks (7%), and non financial corporate businesses (5%). Direct ownership of bonds has decreased over the years as mutual funds have become the investment vehicle of choice for the retail investor. Participation by property and casualty insurance companies (P&Cs) is a function of the underwriting cycle. This investor class has seen a resurgence in demand recently as profitability has returned to many insurance companies. Commercial bank holdings of municipals have decreased by almost 50% since the Tax Reform Act of 1986, as banks are now restricted in their ability to invest in municipals with borrowed funds. The dollar amount of debt outstanding has decreased since 1993, as bonds that have either matured or been called are not being replaced with new borrowings. This is a direct result of the trend towards tighter fiscal policy on the state and local level that is driven by the desire for smaller government. Municipalities continue to borrow. However, they are increasingly facing pressure from the electorate to only fund projects that are absolutely necessary.

The decision to allocate assets to municipal bonds is generally an income question. Both individual investors and P&Cs invest in municipals to the extent they have income to shelter. Seldom does an investor buy municipals for reasons other than the tax preference. However, pension funds and other nontraditional investors occasionally participate in the municipal market when valuations relative to taxables stray from the norm and municipals become cheap. These so-called "crossover" investors, although not always a major participant, can occasionally be among the biggest buyers in the long end of the market.

MUNICIPAL BOND BASICS

Generally speaking, municipal bonds are issued as current coupon securities with ten years of call protection. Noncallable bonds with maturities longer than ten years are issued occasionally, but they do not constitute a critical mass. The lack of a noncallable, credit risk-free bond universe that frequently trades in the secondary market leads to an interesting dilemma. Namely, what should be used as the benchmark yield curve for the market? The taxable market has the benefit of a large amount of Treasury securities which are almost completely credit risk and option free. The Treasury yield curve forms the building blocks of interest rate and option models in the taxable market. The municipal market has no such alternative, and participants are forced to develop a generic yield curve.

Given that most municipal bonds are issued as current coupon bonds with ten years of call protection, and a small proportion of the outstanding debt trades in the secondary market, market participants are forced to approximate a benchmark yield curve from secondary market posts of actual trades, and from new issue offering levels. Once this generic benchmark curve is constructed, many investors compare it with the Treasury curve in order to construct a *yield ratio curve* (simply, municipal yields divided by Treasury yields, across the maturity spectrum). Market participants use this yield ratio curve as a guide to evaluate whether the market in general, or a security in particular, is rich or cheap. Many derivative securities pricing models that apply to municipal bonds utilize this yield ratio approach to construct benchmark curves. The shortcomings of implicitly using the Treasury curve as a benchmark curve in pricing models (basis risk, etc.) is an issue that needs to be addressed before the municipal derivatives market can continue evolve.

Valuation Relative to Treasuries

Using the ratio of municipal yields to Treasury yields serves a useful purpose in evaluating the relative value in each market. The aforementioned crossover buyers typically use yield ratios as thresholds that determine when to enter and exit the market. More traditional buyers use yield ratios as a determining factor in evaluating opportunity within the market by comparing current ratios with historic norms across the yield curve. By doing this, investors can see when a particular part of the curve is being bid up (i.e., 2-year maturities), or weakening (i.e., 30-year maturities) as investor preferences shift from long mutual fund ownership to direct purchases of shorter maturity individual bonds. Whatever the investor uses yield ratios for, one thing is certain: yield ratios do not remain constant. Municipal yield changes are often independent of Treasury yield changes. Yield ratios are a function of supply and demand in both markets, and of risks specific to each market. It is intuitive that yield ratios would fall when municipal new issue supply decreases. There are fewer bonds to go around without a commensurate decrease in demand. Similarly, yield ratios increase when the backbone of the municipal market, the tax preference relative to other fixed income alternatives, is threatened. Double-A rated municipals with ten years of call protection are considered fairly valued when they yield roughly 86% of Treasuries. Similar credit quality 2-year paper is fairly valued at 75% of Treasuries. Exhibit 1 indicates the ratio between the bid side on current coupon double-A rated municipal bonds and Treasury securities from 1994 through 1996. This period was chosen since it gives a good example of how relative valuations between the two markets can change over a relatively short period of time.

Exhibit 1: Aa Municipal Yield/Treasury Yield Ratio

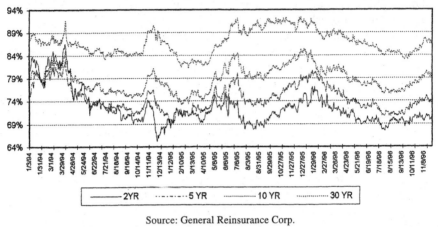

Source: General Reinsurance Corp.

When there is a radical change in the municipal-to-Treasury yield ratio, the cause is usually obvious. For example, municipals cheapened to Treasuries in late November 1994 when Orange County, California flirted with bankruptcy. The surprise with the speed and scope of the credit deterioration of one of the country's wealthiest counties led many to believe that other credits could also be in jeopardy. Additionally, municipals cheapened in 1995 due to rumblings from Washington regarding a possible overhaul of the tax code that would be unfavorable to municipals. Seasonal supply/demand imbalances also put pressure on ratios over the shorter term.

Municipals normally become cheaper to Treasuries the farther out the yield curve. The result of this characteristic is that the municipal yield curve is generally steeper than the Treasury curve. The relative steepness of the municipal curve can be best explained by both the preferred habitat theory and the liquidity preference theory of term structure. Individuals, banks, and trusts account for most of the demand in the front end of the curve. Demand from property and casualty insurance companies generally support the intermediate part of the yield curve, as these company's liability streams dictate buying bonds out to 20 years (although most P&Cs also own bonds longer than 20 years). Mutual funds account for a majority of the demand on the long end of the curve, as that is where the highest yields can be found. Unlike the other investor classes, investment by mutual funds is more volatile, with investors sometimes divesting when interest rates rise. This uncertain demand leads to higher ratios on the long end of the curve. The relative steepness of the curve is also affected by the perceived lack of liquidity in the municipal market and the threat of a change in the tax code. Together, these theories can explain a steeper yield curve.

Valuation Within the Municipal Market

The municipal market is not a homogenous market. Depending on the tax laws in each state (which are the major determinant of demand), and the debt issuance in each state (which determines supply), similarly rated credits from the same sector will trade remarkably different. In order to be entirely precise, an investor has to construct 50 benchmark yield curves every day that takes into account the supply/demand dynamics in each state. In practice, investors construct one benchmark yield curve and apply state specific yield spreads to it, much in the same fashion that quality spreads are used.

Some states (such as New York, California, and Connecticut) allow their residents an exemption from income taxation on debt issued by in state issuers. These states, called "specialty states," tax interest on municipal bonds from out-of-state issuers, creating an increased demand for their paper from in-state investors. Other states (for example, Washington, Illinois, and Indiana) make up what is called the "general market," since they either tax all municipal bond interest (no matter where it originates), or tax none of it. Bonds from specialty states will yield less than general market paper, as it is in higher demand. Institutional investors, such as property and casualty insurance companies, generally receive no state tax preference, and are content collecting the higher income that general market paper offers.

Exceptions to these two classifications do exist. Although Florida lacks an income tax, it is considered a specialty state due to a state intangibles tax, which gives resident's preference to holding in-state bonds at year-end. However, Florida residents possess an unusual penchant for in-state paper that is not fully explained by the tax analysis. As stated earlier, tax preferences, or the lack thereof, are the backbone of the municipal market. It is imperative that investors understand not only how the federal tax code affects the municipal market, but concern themselves with state and local tax laws also.

CREDIT SECTORS

The municipal market is normally broken down into two broad credit classifications: general obligation bonds and revenue bonds. However, not all bonds fall into these two categories: They include appropriation-backed bonds, insured bonds, and prerefunded bonds. Generally speaking, the municipal market is perceived as having a lower level of credit risk than the corporate market. There are sectors, however, where credit risk is real and investors must beware.

General Obligation Bonds

General obligation bonds (GOs) are bonds issued by a municipality which are backed by its full faith and credit. This security pledge includes the ability of the municipality to levy property taxes to pay the principal and interest on these bonds should operating revenue fall short. These bonds are not backed by a specific revenue source, rather, by a general claim on the taxing authority of the issuer. Some investors consider general obligation bonds to be almost default risk free, due to the municipalities unlimited taxing power. However, the market has learned over time that municipalities are often reluctant to increase property taxes in times of fiscal stress, but rather look for other sources of funds to balance their budgets.

General obligation bonds are issued by states, counties, cities, towns, school districts, and any other geographical subdivision with *ad valorem* property taxing authority. In order for a general obligation bond to be issued, the municipality normally has to get voter approval. This type of bond is believed to be the most credit worthy, with very few defaults ever being experienced.

Revenue Bonds

Revenue bonds are bonds issued by a municipality to fund a specific project or enterprise whose cash flows support operations and debt service. An example of a revenue bond is a bond issued by a state turnpike authority which is issued to make road improvements and is supported by vehicle tolls. Investors receive no state guarantee, and if toll revenues were insufficient to cover debt service, the bondholder may face a loss. Investors are secured by protective covenants, such as rate covenants and minimum debt service reserve fund levels. For example, the toll authority will covenant to set tolls at a multiple of debt service (such as 1.25 times), and have on reserve one-times average annual debt service. However, the bondholder is ultimately subject to the economics of the project or enterprise.

Revenue bonds are issued for the benefit of public power utilities, water and sewer enterprises, turnpike authorities, bridge and tunnel authorities, parking authorities, hospitals, and both public and private universities. Any municipal enterprise that utilizes pay-as-you-go financing generally can issue revenue bonds. Given the one dimensional nature of the security source, revenue bonds are considered riskier than general obligation bonds by many investors. Revenue bonds typically yield a bit more than similarly rated general obligation paper due the incremental credit risk. However, given an essential service municipal enterprise with favorable economics, revenue bonds are also very safe investments.

Appropriation-Backed Bonds

With the increased difficulty that municipalities are having with bond elections, public finance officials have had to find creative ways to enter the capital markets without the benefit of voter approval. One such type of financing that has become popular the past decade is the use of appropriation-backed bonds. These bonds do not require voter approval and do not legally constitute debt. They are essentially an off-balance sheet form of financing.

These bonds work as follows. A municipality that wishes to raise debt but does not have the luxury to gain voter approval for general obligation debt sells bonds backed by an annual appropriation from its general fund. The municipality does not covenant to make an appropriation (if it did, this would constitute debt), only to try to appropriate funds each year. It is under no obligation to do so, and if it did not, the bondholder would have no recourse.

On the state level, investors ask for only a modest yield premium over general obligation debt that, on the surface, does not seem commensurate with the incremental credit risk incurred. One explanation that has been put forward for these tight spreads is that states would be denied future access to the capital markets should they default on their appropriation backed obligations. Given that states and their authorities are constantly tapping the markets for funds, failure to honor their appropriation-backed obligations would bring swift punishment from the investor community. Appropriation-backed bonds issued by cities and counties are not considered as stable, as the market perceives an increased probability that these issuers could walk away from their obligations (Brevard County, Florida is a good example). Whether issued by states or other municipal entities, appropriation-backed bonds possess a high degree of political and credit risk that separate them from both general obligations and revenue bonds. Investors need to be cautious when participating in this sector.

Insured Bonds

One sector of the market that has grown over the past decade is the insured sector. In 1995, almost 45% of all new issues were insured, up from roughly 10% in 1986. An insured bond is any municipal bond that has its principal and interest (P&I) payments guaranteed by a third party, called a bond insurer. There are a number of firms who insure bonds, with the market being dominated by three firms: AMBAC, FGIC, and MBIA. Together, these firms account for more than 80% of the insured volume of outstanding bonds. All of these firms have a claims-paying ability rating of triple-A by Moody's and Standard and Poor's. The ratings are based on an analysis of the quality of their insured book of business and their capital adequacy.

Bond insurance works this way. The issuer of a bond pays a premium to the bond insurer in return for its guarantee of P&I and a higher credit rating on its debt. By using bond insurance, the issuer lowers their cost of capital since they can sell their debt on the insured scale, rather than on a lower rated scale. By buying insured bonds, the investor implicitly pays the cost of insurance for the issuer by accepting a lower yield in return for the credit enhancement. Should the municipality default, the investor then hopes to receive the timely payment of P&I from the bond insurer. Note that in the event of default, the bond insurer does not accelerate the payment of P&I. The bondholder is paid according to the original payment schedule.

Although the major bond insurers are rated triple-A, insured bonds do not trade like natural triples. Instead, insured bonds trade a bit cheaper than double-A rated paper, as investors require additional yield to compensate them for the leveraged nature of the bond insurance industry (the average firm has roughly $170 of exposure for every $1 of capital) and the lack of a long-term track record for the industry. However, most bond insurers write to a zero loss tolerance, with claims on their policies occurring so infrequently that one has to wonder whether these bonds should trade better.

Prerefunded Bonds

A unique feature of the municipal market is the ability of issuers to refund their debt in advance of the first call date. Given a material drop in interest rates, and the fact the Treasury bonds yield more than municipal bonds, issuers are able to refinance their original debt long before the first call date by issuing advance refunding bonds. The proceeds from advance refunding bonds are used to buy a portfolio of Treasury securities with cash flows that match the principal and interest payment schedule of their original debt. The portfolio of Treasuries forms an escrow which guarantees that the original debt will be retired on the first call date. Once the escrow is in place, the payment source for the original bonds is transferred to the advance refunding bonds. The net result of this transaction is a lowering of the cost of capital for the municipality, the issuance of new bonds in the marketplace, and a transformation of the original bonds. Upon the instance of an advance refunding, the holder of the original bond is left with the credit risk of a Treasury portfolio and an option-free bond. These bonds are referred to as prerefunded bonds. If the rating agencies are satisfied with the strength of the escrow agreement, the prerefunded bonds will be rated #Aaa by Moody's and AAA by S&P. Due to the Tax Reform Act of 1986, municipalities may now only refund their debt once.

Given the relative risk-free nature of rerated prerefunded bonds, one might expect them to trade better than, or at least on par with, other triple-A rated paper. However, prerefunded bonds generally offer yields similar to double-A rated paper. Prerefunded bonds of certain specialty state issuers (California and New York, specifically) do trade closer to the triple-A scale, but not as well as triple-A paper. The rationale for the cheapness of prerefunded bonds is often explained by the aversion of the individual investor to bonds priced over par. Since prerefunded bonds are created when their options are in-the-money, they are by definition at a premium to par. Many individual investors are not comfortable receiving more interest over time as a trade off for a reduction in principal at maturity. The fact that prerefunded bonds continue to trade like double-A rated paper is testimony to the fact that the individual investor dominates the market.

PORTFOLIO MANAGEMENT

Simply stated, portfolio management entails setting objectives and managing risks. It is imperative that the objectives be clearly defined and a standard to measure performance be selected. Once this framework is in place, the role of the portfolio manager is to outline a strategy that will achieve these objectives. Transactions are then executed that implement the strategy, and the portfolio is continually monitored for further adjustment. In a volatile interest rate environment, portfolio strategy can change frequently. The portfolio management process is a never ending challenge.

Objectives

Nearly all investors in municipal bonds participate in the market in order to shelter income from the government. With the sole determinant for participating in the market being after-tax income, one might think that the potential for capital appreciation opportunities should be of secondary concern, or be ignored entirely. This is because the accumulation of capital gains results in a potential capital gains tax liability. However, municipal bond portfolios are managed for total return by many insurance companies and mutual funds. Is it prudent to think in terms of capital appreciation when you are looking to avoid paying taxes? The answer is yes, because a portfolio's capital gains tax liability can be minimized or even eliminated: capital gains can be offset with capital losses. The goal of every investor should be to maximize after-tax total returns. The desire for sheltered income should not stop the portfolio manager from managing a portfolio's interest rate risk. By managing a portfolio's duration, convexity, yield curve position, sector weightings, and tax liability, material after-tax rewards can be generated.

Pre-tax returns tell the investor or shareholder very little about the true performance of a portfolio or the value added by a manager. Stakeholders need to be concerned with the bottom line, which includes both after-tax income and after-tax capital appreciation. This not withstanding, there are still many investors whose objectives consist solely of maximizing their after-tax income, and those who endeavor to maximize pre-tax total return. Pre-tax total return optimizers generally also try to minimize their portfolio's tax liability. However, due to the absence of market recognized after-tax performance benchmarks, these investors ultimately concern themselves with pre-tax results.

Risks

The risks that a municipal bond portfolio manager face differs only slightly from those faced by taxable portfolio managers. Both groups are concerned with interest rate risk, credit risk, sector risk, and event risk (among other things). However, the primary difference between the two markets concerns securities valuation. With the individual investor being the largest purchaser of municipal bonds, securities valuation lacks a certain sophistication. Individual investors think in terms of maturity, yield-to-worst, and callability, rather than duration, effective yield, and volatility. The municipal market lags the taxable market in its application of quantitative methods. Given this inherent bias towards inefficiency, institutional investors may be at the advantage, since their valuation techniques are more sophisticated. However, rich/cheap analysis is sometimes fruitless in that sectors or securities that are theoretically mispriced may never become fairly valued.

Duration

For our purposes, the term "duration" will refer to the concept of modified duration. Modified duration is used as a measure of a bond or portfolio's sensitivity to parallel shifts in interest rates. The objective of duration management is to adjust the portfolio's sensitivity to parallel shifts in the yield curve by either lengthening or shorting the duration of the portfolio. When higher (lower) interest rates are expected, the modified duration of the portfolio should be shortened (lengthened). While adjusting duration can be easy, correctly anticipating changes in interest rates is not!

In the municipal market, a portfolio's modified duration can be adjusted in two primary ways: cash market operations and derivative market operations. Derivative market operations consist of futures market transactions or interest rate swaps. The municipal futures market is not a well-developed market. The only contract available to go long or short is the Municipal Bond Index Futures Contract. The basis for the contract is the Bond Buyer Municipal Bond Index, which contains 40 long-term municipal bonds. This contract lacks liquidity, with only a nominal number of contracts trading each day. Many investors use Treasury futures as a duration management tool instead. While the use of Treasury futures introduces basis risk, its superior liquidity makes it the more acceptable alternative. The municipal interest rate swaps market also has its shortcomings, as it is in the early stages of development. Given the lack of development of the municipal derivatives markets, cash market operations tend to predominant the duration management process.

Securities in the municipal market trade on a yield-to-worst basis. This means that for a given bond price, its yield is quoted either to maturity or to a shorter call date, whichever date produces the lower yield. Given a positively sloped yield curve, a 30-year bond with a 10-year par call will be quoted on a yield-to-maturity basis when it is trading at a discount, and on a yield-to-call basis when it is trading at a premium. No effort is made to model future interest rates and calculate an effective yield. A by-product of this binary pricing mechanism is that duration is quoted on a duration-to-worst basis, meaning premium bonds pricing to a call have the duration of bonds with a final maturity of the call date. Their interest rate sensitivity is best approximated by assuming that its maturity has shortened to the effective call date. The duration of discount bonds readily approximates their true price performance, since the market assumes that calls will not become effective. The duration to-worst of bonds with call options at or near the money is not a valid approximation of interest rate sensitivity, as these bonds will trade either to the call, or to maturity, should interest rate change even modestly.

Given this pricing mechanism, it is difficult to apply option adjusted duration measures to the portfolio management process since bonds do not trade on an option-adjusted basis. Investors in municipals are best served by concentrating on duration-to-worst in order to approximate interest rate sensitivity. Large swings in interest rates can materially impact a portfolio's duration-to-worst, as bonds shift from trading between their call date and maturity. The duration management process involves not only setting a target duration, but also setting a target for the sensitivity of a portfolio's duration to changes in interest rates.

Convexity

For our purposes, convexity is defined as the property whereby the duration of a security or portfolio increases when interest rates fall, and decreases when interest rates rise. Conversely, *negative convexity* refers to the less desirable trait where duration moves in the same direction as interest rates. Given the impact that convexity positioning has upon duration, its role in the overall interest rate sensitivity management process should not be understated. Positively convex portfolios will have more stable durations than negatively convex ones. Given that the duration of convex portfolios moves inversely with interest rates, more convex portfolios will typically outperform their peer group in volatile interest rate environments, all other risk factors being equal.

Clearly, positive convexity is beneficial to a portfolio. Like anything that provides a benefit to a portfolio, it comes with a cost. In the taxable market, institutional investors dedicate a great deal of time and energy pricing call options. In essence what they are doing is quantifying how much they need to be compensated for selling convexity. As already stated, the municipal market is lacking in its sophistication regarding quantitative methods. The net result of this lack of sophistication is a consistent mispricing of call options and a corresponding misevaluation of the cost of convexity. Securities valuation in the fixed income markets are always a function of supply and demand. In the taxable market, demand comes from educated investors. In the municipal market, demand is dominated by individuals who lack the resources to properly evaluate risk. Institutional investors in the municipal market are at a distinct advantage.

Municipal bonds are generally issued as current coupon bonds (par bonds) with 10 years of call protection. Individual investors demand this structure since it makes their life simple. If the bond is held to maturity, there is no tax event. The interest income is tax free, and there is no capital gain. Even when buying in the secondary market, the individual investor favors par bonds, as discounts can carry with them a potential capital gains tax liability. Premium securities are usually avoided at all costs due to the perceived loss of capital as they amortize to par. Few individual investors can grasp the concept of receiving larger interim cash flows (more coupon interest) in return for a reduction in capital at maturity. The penchant for current coupon callable bonds by the individual investor, provides opportunities for institutional investors to buy more convex structures in the secondary market. Disciplined institutional investors know how to manipulate the individual investor demand profile in order to create an optimal risk profile for their portfolio.

Yield Curve

The final piece of the interest rate sensitivity management puzzle is the yield curve. Earlier we defined modified duration as a measure of a portfolio's sensitivity to parallel shifts in the yield curve. While the yield curve does occasionally move in this fashion, it also moves in a nonparallel way. Yield curve management is related to duration management in that it is how we construct a portfolio's duration profile. There are numerous ways to construct a portfolio with a duration of, say, 7 years. We can buy only those securities with a duration of 7 years (this is a called an extreme bullet maturity structure), or buy a combination of very short and very long maturity securities that when combined, has a duration of seven years (this is an extreme barbell maturity structure). Additional combinations of maturity structures exist between the extreme bullet and the extreme barbell that also will have our target duration.

The goal of yield curve management is to decide the optimal maturity structure for a portfolio. The strategies that portfolio managers employ to benefit from anticipated shifts in the yield curve are the same for all fixed income portfolios. Investors expecting a steeper yield curve generally will favor a bulleted maturity structure. Investors who anticipate a flatter curve will generally favor a barbell structure. The tax exempt market differs from the taxable market less in how yield curve weightings can be manipulated, and more in the opportunities that its characteristic shape present.

The municipal yield curve is normally steeper than the Treasury curve. The steepness is generally concentrated in the first 20 years of the curve, with very little incremental yield being offered for extending past 20 years. Within the first 20 years, interesting yield curve roll opportunities can arise to take advantage of this steepness. *Yield curve roll* is the name given to the feature of price appreciation potential that arises from the seasoning of securities. In a positively sloped yield curve environment, when maturities shorten due to the passing of time (i.e., a 15-year maturity becomes a 14-year maturity), bond prices will increase as they become valued at lower yields. Unlike the Treasury curve, the municipal curve only rolls on an annual basis (after the first of the year), providing ample time for the investor to increase maturity weightings, and increase price appreciation potential. A characteristic of the municipal curve related to the annual roll is that there is generally no yield curve within each year, meaning investors do not differentiate between bonds that mature in the first and the last parts of each year. This is true for all but the shortest maturities (inside of 5 years). As an example, when the spread between two maturities (say 2009 and 2010) is 10 basis points, the spread between paper maturing December 1, 2009 and January 1, 2010 is also ten basis points, even though they differ by only a month. Because of this lack of distinction, investors can give preference to maturities in the first part of the year to receive greater duration-adjusted yields. Other opportunities to take advantage of yield curve biases also exist.

Sector Rotation

Sector rotation is defined as the shifting of assets among distinct sectors of the market in order to potentially benefit from pricing disparities. The primary sectors to manipulate are the ratings quality classes, credit type classes, insured bonds, prefunded bonds, specialty state markets, and market discount bonds. Strategies involve anticipating changes in spreads between sectors. The most common example is swapping between credit rating sectors in anticipation of a movement in quality spreads. For example, single-A rated paper may be trading tight to triple-A rated paper, presenting the opportunity to upgrade credit quality for only a modest cost. Within the credit-type sector, most essential service revenue bonds and general obligations tend to trade generically. The exception to this rule is the more credit intensive areas, such as health care, housing and solid waste. Spreads also fluctuate between the various specialty states, as individual buying behavior can be readily recognized to have an impact on bond prices. While sector rotation generally contributes only modestly to portfolio performance, a sector that dictates more complex analysis is market discount bonds.

Market Discount Bonds

In the municipal market, bonds trading at a discount to par trade on an after-tax basis, such that yields on bonds with a potential future tax liability are increased to compensate the investor for an expected future tax liability. Specifically, given a generic double-A yield curve of 5.50% for 10-year maturities, Exhibit 2 details how the market values three bonds trading at a discount to par such that they all yield 5.50% after-tax.

The pricing mechanism works as follows: the market assumes that all bonds will be held to maturity, at which time the holder will pay either a capital gains tax, an income tax, or no tax on the accretion of discount to par. The pre-tax price of the bond is reduced by the discounted value of the expected future tax liability. The tax liability is calculated using the rates of 28% and 39.6% for capital gains and income taxes, respectively. The market uses these tax rates, since they apply to individuals.

Returning to Exhibit 2, all generic double-A rated bonds with a coupon of 5% and a final maturity of 07/01/2006 must pay the investor 5.50% after taxes are considered. In this example, Bond A is what is known as an *original issue discount* (OID) *bond*, since it was originally sold at a discount to par. The federal government treats the accretion of OID as tax-exempt interest, rather than as a capital gain. In the secondary market, as long as an investor buys an OID bond at a yield equal to or less than its yield at issue, there will be no taxable capital event. Since the going rate for Bond A is its issue yield, there is no difference between Bond A's gross and after-tax yield. Bond B was issued at par and is currently trading as a market discount. When a bond is classified as a market discount, it means that the accretion of its discount to par is taxable on the federal level as income. (A bond is classified as a market discount for federal income tax purposes when its price at purchase is lower than its price at issue, less a *de minimus* exemption of one-quarter points per calendar years to maturity. For a bond issued at par, with 10 years remaining until maturity, it will be considered a market discount if its market price is less than $97.50.)

Exhibit 2: After-Tax Pricing of Aa rated 5s Due 07/01/2006 Priced on 11/01/1996

Bond	Coupon (%)	Maturity	OID Yield (%)	Gross Yield (%)	After-tax Yield (%)	Price
A	5	7/1/2006	5.50	5.50	5.50	96.193
B	5	7/1/2006	5.00	5.65	5.50	95.055
C	5	7/1/2006	5.25	5.55	5.50	95.828

In order for Bond B to have an after-tax yield of 5.50%, it must be priced in the market at 5.65%. The difference in price between Bond A and Bond B is the present value of the expected future tax liability on Bond B. Bond C is an OID bond trading at a yield greater than its yield at issue. Therefore, there will be a taxable event for an investor who holds this bond to maturity. A portion of the accretion of discount will be tax exempt, since it amounts to the accretion of OID. The remaining portion will not be taxed as income, since its discount is not so large as to classify it as a market discount. In contrast to Bond B, the remaining portion will be taxable as a capital gain, since the discount falls within the *de minimus* exception. Since Bond C's expected tax liability is lower than Bond B's, it will not have to yield as much on a gross basis.

The ramifications of the after-tax pricing mechanism on portfolio management are far greater than just the yield implications. In the process of compensating the investor for a future tax liability, the pricing mechanism has dramatically altered the interest rate risk profile of securities and portfolios. Analyzing market discount bonds further, portfolio interest rate risk sensitivity is increased due to the after-tax pricing mechanism because changes in gross yields do not correspond on a one-to-one basis with changes in after-tax yields. As investors require an increase or decrease in after-tax yields due to changes in generic interest rates, gross yields must rise or fall by a greater amount. In essence, the after-tax pricing mechanism increases the duration of the bond and of the portfolio. In Exhibit 3, we see that by calculating the dollar value of 10 basis points for an OID and a market discount, the market discount has far greater interest rate sensitivity.

In this example, Bond B is almost 1.2 times as sensitive to changes in interest rates as Bond A. Unknowing investors in Bond B will actually receive the interest rate sensitivity of a much longer bond. Extending the analysis across the yield curve finds that the incremental interest rate sensitivity is not uniform. All other factors being equal, the shorter the maturity of the market discount bond, the greater the duration extension related to the after-tax pricing mechanism. This is because the discounted value of the expected tax liability becomes larger the closer the bond is to maturity. To accurately value market discount bonds, investors not only have be compensated for potential tax liabilities, but need additional compensation for the increased interest rate sensitivity.

Strategies that manipulate the after-tax pricing mechanism abound. As interest rates change, bonds shift between being classified as market discounts and OIDs. Similarly, their interest rate sensitivity changes in a way not fully explained by the traditional measures of duration and convexity. Given the complexities of these bonds (and the potential for a tax liability), the individual investor normally avoids this sector. For the institutional investor, market discount bonds are used in both the duration management process and to make yield curve bets. Their greater relative interest rate sensitivity make them good candidates for yield curve roll strategies, and duration extension strategies. Investors with an income tax rate of less than 39.6% realize incremental after-tax income by being overcompensated for their future tax liability. The market discount sector presents interesting challenges to the portfolio manager.

SUMMARY

The municipal bond market, although not a major portion of the domestic fixed income market, provides opportunities for investors to generate superior after-tax returns in their fixed income portfolios. The market is dominated by the individual investor (either directly or through mutual funds), with the largest institutional demand coming from property and casualty insurance companies.The chief reason for investing in municipal bonds is the preferential income tax treatment that they enjoy. Other non-traditional investors sometimes buy municipal bonds when valuations to taxable bonds present value. The municipal market lacks the sophistication and the quantitative bent that is characteristic of the taxable bond market. It is because of this feature that insurance company and mutual fund portfolio managers can utilize modern valuation techniques in order to manipulate the demand profile of the individual investor. Although sometimes fruitless, the use of quantitative methods can lead to opportunities to construct portfolios with optimal risk/return characteristics.

Exhibit 3: Calculation of Dollar Value of 10 Basis Points
OID versus Market Discount Bonds
Priced on 11/01/1996

	Coupon	Maturity	OID Yield	Gross Yield	After-tax Yield	Price
				5.40%	5.40%	96.939
Bond A:	5%	7/1/2006	5.50%	5.50%	5.50%	96.193
				5.62%	5.60%	95.311
Average Price Change/ Beginning Price: 0.8140/96.193 = 0.85%

	Coupon	Maturity	OID Yield	Gross Yield	After-tax Yield	Price
				5.52%	5.40%	96.014
Bond B:	5%	7/1/2006	5.00%	5.65%	5.50%	95.055
				5.78%	5.60%	94.110
Average Price Change/ Beginning Price: 0.9520/95.055 = 1.00%
Bond B is 1.18 times more price sensitive than Bond A at these interest rate levels.

About the Authors

J. Thomas Madden, CFA

J. Thomas Madden is an Executive Vice President and Chief Investment Officer of Federated Research Corp., the investment arm of Federated Investors. He oversees portfolio management in the domestic equity, high yield, and asset allocation areas, and contributes to the formation of investment strategy at Federated. Prior to joining Federated in 1977, he was with the Trust Department of Mellon Bank, where he followed the energy service and industrial machinery equity groups. Mr. Madden oversees $10 billion in domestic equity, asset allocation (lifecycle), and high yield funds. He has led Federated's high yield bond unit since the early 1980s, managing and co-managing Liberty High Income Bond Fund, Federated High Yield Trust, and other portfolios through the 1980s. High yield assets grew from $40 million in 1978 to $2.8 billion today. In addition, he has overseen the start-up and management of a variety of Federated funds including mortgage-backed, asset-backed, investment-grade corporates, and asset allocation portfolios. Mr. Madden is a graduate of Columbia University (B.A. Economics) and the Darden School of the University of Virginia (M.B.A., concentration in Finance). He is a past President and current member of the Pittsburgh Society of Financial Analysts.

Joseph M. Balestrino, CFA

Joseph M. Balestrino is a Vice President of Federated Research Corp. He is responsible for research and portfolio management in the corporate fixed income area. Prior to joining Federated in 1986, he was with the Product Development and Operations departments at Federated and IDS/American Express, where he was a financial planner. Mr. Balestrino is a graduate of the University of Pittsburgh (B.A. History) and the University of Pittsburgh Graduate School of Public and International Affairs (M.U.R.P., concentration in Regional Planning). He is a current member of the Pittsburgh Society of Financial Analysts.

Chapter 6

Management of a High-Yield Bond Portfolio

J. Thomas Madden, CFA
Executive Vice President
Federated Investors

Joseph Balestrino, CFA
Vice President
Federated Investors

High-yield bonds are usually defined as bonds rated less than Baa (Moody's) or BBB (Standard & Poor's) or securities of equivalent quality. Such bonds may be called "lower rated" or, more cavalierly, "junk." High-yield bond management is, first and last, the balancing of risk and return. Any investment in subordinated debt of issuers rated less than Baa/BBB with debt to capitalization ratios in the 7:10 to 10:10 range bears significant risk. (Adjusted for intangible assets, some high-yield deals have negative equity.) Issuers may default, postpone payments, force exchanges, or tender for or call debt, depriving the holder of the high coupon. But in return for accepting such risks, investors are paid annual yields that well exceed yields on U.S. Treasury bonds.

Studies of the high-yield market that focus only on default rates, annual or cumulative, without considering returns on specific portfolios, are of little help in evaluating the attractiveness of the market. Such analyses are like describing the risks of a professional football career without ever mentioning the players' salaries. The high-yield bond market studies that address return as well as risk, from the earliest to most recent, provide a strong rationale for high-yield bond investing.

The objective of this chapter is to discuss some of the practical aspects of high-yield bond management in a diversified portfolio. This chapter focuses on the game rules of successful high-yield investment. The ultimate objective is to achieve excess returns — largely in the form of a cash stream — for assuming risk and to compound the investment over time at attractive rates. The portfolio management process we will describe has evolved over nearly two decades. It has been successful in creating superior results for mutual funds, but applies equally well to separate accounts management. We begin by examining portfolio objectives.

DEFINITION OF PORTFOLIO OBJECTIVE

Any portfolio management process is driven by the definition of portfolio objectives. High-yield bonds may be used as components of larger portfolios (for example, as a subset of bond portfolios to boost overall fixed income return) or as substitutes for common stock investments in equity portfolios. The approach we describe assumes a client who desires superior total return on a pure portfolio of lower rated debt. Inclusion of such a portfolio within a larger investment strategy is a separate and complex topic beyond the scope of this chapter. How should such a high-yield portfolio be managed? The first step is the definition of the available universe from which the portfolio can be assembled.

By definition, a portfolio can be assembled only from the universe of buyable securities. Although in excess of 3,000 issuers have used the market in the last decade, perhaps 200 to 250 issues normally trade in the secondary market. The available universe is augmented by new issues. One evaluation a manager must make early on is to consider whether the new issue market is "cheap" or "rich" relative to the secondary market. That is, are new issues higher or lower in yield relative to risk than similar issues in the secondary market?

After defining the array of possible holdings, the portfolio manager moves to create the portfolio. In order to make this process successful, experience teaches some "rules of the road," which we examine next.

SUMMARY OF HIGH-YIELD INVESTMENT STRATEGY

Low Cash Position

We manage high-yield portfolios on a fully invested basis; that is, cash positions are held below 10% of our portfolios. The cash versus market decision is a separate portfolio issue and departs from the most basic reason to own lower rated debt, which is to benefit from the positive net yield spread over reasonable holding periods. We believe that significantly raising or lowering cash within a high-yield portfolio, based on assertions that the high-yield market is cheap or rich relative to higher quality bonds, departs from this primary objective.

Target Securities Rated Single or Double B

Our objective here is to purchase stable to improving credits in the middle range of the lower rated sector. These may be nonrated, but of comparable quality. Recent empirical results suggest that single and double B rated portfolios have provided attractive net returns versus investment-grade bond portfolios over long holding periods.

High Degree of Diversification

Diversification provides the primary method of risk management in the high-yield portfolio, as in any investment portfolio. Our portfolios typically hold 1% to 3%

percent in a single issuer and never over 5% of total portfolio assets per issuer. All academic studies suggesting superior returns assume, in effect, a degree of diversification comparable to the market as a whole. Though we have demonstrated in our portfolios the added value of security selection over time, one large incorrect bet can damage results severely. The portfolio discipline should prevent such bets.

Investors may also want to think about percentage ownership of an issue — in the extreme case, the manager who owns an entire issue is not likely to find much of a trading market. Investors must balance the control that a large position provides in times of trouble with ongoing liquidity. We try to own less than 15% of any given issue, for example, no more than $15 million of a $100 million deal. Today, with liquidity at a premium, much smaller positions are the rule in our portfolios.

Diversification doesn't mean owning a sector of the high-yield market even if that sector has unattractive fundamentals in relation to high leverage or is unanalyzable. As part of our "critical factor" analysis, which we describe more fully later, we ask whether industry fundamentals are congenial to use of high-yield debt. For example, we have for many years sharply limited investments in airline issuers, believing that deregulation of the airlines and subsequent industry consolidation implies constant margin pressure and volatile cash flows, both broadly unfavorable conditions for high leverage. Further, we systematically avoided financial intermediaries (Southmark, Integrated Resources, savings and loans) because analysis of balance sheets appeared difficult if not impossible. Portfolio diversification should never force mechanical investment in unattractive industry sectors.

Intensive Fundamental and Credit Review of Each Issuer

Issuer analysis is worthy of a full-blown separate discussion. The following merely outlines important areas. The analysis should always focus on sources of cash, because cash is ultimately what pays debt service. Fundamental analysis of high-yield issuers begins with examination of an issuer's dominant lines of business and its position relative to competition, as well as industry trends and cyclicality. The seasonality, volatility, and profitability of operations are considered in light of the impact of these variables on operating cash flow before noncash charges, interest, and taxes, often referred to as earnings before interest, taxes, and depreciation or amortization (EBITDA). This is cash flow available for interest, principal repayments, property and equipment expenditures, and working capital additions. EBITDA projection is the heart of high-yield bond analysis.

We prefer to invest in operating companies whose dominant products or services have proprietary or semiproprietary characteristics against an industry backdrop of high-capacity utilization, because these attributes favor stable pricing, higher margins, and more predictable cash flow. We also prefer issuers with strong brand names or product franchises for similar reasons (e.g., Duracell, American Standard, Playtex, and Revlon).

Accounting practices are scrutinized. A smaller or less well known accounting firm is typically a flag for possible trouble. Similarly, a recent change in accountants should be questioned.

Balance-sheet analysis includes an evaluation of working capital requirements, estimated asset values, and the separability of assets or operations for sale.
In effect, the analyst should ask: How much cash does this company need to
invest in inventories, receivables, and other current assets to grow its business?
What could it sell to raise cash if things go wrong? Would such sales be easy or
difficult? If asset sales are built into the financing, as with RJR Nabisco in the late
1980s, the realism of expectations about price and timing are crucial. Evaluation
of intangibles like goodwill can lead to a more realistic view of the balance sheet.

Debt structure may include floating- versus fixed-rate debt; examination
of the schedule of debt amortization, and contingencies affecting that schedule is
critical. Bank line availability and public marketability of the company's equity
are considered. Here, the analyst should ask how appropriate the structure is to
the company's business plan. Is too much debt repayable too soon? If zero-coupon bonds are used, what happens when they "go cash-pay"? How much does
debt repayment depend on asset disposition instead of cash from the operating
cycle? Can the company borrow more from its banks?

Also important are environmental and legal issues, union contracts (if
applicable), and contingent liabilities, including self-insurance and underfunding
of pension and other liabilities. The recent experience of Mid-American Waste
Systems shows the critical nature of good analysis of nonfinancial risk.

Overt judgments about management are of critical importance: character,
experience, past performance, knowledge of the business, ability to state its business plan clearly, and degree of management equity ownership are evaluated. We
like deals where management has significant personal wealth at stake below the
subordinated debt.

Willingness to assume risk and ability to manage in financially risky circumstances are not always coupled. Management's motivation for underwriting a transaction should be examined. Is the deal "ego driven" or based on financial opportunity?
Is the business forecast on which the transaction is based realistic or "pie in the sky"?
These analytical elements form the backdrop for calculation of cash interest, total
interest, and debt service coverages. Most of our holdings cover cash interest 2.0 to
2.5 times, when EBITDA — earnings before depreciation, amortization, interest, and
taxes — is divided by annual charges. With such narrow margins, stability of cash
flow is critical. Our forecasts have a time frame of no longer than two years. Experience teaches that outlooks beyond the 2-year area are guesses, not analyses.

Market Analysis

Our objective in market analysis is to understand risks associated with indenture
covenants; call, exchange, and sinking fund provisions; interest rate resets, and
other elements of the issue's structure and provisions. In addition, the investment
banker creating and distributing the deal should be examined both from the standpoint of (1) due diligence, and (2) sale/ trading commitment and capability. Both
issues deserve careful consideration. With newer forms of financing that include

zero-coupon, pay-in-kind, and other deferred interest bonds (DIB), careful attention is paid to calculation of internal rate of return, security ranking, put characteristics, reset characteristics, and other structural elements.

Additionally and critically, market analysis also includes evaluation of the record of the underwriter, with attention to historical effectiveness of due diligence on past issues, support for issues in the secondary market, knowledge of investment bankers, responsibility for the issue, and overall corporate strategy of the underwriter toward the high-yield market. Federated Investors, Inc., has found specific consideration of these issues to be critical, as high-yield investment banking and trading performance varies sharply among firms and over time. A separate section discussing the analysis of investment bankers follows later.

Critical Factor Determination

The objective here is to identify those specific aspects of the deal that have the largest impact on risk and return. Results of sector, fundamentals, and market analysis are evaluated to determine the most important issues determining bond performance (Critical Factor Identification). We have learned that in successful high-yield bond management, the ultimate challenge is to analyze what's important to an investment outcome, not every attribute of the issuer. This is the Pareto principle, or "80/20" rule, applied to high-yield analysis. No matter what the process is termed, we believe it is crucial to rank order analytical insights to focus attention on those that carry most weight for the issuer's performance. In the early 1980s, for many high-yield issuers, the critical factor was the trend in oil prices. Today, it may well be the impact of a recession on an issuer's major operations. Analyze the critical, not the trivial.

Simple Sell Disciplines

With this approach, we strive to sell issues when yields improve to an effective BB to BBB equivalent or when issuer fundamentals appear to be deteriorating. We strive to be early sellers: our rule is "first sale, best sale."

ANALYZING THE HIGH-YIELD INVESTMENT BANKING PROCESS

The investment banker is critically important in the creation of a successful high-yield issue. While issuer objectives for a high-yield transaction are important, it's the investment banker as intermediary who typically structures and engineers the transaction in its final form.

Ideally, the banker has performed extensive due diligence on the issuer, thought carefully about how the high-yield financing will fit the issuer's business and financing objectives, and helped the issuer plan the role of the deal in the issuer's overall strategy. What will the size of the issue be? What term will apply?

Will the coupon be fixed, floating, adjustable, or increasing? Will the issue be a single financing or complex and multilayered? Will the issue convert to common stock? Will warrants for common stock be attached, or is there some other form of equity kicker required to make the deal a success? What will the call and refunding provisions be? What covenants will be included in the indenture? Will the transaction be protected against event risk — that is, the releveraging of the enterprise at some later date with an adverse effect on current creditors? Will financing covenants be included? (For example, pledges as to minimum levels of interest coverage or net worth.) These examples are but a fraction of the issues the investment banker deals with when negotiating between high-yield buyers and the issuer.

The intelligent high-yield buyer will attempt to test the investment banking process within the analysis. Conversations with underwriters may cast light on the thoroughness of the due diligence. Questions to management may illuminate the appropriateness of the deal and its structure. For example, the high-yield buyer should ask whether the valuation process makes sense if assets are being acquired with bond proceeds: Have peak cycle operating earnings been discounted, with allowance for the down cycle? How does the equity market value similar businesses? Do competitors think the deal is fair, or is the issuer going to overpay? If cost savings will help repay the debt, are such savings realistic? Are capital expenditures being unrealistically reduced? A reasonable approach may be for the high-yield investor to stand in the shoes of the banker and then ask how he or she might have put the transaction together. Seen from the "sell side," the transaction may appear to change form. The presence of obscure covenants may become clear and the likelihood of developments adverse to the high-yield buyer may be clearly discerned. One additional rule of thumb: a thick, overly complex, poorly organized offering circular may signal an overly complex and poorly organized financing.

Evaluation of the deal and its structure is only part of the buyer's analysis. The buyer must also consider the history and reputation of the investment banker. Among questions the buyer should ask are: What continuing commitment, if any, will the banker have to the deal after it is placed? Does the investment banker have a record of supporting high-yield transactions in the secondary market — will it bid in the secondary market for its own deals? If a transaction runs into trouble, will the banker actively work to restructure the deal or will it leave this task to bondholders and their attorneys and advisors?

Perhaps more broadly, the high-yield buyer should consider what appear to be the investment banker's general objectives for its high-yield operation. In the 1980s, to many observers, some Wall Street firms appeared to participate in the market on a deal-by-deal basis. These firms seemed to examine each transaction on its own merits without a sustained commitment to the market. Other firms lacked commitment to the high-yield market at the most senior level. High-yield market observers recognize that the policy toward lower rated debt at these firms was a cause of much disagreement and rancor with high personnel turnover. More recently, major firms have confined their high-yield efforts to a highly successful leveraging of their historical client base, focusing intelligently on industries with stable cash flow characteristics. Senior managers of one such firm have stated emphatically their intent to transact as principals, not on an agency basis, in their high-yield activities. Their well-articulated strategy focuses on diversified equity investment by the firm for its own account using high-yield bonds as one financing tool. This firm's high-yield debt issuance has been favorable for both buyers and sellers.

The successful high-yield manager will be both thoughtful regarding the difference between high-yield investment banks and knowledgeable about their track records in the market, since continuity and consistency have been scarce commodities. In the current climate, the focus appears largely transactional. High-yield issuers switch investment bankers on a deal-by-deal basis. Corporate finance and sales and trading units swap personnel like professional sports franchises. Several well-known high-yield broker/dealers have experienced severe illiquidity as a result of over-aggressiveness in bridge financing transactions.

Thoughtful assessment of all of these issues as they bear on a specific purchase candidate is critical. Again, a useful analytical technique is to place oneself in the shoes of the issuer and its corporate finance advisor. Failure to address the history, intent, and objectives of the high-yield investment banker is a hallmark of incomplete analysis.

In the next section, we discuss issues concerning problem credits. Though it is certainly among the least attractive aspects of high-yield investments, an alert and aggressive approach to problem credits presents an area of added value provided by a high-yield manager.

ISSUES OF PROBLEM CREDITS

Most investors in high-yield bond portfolios will eventually encounter the complex problems of deteriorating credits. Various well-publicized studies of high-yield default experience suggest that between 1% and 2% of a representative high-yield portfolio will default in any given year. Several recent studies have looked at cumulative default experience for high-yield portfolios, and although the results may differ to some extent, all such studies show a tendency for high-yield issues to become more susceptible to credit problems with the passage of time. Hence, any effective approach to the management of lower rated bond portfolios must include a specific strategy for deteriorating and defaulted deals.

Early Detection and Sale Is the Best Defense

Our approach begins with the doctrine of "first sale, best sale." The mathematical advantage of taking a small loss on a position, selling that position with accrued interest, and reinvesting proceeds in a more attractive high-yield bond is instantly apparent when compared with holding a security through a work-out period of one to two years, during which the investment stops paying interest. Use of present value analysis in making the decision to exit a troubled issue at a loss is frequently helpful. Proceeds of a bond sale, even at a deep discount, can be reinvested at currently very high yield' and immediately begin compensating for the difference between today's price and some hoped-for higher value in the future.

A full description of methods for detecting deteriorating credit worthiness is beyond the scope of this chapter. However, several major causes of such deterioration are summarized below.

Secular Deterioration in the Issuer's Principal Product or Service

Energy and energy services companies' inability to escape collapsing oil prices in the early 1980s provides a clear-cut example. Only a handful of such companies with high leverage could avoid debt service problems as oil prices plummeted from in excess of $30.00 per barrel to an eventual low of $7.00 $8.00 per barrel over the period 1981-1985. Early perception of the macro premise that the demand for hydrocarbons was elastic should have spurred high-yield managers to wholesale elimination of energy-related bonds from portfolios.

Inadequate Financing Controls

It is imperative for any issuer operating with high leverage to have a clear and timely way to monitor cash. Among the causes for the Chapter 11 filing of Revco Drug Stores were inadequate management accounting and inventory control systems. Rapid growth through acquisition by Northern Pacific similarly led to inventory management problems. This area should rank high among analyst concerns.

Initial or Second Stage Overleveraging

The problem of high-yield financings by Robert Campeau (Federated-Allied Stores) and by the Thompson family (Southland) are straightforward results of overpaying for operating assets.

Given that perpetuals went out of style during Napoleon's time, one way to look at determining whether growth in earnings or cash flow and exit valuation are important in realizing the return on debt claim is to look at how long it would take to recover your investment from internally generated cash flow. The assumption here is that most lenders will not rent their money for longer than 20 or 30 years.

Fraud and Criminal Activity by Management

The most difficult cause of a deteriorating credit to detect or avoid comes from malfeasance in the management of highly leveraged companies. Issuers like Saxon Industries, Flight Transportation, ZZZZ Best, and Wedtech are examples of high-yield transactions where managements systematically defrauded creditors while misleading investment bankers and accountants. The importance of thorough due diligence by high-yield underwriters cannot be overemphasized. Further, any suspicions by analysts or managers should be highlighted and discussed routinely. A sense of unease may provide the best signal to sell. Visits to production facilities and other operating assets financed by the issue should also be emphasized. A refusal by management to accommodate such visits is a danger signal.

Restructuring the Troubled Issuer

This section proposes a few summary observations derived from practical experience. The sharp rise in corporate debt use has been accompanied by deterioration in the rights and remedies of creditors. Recent changes in bankruptcy statutes provide growing flexibility for the troubled debtor. Leveraging of investment-grade bond issuers like R.J. Reynolds has incorporated the deliberate exploitation of weak indenture covenants in older investment-grade bond offerings. High-yield borrowers have become, in the last 15 years, ever more ready to propose out-of-court exchanges of new securities for old, usually involving reductions in claims and attempted preservation of large equity stakes by underperforming managements or investors. One recent example, blocked eventually by bondholders, is Marvel Group. Over the last several years these trends have been met by increased militancy on the part of high-yield bondholders. Some attributes of successful restructurings are set forth below; these appear to be increasingly embraced by high-yield creditors:

Out-of-Court Exchanges Must Be Guided by the Intent of the Bankruptcy Statutes

In brief, this means that a company that fails to pay as agreed must sacrifice its equity to preserve creditor wealth. A high-yield company that cannot service its debt belongs to its senior and subordinated lenders. Restructurings that seek to escape this outcome are increasingly unsuccessful. Much time and energy can be saved in negotiations with issuers if all sides understand that an out-of-court proposal, which is inferior to the likely outcome of a court-supervised reorganization, is likely to be a nonstarter.

Aggressive, Concerted Action by Bondholders Is a Necessity

The successful high-yield bond manager must be prepared to intervene early and forcefully in a deteriorating situation. Uncovering the list of issue holders and conferencing on the intent and objectives of the creditor group is paramount. Any negotiation with a troubled issuer is likely to be more efficient and successful when a large percentage of bondholders are negotiating within a united front. Knowledge of the general purpose and mechanisms of the bankruptcy laws and the ability by bondholders to retain top quality legal advisors are critical. The reader can immediately grasp the advantages of scale and institutional resources in a reorganization negotiation. The small-scale bondholder is disadvantaged compared to the institutional high-yield manager in a difficult negotiation with troubled issuers. Legal fees and travel expenses in a restructuring can mount quickly.

Further, the bondholder group must be alert to the prospect for restoring the investment through litigation, not only against the issuer, but also against parties involved in the initial transaction, such as managements and boards of directors, as well as individuals. Accounting firms should also be scrutinized. The rise of lawsuits involving fraudulent conveyance is one example of a growing interest in a variety of litigation strategies. One seminar on this topic listed breach of covenant litigation, RICO liabilities, direct liability, and the class action lawsuit among important considerations for creditors.' The effective high-yield manager needs to understand such concepts as equitable subordination, constructive trust, and lender liability in order to successfully integrate with other bondholders and litigators. Note again the disadvantage suffered by the odd-lot bondholder and stand-alone money manager or investment advisor in this increasingly complex arena.

The importance of an aggressive and forceful approach in troubled negotiations, in or out of bankruptcy court, can be scarcely overemphasized. The insolvent or illiquid debtor is aided by the passage of time during which he is failing to pay debt service. Protracted negotiations over minor details and less important issues is an effective debtor strategy, as is dividing the creditor group and conducting separate negotiations with group members. Most effective resolutions are likely to result from the appointment of leadership among creditors and the delegation of authority to negotiate to those leaders.

The Importance of Not Liquidating at the Bottom

Given the complexity of troubled debt negotiations, along with the expense and time involved in moving such negotiations forward successfully, the student of high-yield management may wonder whether a quick sale of the defaulted issue may not prove the better alternative. While each investment must be individually analyzed, strong empirical evidence exists suggesting the perils of early sale of defaulted bonds. One of the most powerful conclusions from the Hickman study is the high return enjoyed by investors who purchased corporate bonds at deeply depressed levels in the trough of the Great Depression. Prices of high-yield bonds following the initial announcement of grave financial difficulties appear to overly discount the impact of such problems.

Exceptions to this rule exist of course, but such exceptions typically emanate from deals that financed assets of very limited economic usefulness (for example, the ultralarge and slow-steaming container ships of McLean Industries). Another exception is where the business is acquired for a price well in excess of the economic value of its operating units (e.g., Southland, Federated-Allied). But in many instances aggressive negotiations may be handsomely rewarded. A rule of thumb that has prevailed since the early years of this century is that the subordinated debt of troubled issuers ultimately provides a worth of approximately 40 cents on the dollar. This outcome is suggested in the Hickman report as well as in several studies by Edward Altman of New York University. Money managers use this benchmark to begin consideration of restructuring outcomes.

CONCLUSION

Seeing an erroneous obituary in 1897, Mark Twain quipped to a correspondent that the report of his death had been greatly exaggerated. A similar exaggeration was the widely reported demise of the high-yield market in the late 1980s — in the late 1990s, this market is a primary financing source for thousands of growing businesses, with dozens of major financial institutions, banks, and brokers alike issuing and trading lower rated debt. But the practical rules for successful high-yield money managers have altered little in the past several decades. Thorough diversification, careful credit and market analysis, early sales when trouble approaches, and aggressive, prompt action when restructuring is required, all will apply in the coming millenium as they did in the 1990s, 1980s, and, we suspect, the more distant past.

About the Authors

Christopher B. Steward, CFA

Christopher B. Steward is a Vice President and global bond portfolio manager at Scudder, Stevens and Clark. His responsibilities include both research and portfolio management. Upon joining Scudder in 1992, he served as a market analyst specializing in non-dollar structured notes before assuming responsibilities as a portfolio manager. Prior to joining Scudder, Mr. Steward worked in the Foreign Exchange Analysis Department at the Federal Reserve Bank of New York where he provided regular reports to the Federal Open Market Committee on developments within the European Monetary System. He holds an M.A. in economics from Cambridge University and a B.A. from Vassar College. A Chartered Financial Analyst, he co-authored two chapters in the fifth edition of *The Handbook of Fixed Income Securities*, one on international fixed income markets and another on international fixed income portfolio management.

J. Hank Lynch, CFA

Hank Lynch is a Vice President at Scudder, Stevens and Clark. He serves on the firm's global bond management team with a focus on portfolio allocation and quantitative strategy. Mr. Lynch had worked in quantitative bond research where he was responsible for U.S. yield curve strategy and relative value analysis of debt instruments with non-traditional cash flows. His work included analysis of derivatives and structured notes linked to foreign markets, emerging market debt, and currencies. More recently, Mr. Lynch has been weighing expected risks and returns of bond market, currency, and option-based strategies for Scudder's international and global bond portfolios. He holds a B.A. from Amherst College and is a Chartered Financial Analyst.

Chapter 7

International Bond Portfolio Management

Christopher B. Steward, CFA
Vice President
Scudder, Stevens and Clark

J. Hank Lynch, CFA
Vice President
Scudder, Stevens and Clark

INTRODUCTION

Management of an international bond portfolio poses more varied challenges than management of a domestic bond portfolio. Differing time zones, local market structures, settlement and custodial issues, and currency management all complicate the fundamental decisions facing every fixed income manager in determining how the portfolio should be positioned with respect to duration, sector, and yield curve.

The following fundamental steps in the investment process apply to domestic and international investing alike:

1. setting investment objectives
2. establishing investment guidelines
3. developing portfolio strategy
4. constructing the portfolio
5. monitoring risk and evaluating performance

The added complexities of cross-border investing magnify the importance of a well defined, disciplined, investment process. The chapter is organized to address each of these challenges in turn.

INVESTMENT OBJECTIVES

Most investors are attracted to global bonds as an asset class because of their historically higher returns than U.S. bonds. Others are drawn to global bonds because of their diversification value in reducing overall portfolio risk. The investor's rationale for investing in international bonds is central to developing appropriate return objectives and risk tolerances for a portfolio. Broadly speaking, investor objectives can be divided into four categories: total return, diversification or risk reduction, current income, and asset/liability matching. Each of these investment objectives has implications for the management of an international bond portfolio and should be reflected in the investment guidelines. At a minimum, investment guidelines should include return objectives, risk tolerances, benchmark selection, and an appropriate time horizon for judging performance.

Benchmark Selection

Benchmark selection for an international bond portfolio has many ramifications and should therefore be done carefully. As is the case when choosing an international equity benchmark index, the choice of a pure capitalization (market value) weighted index may create a benchmark that exposes the investor to a disproportionate share in the Japanese market relative to the investor's liabilities or diversification preferences. While international equity indices chosen for benchmarks are most often quoted in the investor's local currency (i.e., unhedged), international bond benchmarks may be hedged, unhedged, or partially hedged depending on the investors objectives. The choice of a hedged, unhedged, or hybrid benchmark will likely alter the risk and return profile of the resulting investment portfolio and should thus be done with careful consideration of the primary rationale for investing in international bonds.

Benchmarks can be selected from one, or a combination, of the many existing bond indices: global, international (ex-U.S.), currency-hedged, G7 only, 1-3 year, 3-5 year, 7-10 year, emerging markets, Brady bonds, etc., or a custom index can be created. The most frequently used benchmarks are the J.P. Morgan Global Government Bond Index, or the Salomon Brothers World Government Bond Index, although many other investment houses such as Merrill Lynch, Lehman Brothers, Goldman Sachs, and UBS offer full index services as well. The benchmark often provides both the return objective and the measure of portfolio risk.

Benchmark Currency Position

Currency management is a matter of much debate in the academic literature. The natural currency exposures incurred through international investing require portfolio managers to adopt either an active or passive approach to currency management. Many managers are attracted to active currency management because of the large gains that can be attained through correctly anticipating currency movements. Some international fixed income portfolio managers, however, prefer not to actively manage currency exposures. This may reflect doubts about their own ability to add value through active currency management, or a belief that no one can forecast currency movements with any degree of reliability. The former often hire outside currency overlay managers to manage the residual currency risk determined by the bond allocation, the latter often run fully hedged or unhedged portfolios as a matter of policy.

Exhibit 1: Returns and Standard Deviation of Returns of the Salomon Non-U.S. Government Bond Index and Lehman Aggregate Index (Monthly Data, Unhedged, and Hedged Basis)

	1985-96	1985-88	1989-92	1993-96	1989-96
Annualized Total Return					
Unhedged Index	14.45%	25.15%	7.91%	11.00%	9.45%
Hedged Index	8.75	10.23	6.60	9.45	8.02
50% Hedged	11.26	16.93	7.00	10.09	8.53
U.S. Aggregate Index	10.10	11.76	11.66	6.94	9.28
Standard Deviation of Returns					
Unhedged Index	10.97%	13.34%	11.21%	6.89%	9.31%
Hedged Index	3.77	4.23	3.39	3.56	3.50
50% Hedged	6.65	8.28	6.57	4.17	5.52
U.S. Aggregate Index	4.86	5.90	4.12	4.24	4.22
Sharpe Ratio					
Unhedged Index	0.77	1.37	0.12	0.93	0.42
Hedged Index	0.73	0.80	0.00	1.37	0.70
50% Hedged	0.79	1.22	0.60	1.33	0.54
U.S. Aggregate Index	0.84	0.84	1.23	0.56	0.87

Most of the academic research on currency hedging for U.S. dollar-based investors suggests that a partially hedged benchmark offers superior risk-adjusted returns as compared with either a fully hedged or unhedged benchmark. This research has led some to recommend a 50% hedged benchmark for either a passively managed currency strategy, or as a good initial hedged position for an active currency manager. In addition to selecting an appropriate benchmark, a suitable currency hedge position, or benchmark hedge ratio, needs to be determined. For example, a U.S. dollar-based fixed income investor whose primary goal is risk reduction might adopt a hedged or mostly hedged benchmark as the diversification benefit has historically been greater from hedged international bonds. Despite a higher correlation with the U.S. bond market than unhedged international bonds, hedged international bonds offer better risk reduction due to a lower standard deviation of return than even the U.S. market. In addition, this lesser volatility of hedged international bonds results in more predictable returns. Conversely, an investor who has a total return objective, and a greater risk tolerance, would be more likely to adopt an unhedged, or mostly unhedged benchmark and allow more latitude for active currency management.

International bonds have historically provided higher returns than U.S. bonds. As seen in Exhibit 1, over the 12 years through 1996, the Salomon Non-U.S. Government Bond Index has outperformed the Lehman Aggregate Bond Index by an average of 435 basis points per annum. When looked at on a hedged basis, however, the non-U.S. index lagged the U.S. performance by 135 basis points. The standard deviation of returns for the non-U.S. unhedged index is substantially higher than the standard deviation of U.S. returns. However, the standard deviation of returns for the hedged index is lower than the standard deviation of U.S. returns during all periods. Using Sharpe ratios to compare returns on a risk-adjusted basis,[1] both the hedged and unhedged non-U.S. index underperformed the U.S. over the 12-year period. However, the results for each of the three 4-year periods are too variable to draw a firm conclusion about which provides the better risk-adjusted return.

Although the unhedged non-U.S. bond index often provided higher returns than the hedged index, the nearly 15 percentage points in annualized out-performance of the unhedged over the hedged index from 1985 through 1988 was extremely unusual. This was due to the dollar's rapid decline from its 1984 peak. If instead only the eight years from 1989 through 1996 are analyzed, the picture changes dramatically with the unhedged index outperforming the hedged index by 143 basis points. The Sharpe ratios for this period are 0.42 for the unhedged index and 0.70 for the hedged index, compared with 0.87 for the Lehman Aggregate index. According to the data in Exhibit 1 the argument for international bonds as an asset class for U.S dollar-based investors hardly seems compelling. However, it is the correlations of different asset classes that provide the diversification ben-efit, and when international bonds are included as a component of a U.S. dollar-based fixed income portfolio, the analysis provides dramatically different results.

Exhibit 2 shows that when the same analysis used in Exhibit 1 is applied to a portfolio composed of a 30% allocation to international bonds, the risk-adjusted returns improve substantially. Over the 12-year period, the portfolio with an allocation to unhedged bonds provided 130 basis points of added return over a domestic-only portfolio while slightly lowering overall portfolio volatility. Although the portfolio including hedged international bonds returned 41 basis points less than the domestic-only portfolio, its Sharpe ratio was higher than the domestic-only portfolio because its standard deviation was 25% lower than that of the domestic-only portfolio. In fact, the domestic-only portfolio had the highest standard deviation of any of the four portfolios, giving it the lowest Sharpe ratio.

As shown above, returns from currency have been highly variable depending on the time period chosen. The academic literature, and the data in Exhibits 1 and 2, support adopting a partially hedged currency benchmark. A benchmark currency position should be established in accordance with careful consideration for risk tolerances and return objectives.

Returns of those portfolios with a 30% international bond allocation over the 1989 to 1996 period are lower than the full 12-year performance figures, but the risk-adjusted performance of each of these portfolios remains higher than the domestic-only portfolio. The return on the portfolio including a 30% allocation to unhedged

---

[1] The Sharpe ratio measures returns in excess of the risk-free rate, per unit of standard deviation. The formula is $(R_p - RFR)/\sigma_p$ where R_p is the return on the portfolio, RFR is the risk-free rate, and σ_p is the portfolio standard deviation. The U.S. Treasury bill component of the Salomon Brothers World Money Market Performance Index was used as the risk-free rate.

international bonds of 9.33 was five basis points higher than the domestic-only portfolio, and its standard deviation of 4.12% was ten basis points lower than the domestic-only portfolio, giving it a Sharpe ratio of 0.91 compared to the domestic portfolio's 0.87. The Sharpe ratios for the other two portfolios that include hedged and 50% hedged international bonds are even higher at 1.04 and 1.01 respectively.

Risk Limits

Many investment guidelines will include explicit risk limits on bond and currency positions as well as duration and credit risk. Exposure limits can be either expressed as absolute percentages, or portfolio weights relative to the benchmark. Expressing limits in terms of trading blocs, which exhibit a high degree of correlation, allows the portfolio manager more scope for shifting exposures without adding significantly to overall portfolio risk. Bond markets can be divided into five trading blocs: the *dollar bloc* (the U.S., Canada, Australia, and New Zealand), *core Europe* (Germany, France, Holland, and Belgium), *peripheral Europe* (Italy, Spain, the U.K., Denmark, Sweden, Finland, and Portugal), Japan, and the *emerging markets*. These dividing lines, however, are somewhat subjective. For example, the U.K. often trades more closely with dollar bloc than European markets, and many might place Denmark with the core European countries. Limits on investment in countries outside the benchmark should also be specified at the outset. Despite the pitfalls of using duration to measure interest rate risk across countries, risk limits on duration are nonetheless useful and should be established.

Exhibit 2: Returns and Standard Deviation of Returns of a Portfolio with 30% International Bonds and 70% Domestic Bonds (Monthly Data)

	1985-96	1985-88	1989-92	1993-96	1989-96
Annualized Total Return					
Unhedged Index	11.40%	15.78%	10.54%	8.16%	9.33%
Hedged Index	9.69	11.30	10.14	7.70	8.90
50% Hedged	10.45	13.31	10.26	7.89	9.05
U.S. Aggregate Index	10.10	11.76	11.66	6.94	9.28
Standard Deviation of Returns					
Unhedged Index	4.79	5.82	4.51	3.63	4.12
Hedged Index	3.64	4.38	3.10	3.20	3.18
50% Hedged	4.00	4.89	3.56	3.25	3.44
U.S. Aggregate Index	4.86	5.90	4.12	4.24	4.22
Sharpe Ratio					
Unhedged Index	1.13	1.54	0.87	0.43	0.91
Hedged Index	1.02	1.02	1.14	0.98	1.04
50% Hedged	1.11	1.33	1.03	1.02	1.01
U.S. Aggregate Index	0.84	0.84	1.23	0.56	0.87

Exhibit 3: Examples of Bond and Currency Risk Limits for an International Bond Portfolio

Bond Exposures

Currency Bloc	Benchmark	Minimum	Maximum
Yen	32%	15%	45%
U.S.	0%	0%	15%
Dollar Bloc	6%	0%	18%
Core Europe	47%	30%	65%
Peripheral Europe	16%	0%	35%
Other Markets	0%	0%	15%
Total Duration as a % of Index	100%	80%	120%

Currency Exposures

Currency Bloc	Benchmark	Minimum	Maximum
Yen	32%	10%	40%
U.S.	0%	20%	95%
Dollar Bloc	6%	0%	20%
Core Europe	47%	15%	55%
Peripheral Europe	16%	0%	25%
Other Markets	0%	0%	10%
Total Foreign Currency Exposure	100%	5%	80%

The risk limits in Exhibit 3 might be appropriate for a moderately risk averse investor. Note that in Exhibit 3 the range of allowable exposures is wider for bond exposures than currency exposures and that the minimum U.S. dollar exposure is 20%.

Derivatives

Investment guidelines should specify the permitted use of derivatives in the portfolio. Although derivatives are required to hedge currency exposures, they are a useful, but not necessary, tool for duration management. Guidelines will usually place limitations on the leverage[2] that can be obtained through use of derivatives, for example by requiring cash to be set aside equal to the notional amount of a long futures position, or by prohibiting the writing of uncovered put or call options. Structured notes, which combine derivatives, such as swaps and options, with a certificate of deposit or medium-term note to create a specific exposure to interest rates or currencies, should be subject to the same limitations on leverage. Many structured notes were engineered to have risks commensurate with, or less than, plain vanilla bonds. The separation of coupon and principal payments in most structures notes gives them a similar appearance to fixed income securities.

[2] Implicit in most derivatives, both fixed income and currency derivatives, is an exposure to shifts in short-term interest rates.

However, structured notes, like the derivatives of which they are composed, can also be highly levered. The risk to capital incorporated in some of these securities, if poorly understood, can result in substantial losses. Thus, the use of structured notes need not be prohibited, but guidelines for their use should contain criteria consistent with those applied to the derivatives of which they are composed.

PORTFOLIO STRATEGY

Once the investment guidelines have been established, the portfolio manager needs to develop a portfolio strategy appropriate to the investor's objectives and risk tolerances. Just as in many other areas of investment management, portfolio managers often subscribe to different management styles, or investment disciplines. As the performance of most portfolio managers is judged against the benchmark return, they are constantly seeking opportunities to outperform the benchmark. There are a number of means by which portfolio managers can add to returns, however, the bulk of excess returns relative to the benchmark come from broad bond market and currency allocation decisions. A disciplined investment approach, based upon fundamental economic factors and market indicators of value, can facilitate the market and currency selection process. Because of the historically high volatility of currency returns, the approach to currency management should be of primary concern.

Styles of International Bond Portfolio Management

The image that many people have of international bond managers is that of a jet fighter pilot: well seasoned, cool under fire, and ready to pit his nerve and skill against the market. However, the metaphor that best describes the international bond manager is not that of the fighter pilot, but the captain of a 747. Rather than "pushing the envelope" of his machine's performance, the jumbo jet pilot relies more on checklists and management of computer flight and navigation systems than piloting skill. The modern jetliner is an extremely complicated piece of machinery that requires a depth of experience and skill in managing the wealth of resources available on the flight deck. The pilot, in addition to drawing from his own years of experience, relies on other inputs as well; some from other members of the crew, and some from talking to controllers and meteorologists on the ground. Like managing a portfolio, piloting a jetliner involves managing risks, and a safe arrival is better achieved by avoiding dangerous situations than by deft manipulation of the controls in an emergency.

International bond managers utilize one or more different management styles. These can be divided into four general categories:

- *The Experienced Trader.* These managers use experience and intuition to identify market opportunities. They tend to be active traders, trying to anticipate the next market shift by international fixed income and hedge fund managers. The basis for these trades is derived from estimates of competitors' positions and risk tolerances bolstered by observation of market price movements and flow information obtained from brokerage houses. The experienced trader is often a contrarian, looking to profit from situations where many investors may be forced to stop themselves out of losing positions.

- *The Fundamentalist.* This management style rests upon a belief that bonds and currencies trade according to the economic cycle, and that the cycle is forecastable. These managers rely mostly upon economic analysis and forecasts in selecting bond markets and currencies. These managers tend to have less portfolio turnover as the economic fundamentals have little impact on short-term price movements.

- *The Black Box.* The quantitative manager believes that computer models can identify market relationships that human beings cannot. These models can rely exclusively on economic data, price data, or some combination of the two. Quantitative managers believe that use of computer models can create a more disciplined investment approach which, either because of other managers' emotional attachment to positions, their lack of trading disciplines, or their inability to process more than a few variables simultaneously, will provide superior investment results.

- *The Chartist.* Some investors may rely primarily on technical analysis to determine which assets to buy or sell. Chartists will look at daily, weekly, and monthly charts to try to ascertain the strength of market trends, or to identify potential turning points in markets. Trend following approaches, such as moving averages and stochastics aim to allow the portfolio manager to exploit market momentum. Counter-trend approaches, such as relative strength indices and oscillators try to identify when recent price trends are likely to reverse.

Very few international bond portfolio managers rely on only one of these management styles, but instead use some combination of each. Investment managers that rely on forecasts of the economic cycle to drive their investment process will from time to time take positions contrary to their medium-term strategy to take advantage of temporary under or overvaluation of markets identified by technical analysis, or estimates of market positions. Even "quant shops" that rely heavily on computer models for driving investment decisions will sometimes look to other management styles to add incremental returns. Regardless of the manager's investment style, investment decisions must be consistent with the investor's return objectives and risk tolerances, and within the investment guidelines.

Sources of Excess Return

The baseline for any international bond portfolio is the benchmark. However, in order to earn returns in excess of the benchmark, after management fees, the portfolio manager must find ways to augment returns. These excess returns can be generated through a combination of five broad strategies: bond market selection, currency selection, duration management/yield curve plays, sector/credit/security selection, and, if permitted, investing in markets outside the benchmark. Each of these strategies can add to returns, however, currency and bond market selections generally provide the lion's share of returns.

Bond Market Selection

Incremental returns from overweighting the best performing bond markets can be extremely large. Annual local currency return differentials between the best and worst performing bond markets ranged from 7% to 39%, with an average difference of 17 percentage points according to the 18 years of annual return data from the Salomon Brothers World Government Bond and Bond Performance Indices which include only developed markets. When currency movements are added, the return differentials nearly double. As shown in Exhibit 4, in U.S. dollar terms, the smallest range between the best and worst performing market was 14% and the widest was 65% with an average differential of 31 percentage points. Thus, international bond portfolio managers can significantly enhance returns by overweighting the better performing bond markets, and currencies, in the index.[3]

Currency Selection

Regardless of the initial portfolio hedge ratio, most guidelines will allow for some active management of currency exposures. The attraction of active currency management is strong because the potential gains are so large. However, as the volatility of currency returns is generally higher than that of bond market returns, the incremental returns gained from currency exposures must be evaluated relative to the additional risk incurred. For an active currency management strategy to consistently provide superior risk-adjusted performance, a currency forecasting method is required that can predict future spot rates better than forward foreign exchange rates. As shown later, forward foreign exchange rates are not forecasts of future spot foreign exchange rates, but are determined by short interest rate differentials.

Academic studies have shown that several strategies have been successful in generating consistent profits through active currency management. The fact that forward foreign exchange rates are poor predictors of future spot exchange rates is well known. Historically, discount currencies (i.e., those with higher interest rates than the base currency) have depreciated less than the amount implied by the forward rates, providing superior returns from holding unhedged positions in currencies with higher interest rates. Overweighting of currencies with high real interest rates versus those with lower real interest rates has also been shown to provide incremental returns. In addition, currency movements are not a random walk, but exhibit serial correlation, or a tendency to trend. Thus,

---

[3] As of this writing, it appears likely that at least several countries will adopt the Euro as a common currency when European Monetary Union is scheduled to commence in January 1999. Although the impact of this event is a matter of some debate, the bond markets in the countries which have adopted the single currency will trade much more closely than before.

simple technical trading rules, such as the crossover of a short and long moving average, can provide opportunities for incremental currency returns. These findings, demonstrating that excess currency returns can be generated consistently, provide a powerful incentive for active currency management.

Duration Management

Although closely aligned with the bond market selection decision, duration management can also enhance returns. Bullet versus barbell strategies in a curve steepening or flattening environment can enhance yield and total return. In addition to these strategies that are also available to domestic portfolio managers, the international fixed income portfolio manager has the option of shifting duration between markets while leaving the portfolio's overall duration unchanged. Likewise, duration-neutral positions across markets can be achieved by targeting preferred sectors of the yield curve.[4]

Duration management, however, is more difficult in international bond investing as very few foreign bond markets have liquid bond issues with an original maturity longer than 10 years. Most foreign bond markets also lack the broad range of instruments, such as strips and repos, that allow for low-cost, active management of duration. Recent progress on these fronts is being made in the U.K., Italy, and Germany. Interest rate futures, available in most markets, offer a very liquid and low cost vehicle for changing duration or market exposure quickly. The interest rate swaps market is generally very liquid across international bond markets; however, counterparty credit, technical, and operational barriers limit effective participation in this market to large institutional investors.

Exhibit 4: U.S. Bonds and Non-U.S. World Index versus Best and Worst Performing Markets

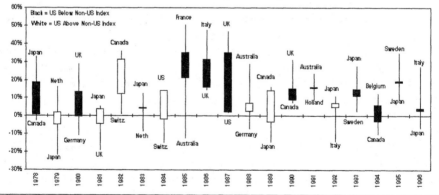

[4] As discussed later, a duration-neutral position to the benchmark would mean having the same contribution to duration from each country as the benchmark. Contribution to duration, measured as the weight times duration of a given market can be achieved with a large market weight of short duration bonds or a small market weight of long duration bonds.

Sector Selection

Investing in non-government bonds can also enhance returns as most indices include only government bonds. However, options are more limited as government and government-guaranteed issues account for 62% of all bond issues outstanding compared with 12.7% for the corporate bonds. If the U.S. is excluded, where corporate bonds account for one third of all U.S. dollar-denominated bonds outstanding, the figure drops to only 4.2%. Corporate bonds account for less than 15% of the market capitalization in all other bond markets — except for a 26% share in the Netherlands. In several large countries, such as Germany and Italy, non-financial corporate bonds are virtually nonexistent. This scarcity of corporate bond markets outside the U.S. is due to a policy of discouraging the raising of capital through bond issuance in favor of bank financing and equity issuance in many countries. Other instruments are also available in selected markets including Eurobonds, mortgage bonds, and inflation indexed bonds.

Investing in Markets Outside the Index

If allowed by portfolio guidelines, allocating assets to markets outside the index can significantly enhance returns without dramatically altering the risk profile of the portfolio. For example, Finland was one of the best performing bond markets during 1995, but, because of its small size, was not included in the Salomon Brothers World Government Bond Index (WGBI) until June 1996. Similarly, New Zealand's very attractive U.S. dollar return of 18% during 1996 would have ranked it as the fourth best performing market in the WGBI. For those investors with a higher risk tolerance, exposure to emerging markets can significantly add to returns. For example, a portfolio composed of 80% exposure to the Salomon Non-U.S. Government Bond Index and 20% exposure to the Salomon Brady Bond Index from 1991 through 1996 would have added 186 basis points to the return of the international index and *reduced* the standard deviation of returns by 13%.

A Fundamental-Based Approach to Investing

The portfolio strategy is often composed of both a medium term *strategic* allocation, and a shorter term *tactical* allocation. The strategic allocation is composed of positions designed to take advantage of longer term economic trends designed to be held for one to three months, or longer. The tactical allocation generally relies on technical analysis or flow information to identify shifts in market prices that are likely to occur within a few days to several weeks. Tactical allocations are often contrarian in nature, driven by expectations of a reversal in a recent price trends; however, tactical allocations can also be momentum following, especially if a breakout of a technical range appears likely. The strategic allocation can be compared to the course set by a sailing ship. The tactical allocation may result in substantial divergence from the course setting at times, much as a ship must tack when sailing into the wind. The trick, however, is to be able to identify when changing conditions warrant a change in the set course, or only a small detour.

Exhibit 5: G7 Industrial Production and Change in Bond Yields

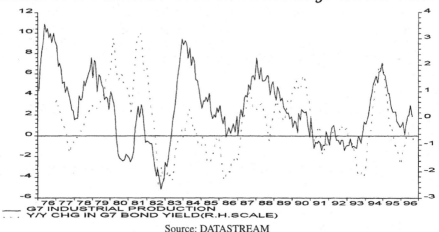

G7 INDUSTRIAL PRODUCTION
... Y/Y CHG IN G7 BOND YIELD(R.H.SCALE)

Source: DATASTREAM

The strategic decision of which bond markets and currencies to over-weight usually begins with an outlook for the economic cycle and bond and currency forecasts in each of the markets to be considered for investment. As shown in Exhibit 5, the long-run economic cycle is closely correlated with changes in bond yields, and trends in both the economic cycle and bond yields tend to persist for a year or longer. The millions of dollars spent each year by money management firms, banks, and brokerage houses in forecasting economic trends is testimony to the potential returns that can be achieved by correctly forecasting economic growth, especially turning points in the economic cycle. Forecasting interest rates, however, is extremely difficult and the academic literature generally holds that interest rate forecasts are unable to generate consistent risk-adjusted excess returns. This is partly because market prices can deviate substantially over the short term from the level consistent with the economic fundamentals which only impact bond and currency prices over the medium to long term. Also, the volatile nature of certain economic data series may result in an exaggerated market reaction to an individual data release that may be at odds with the actual trend in the economy. These deviations may persist for several months until either the initial figure is revised, or several subsequent data releases reveal the error in the initial interpretation.

The creation of an independent economic outlook can be useful in several ways. It can help identify when market interpretations of the economic data are too extreme, or add value through correctly anticipating economic shifts not reflected in the market consensus. Also, as it is often not absolute changes in interest rates, but changes in interest rates relative to other markets that determines the margin of performance in international fixed income investing, an independent economic outlook does not require accurate growth forecasts for each individual market, but only economic growth differentials to be able to add value. Whether the portfolio will invest in U.S. bonds or not, the large influence of the

U.S. dollar and the Treasury market on foreign markets underlines the importance of an independent outlook on the U.S. economy.

Thus, the economic outlook forms the foundation for the *strategic* allocation for bonds and currencies. The economic outlook should also include an indication of the relative conviction regarding the economic view for each country to assist in ranking the relative attractiveness of markets. However, even though economic fundamentals in a particular country may be extremely bond supportive, bond prices may be too high to make it an attractive investment. Likewise, bonds are sometimes excessively cheap in countries with poor economic fundamentals thus providing an attractive investment opportunity. Thus, the economic outlook must be compared with either consensus economic forecasts, or some measure of market value to identify attractive investment opportunities. In addition, the volatilities and correlations of the various bond and currency markets should be used to assess the incremental impact of any position on overall portfolio risk compared with its expected return.

The strategic allocation decision of which markets to over or underweight relative to the benchmark is thus a complex interaction of expected returns derived from assessments of economic trends, technical and value factors, and risk factors, estimated from historical volatilities and cross-market correlations.

Fundamental Economic Factors

The seven main categories of fundamental economic influences are: cyclicals, inflation, monetary policy, fiscal policy, debt, the balance of payments, and politics. Each factor needs to be evaluated against market expectations to determine its likely impact on bond and currency prices. For example, a drop in inflation in a country such as Germany which has a history of low inflation may have a much lesser impact on bond prices than a drop in Italian inflation.

Value and Technical Indicators

Identification of trends in economic fundamentals can help identify attractive investment opportunities in markets, but without some yardstick with which to measure value, we are like Archimedes with his lever but with no fulcrum on which to rest it. The determination of relative value is highly subjective. Most investors have preferred measures for assessing market over or undervaluation, however, even the most respected market strategists often get it wrong.

PORTFOLIO CONSTRUCTION

Translating the strategic outlook into a portfolio allocation requires a framework for assessing expected returns against incremental portfolio risk. The following discussion on sources of return illustrates how returns can be separated into three components: excess returns on bonds, excess returns on currencies, and the risk-free rate. This methodology can assist in identifying where market prices are most out of line with the strategic outlook and whether bond market exposures should be hedged or left unhedged. However, the potential for higher returns is often associated with greater risk, and reference to market correlations can help estimate the incremental risk posed to the portfolio by any change in allocation. A brief discussion of other tools for portfolio construction, such as breakeven analysis and forward curves close this section.

Components of Return

The total return of an unhedged international bond portfolio for a U.S. dollar based investor can be expressed in the following equation:[5]

$$R_\$ \approx \sum w_i(r_i + \varepsilon_{\$,\,i}) \tag{1}$$

where

$R_\$$ = total portfolio return in U.S. dollars
r_i = bond market return for country i in local currency
$\varepsilon_{\$,i}$ = percentage change of the dollar exchange rate with country i
w_i = weight of the bonds of country i in the overall portfolio

Thus, the expected return on the portfolio is a function of the expected returns on the bonds and currencies in each market and their weights in the portfolio. However, in order to fully comprehend the impact of currency exposures on returns, the mechanics of currency hedging must first be understood.

Mechanics of Currency Hedging

Hedge costs are driven by short-term interest rate differentials. The covered interest rate parity theorem, associated with Keynes and Fisher, states that the forward foreign exchange rate for a fixed period must be equal to the interest rate differential between the two countries, otherwise riskless arbitrage would occur to bring the two back into equilibrium.[6] The formula is:

$$F = S_0\!\left(\frac{1 + c_d}{1 + c_f}\right) \tag{2}$$

---

[5] The structure of this discussion is taken from Brian D. Singer and Denis S. Karnosky, *The General Framework for Global Investment Management and Performance Attribution* (Charlottesville, VA: The Research Foundation of the Institute of Chartered Financial Analysts, 1994). An abridged version also appeared in *The Journal of Portfolio Management* (Winter 1995), pp. 84-92. The relationship in equation (1) is approximate because bond market and currency returns of a foreign investment is more accurately expressed as the compounded gain of the two components: $(1 + r_i) \times (1 + \varepsilon_{\$,i}) - 1$.

[6] Uncovered interest rate parity would hold if the forward rates were an unbiased indicator of future foreign exchange rates, which was shown to be false in the portfolio strategy section. For an excellent introduction to currency terminology and the calculation of forward exchange rates see Chapter 1 of Roger E. Clarke and Mark P. Kritzman, *Currency Management: Concepts and Practices* (Charlottesville, VA: The Research Foundation of the Institute of Chartered Financial Analysts, 1996).

where F is the forward foreign exchange rate, S_0 is the spot foreign exchange rate, and c_d and c_f are the domestic and foreign cash returns, or short-term (risk-free) interest rates, which match the maturity of the forward contract. By rearranging equation (2), the forward discount or premium f (or the percentage change of the forward rate from the spot exchange rate), becomes approximately the differential between the risk-free rates.[7]

$$f = F - S_0 \approx c_d - c_f \tag{3}$$

The forward rate can also be expressed in "points" or the difference between the forward and spot rate, $F - S_0$. When interest rates are lower in the foreign country (i.e., the forward points are positive), the forward foreign exchange rate trades at a premium. That is, for the return on cash deposits to be equal in both currencies, the lower interest rate currency must appreciate to the forward foreign exchange rate. For example, as German rates are presently lower than U.S. rates, the forward points are positive for the U.S. dollar against the German mark. Thus, if cash returns are to be the same in both currencies, the percent appreciation of the German mark against the U.S. dollar would have to be exactly equal to the forward premium.

The Currency Hedge Decision

If the possibility of hedging using currency forwards is allowed, the portfolio return of equation (1) changes. The currency term would be left unhedged if the percentage return from currency is expected to be greater than the forward discount or premium, $\varepsilon_{\$i} > f_{\$,i}$, or hedged with forwards if the expected currency return is expected to be less than the forward discount or premium $\varepsilon_{\$i} < f_{\$,i}$. Thus the equation for a hedged portfolio becomes:

$$HR_\$ = \sum w_i(r_i + f_{\$,i}) \tag{4}$$

As equation (3) showed, the forward premium or discount is effectively equal to the short-term interest rate differential; thus, $f_{\$,i} = c_\$ - c_i$. By substituting this identity for the forward hedge, the equations for individual country unhedged and hedged returns become:

$$R_{\$i} = r_i + \varepsilon_{\$,i} \qquad \text{(unhedged return)} \tag{5}$$

$$HR_{\$i} = r_i + f_{\$,i} = r_i + (c_\$ - c_i) \qquad \text{(hedged return)} \tag{6}$$

---

[7] Equation (2) assumes that exchange rates are quoted in "direct terms," i.e., the U.S. dollar value of one foreign currency unit, though quote conventions vary by market. Futures and options on currencies traded on the Chicago Mercantile Exchange are all quoted in direct terms; however, over-the-counter forward contracts use market convention, most of which are in indirect terms (foreign currency units per U.S. dollar). Using indirect terms, the forward discount *or* premium in equation (3) becomes $f = c_f - c_d$. To avoid the complexities of compounding, the time period is assumed to be one year.

where $R_{\$i}$ is the unhedged returns from country i for a U.S. dollar-based investor and $HR_{\$i}$ is the hedged return. There remain, however, two further options: cross hedging and proxy hedging. Cross hedging replaces the currency exposure to country i with currency exposure in country j, $(\varepsilon_{\$,j})$, through a cross forward rate, $(f_{j,i})$. Proxy hedging keeps the currency exposure in country i, but creates a hedge by establishing a short position in country j's currency $(-\varepsilon_{\$,j})$. These strategies would normally be considered only where the currencies of country i and j are highly correlated, and the hedge costs in country j, are lower than in country i.

$$CR_{\$i} = r_i + (f_{j,i} + \varepsilon_{\$,j}) \qquad \text{(cross-hedged return)} \qquad (7)$$

$$PR_{\$i} = r_i + \varepsilon_{\$,i} + (f_{\$,j} - \varepsilon_{\$,j}) \qquad \text{(proxy-hedged return)} \qquad (8)$$

By substituting short term interest rate differentials for the forward returns and rearranging equations (5), (6), (7), and (8), it becomes apparent that the difference in return among the three strategies is entirely due to short term interest rates and currency exposure. The bond component of returns thus becomes the bond return minus the domestic short term interest rate, rather than the full measure of return.

$$R_{\$i} = (r_i - c_i) + (c_i + \varepsilon_{\$,i}) \qquad \text{(unhedged return)} \qquad (9)$$

$$HR_{\$i} = (r_i - c_i) + c_\$ \qquad \text{(hedged return)} \qquad (10)$$

$$CR_{\$i} = (r_i - c_i) + (c_j + \varepsilon_{\$,j}) \qquad \text{(cross-hedged return)} \qquad (11)$$

$$PR_{\$i} = (r_i - c_i) + (c_i + \varepsilon_{\$,i}) + [(c_\$ - c_j) - \varepsilon_{\$,j}] \quad \text{(proxy-hedged return)} \qquad (12)$$

Equations (9), (10), (11), and (12) show how integral the short-term interest rate differential is to the currency hedge decision. Hence, the short-rate differential should be attributed to the currency decision, and bond market returns should be calculated minus the domestic short-term interest rate. This can be made explicit by adding and subtracting the U.S. cash rate from each of the four equations above. This allows the forward premium $(f_{\$,i} = c_\$ - c_i)$ to be inserted into the currency term creating three distinct components of return: the risk free rate $(c_\$)$, the excess bond return $(r_i - c_i)$, and the excess currency return, either hedged, unhedged, cross-hedged, or proxy hedged.

$$R_{\$i} = c_\$ + (r_i - c_i) + (\varepsilon_{\$,i} - f_{\$,i}) \qquad \text{(unhedged return)} \qquad (13)$$

$$HR_{\$i} = c_\$ + (r_i - c_i) \qquad \text{(hedged return)} \qquad (14)$$

$$CR_{\$i} = c_\$ + (r_i - c_i) + (\varepsilon_{\$,j} - f_{\$,j}) \qquad \text{(cross-hedged return)} \qquad (15)$$

$$PR_{\$i} = c_\$ + (r_i - c_i) + [(\varepsilon_{\$,i} - \varepsilon_{\$,j}) - f_{j,i}] \quad \text{(proxy-hedged return)} \qquad (16)$$

Thus, the excess currency return becomes the currency return in excess of the forward premium (or discount). It can be seen that the bond decision is purely a matter of selecting the markets which offer the best expected excess return and that the bond and currency allocation decisions are entirely independent. This method of analyzing sources of return in effect treats bond and currency returns as if they were synthetic futures or forward positions. Equations (13) through (16) could be applied to a purely leveraged investor, such as a hedge fund, by simply omitting the risk free rate term. Cash investors with limited ability to take currency exposures independently of bond positions may find equations (9) through (12) more useful where the risk free rate is treated as an integral part of the currency hedge decision.

This methodology of attributing cash returns to the currency decision, and the excess return over cash to bonds, has implications for how allocation decisions are made. The returns of higher yielding markets, or those with inverted yield curves, will look somewhat less attractive when analyzed net of the cash interest rate. For example, at the beginning of 1996, Italian 10-year bond yields were 10.70% and 1-year Italian interest rates were 10.10%, thus the running yield that could be attributed to bond performance was only 60 basis points. In order to gain the additional 10.10% in running yield, the position would have to be run unhedged. One-year interest rates in the U.S. were 6% resulting in 410 basis point differential with Italy. Thus, it would have cost a U.S. dollar-based investor 4.1% to hedge exposure to the Italian lira over 12 months using currency forwards. In other words, hedging the Italian lira exposure in essence would have substituted the U.S. cash yield (or risk-free rate) of 6% for the Italian cash yield of 10.10%. Thus, if the Italian lira depreciated by less than the 4.1% against the U.S. dollar implied by the forward rate over 1996, the unhedged lira position would have added value over a hedged position.

In actuality, the Italian lira appreciated by 4.3% against the dollar during 1996, and the Italian bond component of the Salomon Brothers World Government Bond Index returned 27.2% in U.S. dollar terms. Thus, it might seem that 4.3% of the return from holding unhedged Italian bonds should be attributed to currency gain, and 22.9% to bond returns. However, following the methodology laid out in equations (13) and (14), the 4.1% Italian/U.S. 1-year interest rate differential should be added to the currency component of return because it was the decision not to hedge that allowed the manager to earn that full measure of return. The Italian 1-year interest rate should then also be subtracted from the Salomon Index's Italian bond market return of 21.9% in local currency terms. Thus, less than half of the gain from holding unhedged Italian bonds, 8.4%, came from excess currency returns, and 11.8% came from excess bond returns. The hedged return would have been only 17.8%, calculated from the Italian bond excess return of 11.8% plus the U.S. 1-year cash return of 6%.[8]

Market Correlations

Two factors that aid in assessing the incremental risk of changes to a portfolio are the volatility of returns and the correlation (or covariance) of returns with the

---

[8] Due to compounding of the bond and currency returns, the sum of the currency and local bond market return figures is 1% less than the U.S. dollar-based total return figure (i.e., 4.3% currency gain × 21.9% local currency bond return = 1%). The Salomon U.S. dollar-hedged index return for Italian lira bonds, based on a rolling 1-month hedge, was 17.5%.

portfolio as a whole. Normally when a decision is made to overweight a market, a less attractive market will be identified to be reduced by the same amount. Otherwise the trading costs associated with keeping all other markets in the same relative proportion to each other would be excessively high.[9] Thus, two risks, rather than one, need to be evaluated: the portfolio risk incurred from the overweight position, and that from the underweight position. A more rigorous approach involves an estimate of the impact on total portfolio risk from each hypothetical change in allocation. A model that utilizes the variance/covariance matrix of portfolio assets can be used to explicitly calculate the incremental impact on portfolio volatility (value at risk and similar models are examined in the final section). Nonetheless, a reasonable estimate of the impact on portfolio risk can be obtained by taking account of the historical volatility and correlations of the two markets to each other through the use of a correlation matrix like the one in Exhibit 6.

Market correlations for both bonds and currencies within trading blocs are much higher than across trading blocs. For example, correlations for the core European bond markets of Belgium, France and the Netherlands with Germany are an extremely high 89%, 80%, and 93%, respectively. Currency correlations among these four markets are all close to 100%. Bond market correlations with Germany for the peripheral European markets of Italy, Spain, Sweden, and Denmark are not quite as high, but still significant, ranging from 46% to 64%. Correlations of peripheral European currencies with the German mark range from 83% to 99%. At the same time, standard deviation of return in European bond and currency markets are fairly similar. Thus, shifting exposure from one of these markets to another to take advantage of tactical trading opportunities should have a minimal impact on a portfolio's overall risk or variance profile, especially within the core European markets.

Forward Rates and Breakeven Analysis

Comparisons of forward interest rates can be instrumental in identifying where differences between the strategic outlook and market prices may present investment opportunities. Forward interest rates, which use the shape of the yield curve to calculate implied future bond yields, allow a quick comparison of what is required in terms of yield shifts for bonds in each market to provide a return equal to the risk free rate (a zero excess return). This would correspond to a bond excess return of zero in equations (9) through (16), or $(r_i - c_i) = 0$. Forward interest rates represent a breakeven rate, not across markets necessarily, but within markets. The strategic bond allocation can then be derived by increasing exposure to markets where the expected return of bonds over the cash rate is most positive, that is where the expected bond yield is furthest below the forward yield. Forward rate calculators are also available on systems such as Bloomberg as can be seen in the graph of German forward rates in Exhibit 7.

---

[9] In other words, if a particular market is selected for a 1% overweighting relative to the benchmark, it is often too costly to reduce all other markets by an equal fraction of that 1% to raise the money for the new purchase.

Exhibit 6: Bond and Currency Correlation Matrix

	AUD	BEF	CAD	DEM	DKK	ESP	FRF	GBP	ITL	JPY	NLG	SEK	AUD Bond	BEF Bond	CAD Bond	DEM Bond	DKK Bond	ESP Bond	FRF Bond	GBP Bond	ITL Bond	JPY Bond	NLG Bond	SEK Bond	USD Bond
AUD	1.00																								
BEF	0.10	1.00																							
CAD	0.06	-0.32	1.00																						
DEM	0.12	0.99	-0.33	1.00																					
DKK	0.14	0.99	-0.33	0.99	1.00																				
ESP	0.14	0.98	-0.34	0.98	0.98	1.00																			
FRF	0.04	0.97	-0.34	0.97	0.97	0.96	1.00																		
GBP	0.43	0.37	0.00	0.39	0.41	0.36	0.31	1.00																	
ITL	0.30	0.84	-0.34	0.84	0.85	0.85	0.84	0.48	1.00																
JPY	-0.25	0.45	-0.20	0.45	0.43	0.45	0.42	-0.09	0.25	1.00															
NLG	0.11	0.99	-0.34	1.00	0.99	0.98	0.97	0.38	0.84	0.45	1.00														
SEK	0.20	0.82	-0.26	0.83	0.84	0.84	0.83	0.33	0.77	0.28	0.83	1.00													
AUD Bond	-0.20	-0.18	-0.03	-0.16	-0.15	-0.14	-0.18	-0.11	-0.17	0.08	-0.17	-0.06	1.00												
BEF Bond	0.22	-0.56	0.22	-0.54	-0.52	-0.53	-0.56	-0.04	-0.39	-0.29	-0.54	-0.37	0.09	1.00											
CAD Bond	0.16	-0.27	0.59	-0.27	-0.26	-0.30	-0.30	0.20	-0.21	-0.33	-0.28	-0.11	-0.04	0.46	1.00										
DEM Bond	0.20	-0.53	0.35	-0.50	-0.50	-0.50	-0.55	0.00	-0.39	-0.27	-0.51	-0.36	0.03	0.89	0.58	1.00									
DKK Bond	-0.04	-0.62	0.19	-0.60	-0.59	-0.56	-0.62	-0.27	-0.53	-0.20	-0.60	-0.40	0.29	0.70	0.17	0.64	1.00								
ESP Bond	0.06	-0.50	0.27	-0.51	-0.49	-0.47	-0.47	-0.09	-0.37	-0.29	-0.51	-0.30	0.08	0.66	0.35	0.62	0.49	1.00							
FRF Bond	0.08	-0.65	0.30	-0.63	-0.63	-0.60	-0.64	-0.18	-0.54	-0.26	-0.63	-0.46	0.21	0.82	0.37	0.80	0.82	0.62	1.00						
GBP Bond	0.28	-0.28	0.13	-0.29	-0.28	-0.26	-0.31	-0.01	-0.15	-0.37	-0.29	-0.09	0.04	0.64	0.50	0.63	0.34	0.59	0.53	1.00					
ITL Bond	0.10	-0.45	0.11	-0.44	-0.43	-0.37	-0.42	-0.18	-0.32	-0.13	-0.45	-0.25	0.33	0.62	0.18	0.55	0.58	0.65	0.62	0.47	1.00				
JPY Bond	0.13	-0.25	-0.13	-0.22	-0.21	-0.22	-0.22	0.07	-0.17	-0.30	-0.22	-0.19	0.26	0.33	0.06	0.24	0.32	0.04	0.32	0.14	0.30	1.00			
NLG Bond	0.21	-0.56	0.28	-0.55	-0.54	-0.53	-0.58	-0.08	-0.41	-0.36	-0.56	-0.36	0.06	0.92	0.52	0.93	0.69	0.66	0.81	0.67	0.60	0.29	1.00		
SEK Bond	0.00	-0.56	0.18	-0.56	-0.55	-0.54	-0.55	-0.16	-0.47	-0.33	-0.56	-0.36	0.03	0.51	0.17	0.46	0.65	0.55	0.64	0.33	0.48	0.19	0.55	1.00	
USD Bond	0.16	-0.22	0.31	-0.21	-0.21	-0.21	-0.21	-0.03	-0.14	-0.20	-0.22	-0.12	-0.13	0.52	0.71	0.59	0.16	0.43	0.39	0.54	0.36	0.02	0.59	0.10	1.00

Source: JP Morgan Riskmetrics as of 12/19/96. Bond markets are estimated using 5-year government zero-coupon bond equivalents in each market.

Exhibit 7: Forward Yield Curve Analysis

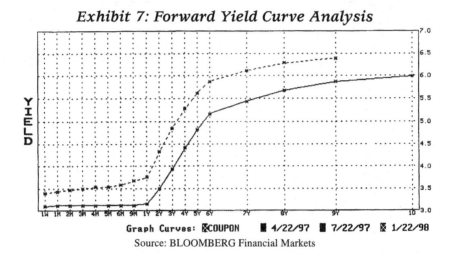

Graph Curves: ⬛COUPON ⬛ 4/22/97 ⬛ 7/22/97 ⬛ 1/22/98

Source: BLOOMBERG Financial Markets

Exhibit 8: 10-Year Benchmark Bond Yield Spreads

0000	JP MORGAN COUNTRY		BENCHMARKS ISSUE		PRICE	CNV YLD	JP MORGAN O/UST	MEUR O/GER
1154	US	6.50	15-10-06	T	98.95-99	6.64		
1154	JAPAN	2.90	20-12-06	JGB	102.28-28	2.61	-410	-326
1154	GERMANY	6.00	04-01-07	BUND	100.60-66	5.91	-84	
1154	FRANCE	5.50	25-04-07	OAT	97.04-18	5.88	-87	-3
1154	UK	7.50	07-12-06	GILT	99.02-02	7.64	+103	+187
1154	ECU	7.00	25-04-06	ECU	105.61-71	6.17	-58	+26
1154	ITALY	8.75	01-07-06	BTP	108.73-93	7.57	+82	+166
1154	SPAIN	8.80	30-04-06	BONO	112.99-14	6.84	+9	+93
1151	BELGIUM	6.25	28-03-07	OLO	101.53-63	6.03	-72	+12
1151	HOLLAND	6.00	15-01-06	DSL	101.71-79	5.75	-101	-17
1151	SWEDEN	6.50	25-10-06	SGB	98.22-42	6.74	-2	+82
1154	DENMARK	8.00	15-03-06	DGB	109.52-62	6.57	-18	+82

The forward foreign exchange rate represents a breakeven rate between hedged and unhedged currency returns as shown above in the analysis on components of return. In terms of equations (11) through (14), currency excess return is zero when the percentage change in the currency equals the forward premium or discount. As forward foreign exchange rates are determined by short term interest rate differentials, they can be estimated from Eurodeposit rates as in equations (2) and (3), or obtained from market data services such as Bloomberg and Reuters.

Breakeven analysis provides another tool for estimating relative value between markets. Because the prices of benchmark bonds are influenced by coupon effects and changes in the benchmark, many international fixed income traders and portfolio managers find it easier to keep pace with changes in yield relationships than price changes in each market. Exhibit 8 displays page MEUR from Reuters' market information service which provides 10-year conventional yields and yield spreads to both the U.S. and Germany expressed on an annual-pay basis.[10] A constant spread between markets when yield levels are shifting, however, may result in a variation in returns as differing maturities and coupons of benchmark bonds result in a wide spread of interest rate sensitivity across markets. For example, of the benchmark 10-year bonds listed in Exhibit 8, the modified duration ranges from a low of 6.13 in Spain to 8.56 in Japan where yields are less than half that of the next lowest yielding market. Thus, market duration must be taken into account in determining breakeven spread movements.

For example, calculation of the breakeven yield spread of Italy to Germany over a 3-month time horizon, requires an analysis of the price changes in both bond markets, as well as the difference in yield earned over the period. The spread differential of 166 basis points equates to 41 basis points of additional income over a three month period. The modified duration of the Italian 10-year benchmark bond of 6.21 implies that this yield "cushion" provided by the higher yield of Italian bonds over German bunds translates to less than 7 basis points of spread widening over a 3-month period (6.21 times -0.07 is approximately equal to 41 basis points). This is not much of a cushion given that 7 basis points is far less than the average weekly volatility of Italian bond yields. The breakeven spreads of Spain and Sweden to Germany are even tighter at 4 and 3 basis points. Thus, the anticipated direction of bond market movements is of paramount importance in the portfolio allocation decision.

MEASURING RISK AND EVALUATING PERFORMANCE

Once the portfolio has been created, it must be monitored to assess how changing market conditions affect the portfolio's performance and risk profile; hence, a system for tracking portfolio positions and measuring returns is needed. One of the most basic portfolio monitoring tools is the *position report*, which breaks down the interest rate and currency risk market by market. More technically demanding is a portfolio variance approach such as value-at-risk, which estimates potential losses based upon statistical analysis of historical volatilities and correlations. The value-at-risk approach can also be translated into a *tracking error report* that evaluates portfolio risks against the benchmark. These risk models can be used together with performance attribution to assist the portfolio manager in identifying the strengths or weaknesses of his portfolio strategy.

---

[10] U.S. bonds, and most other dollar bloc bonds, pay coupons semiannually, whereas in Japan, and the European markets (except for the U.K.) bonds pay interest annually. This difference in market convention understates the yield of dollar bloc bonds when compared to Japanese or European bonds, so when calculating the yield spread, semiannual yields are converted to annual yields using the formula:

Annual yield = $(1 + \text{Semiannual yield}/2)^2 - 1$

Portfolio Profile

A portfolio profile is usually designed to monitor exposures to the two major sources of risk in international bond portfolios: currency risk and interest rate risk. These market-by-market breakdowns are also useful in estimating how positions will affect portfolio performance versus the benchmark. A sample portfolio profile versus the Salomon Brothers Non-U.S. Government Bond Index is provided in Exhibit 9. The profile shows the percentage allocation to bonds and currencies for each country, as well as the duration, relative to the index. A breakdown by duration cell of each bond market allocation is provided to highlight any yield curve positions. (The country breakdown by duration cell for the index, which has been excluded for simplicity of presentation, would be extremely helpful in identifying where yield curve positions differ from the index.) Finally, the portfolio profile provides a measure of duration weighted exposure (from equation (17)), and currency exposure net of hedges, relative to the index. Summary exposure figures for each of these categories, broken down by trading bloc, are provided at the bottom of the report.

The measure of portfolio interest rate risk in each individual market is a combination of its weight in the portfolio and its duration relative to the duration of the index for that country. For example, the U.K.'s contribution to duration is neutral to the index (i.e., a relative weight of zero percent) despite the higher percentage allocation to U.K. due to the portfolio's shorter U.K. duration. The larger-than-index market weighting in the U.K. is unhedged as indicated by the equivalence of the market weight and the currency exposure, 11.9%, and represents a nearly 4% portfolio overweight position in pound sterling relative to the index.

The summary figures in the bottom right hand corner of the portfolio profile suggest that the sample portfolio's greatest bond market underweight is in peripheral Europe. The 16.8% underweight position there is larger than the sum of the overweight positions in the dollar bloc and core Europe, leaving the portfolio 9.5% underweight duration, or 90.5% of the 4.9 year benchmark duration or 4.4 years. In currencies also, the largest deviation from the benchmark is in peripheral Europe where exposures are 9.7% underweight the index. The overweighting in the yen, and underweighting in core Europe and dollar bloc are largely offsetting in this framework. The overall portfolio is 9% underweight currency exposure, or 9% hedged relative to the unhedged benchmark.

As helpful as they are in quantifying risk within individual markets, the traditional risk measures of duration and percent currency exposure have significant shortcomings when aggregated as a measure of portfolio risk. These shortcomings are explored in more detail below, along with some complimentary approaches to risk measurement that can be instrumental in addressing them.

Exhibit 9: Sample Portfolio Profile
Portfolio Profile versus Salomon Non-U.S. Government Bond Index

Market	Market Weight (%)		Average Duration (Yrs)		Currency Exposure (%)	Portfolio MV% by Duration Cell					Relative Weights (%)	
	Index	Portfolio	Index	Portfolio	Portfolio	0-2	2-4	4-6	6-9	9+	Duration	Currency
Austria	1.3		4.1								-1.1	-1.3
Australia	1.5		4.3								-1.3	-1.5
Belgium	3.9	3.0	4.8	6.0	3.0				3.0		-0.2	-0.9
Canada	4.6	4.6	5.2	11.7	4.6					4.6	6.1	0.0
Switzerland	0.7		5.2								-0.7	-0.7
Germany	14.9	18.0	4.2	6.6	15.0				18.0		11.4	0.1
Denmark	2.6	8.0	4.3	6.0	8.0				8.0		7.5	5.4
Spain	3.7		3.8								-2.9	-3.7
Finland	0.7		4.3								-0.6	-0.7
France	11.4	5.0	5.1	2.7	5.0		5.0				-9.1	-6.4
U.K.	8.1	11.9	5.9	4.0	11.9			11.9			0.0	3.8
Italy	9.5	15.0	3.3	2.0	15.0	15.0					-0.4	5.5
Japan	29.1	30.0	5.7	3.4	24.0		30.0				-13.2	-5.1
Netherlands	5.2	2.0	5.0	3.2	2.0		2.0				-4.0	-3.2
Sweden	2.6	2.5	4.2	2.9	2.5		2.5				-0.8	-0.1
Other												
Total	100.0	100.0	4.9	4.4	91.0	15.0	39.5	11.9	29.0	4.6	-9.5	-9.0

Currency Bloc	Index	Portfolio	Index	Portfolio	Potfolio	0-2	2-4	4-6	6-9	9+	Duration	Currency
Japan	29.1	30.0	3.3	2.0	24.0		30.0				-0.4	5.5
Dollar Bloc	6.1	4.6	5.0	11.7	4.6					4.6	4.7	-1.5
Core Euro	38.1	28.0	4.7	5.6	25.0				29.0		3.0	-3.2
Periph Euro	26.7	37.4	4.4	3.5	37.4	15.0	9.5	11.9			-16.8	-9.7
Other												
Total	100.0	100.0	4.2	4.0	91.0	15.0	39.5	11.9	29.0	4.6	-9.5	-9.0

Contribution to Duration

Many international fixed income portfolio managers measure their bond market exposures in terms of the simple percentage allocation to each particular market. However, a better measure of exposure to any individual bond market is one that combines the percentage of portfolio assets allocated to that market with the duration of that exposure. As seen in equation (17), contribution to overall portfolio duration for each market is the weighted duration in that market multiplied by the percentage weight of that market in the portfolio where D is the duration and w percentage weight of market i in the overall portfolio. Thus, the sum of the contribution to duration of each market will equal the portfolio's overall duration. The duration weighted exposure is calculated by dividing the contribution to duration in each market by the total benchmark duration, D_B as shown in equation (18). The duration weighted exposure figure can then be compared directly with the benchmark composition, providing a more useful gauge of market risk than percent allocation. The sum of the weighted duration figures may add up to more or less than 100%.

Contribution to Duration: $CD_i = D_i \times w_i$ (17)

Duration Weighted Exposure: $WD_i = CD_i/D_B$ (18)

Duration can be a helpful measure when comparing a portfolio's allocation relative to the index, however, its inability to capture the effect of non-parallel shifts in rates is compounded by further shortcomings when used as a measure of interest rate risk in a global setting. Portfolio interest rate exposure will not be equal to a simple sum of the duration weighted exposures from equation (18) in each market as interest rate movements in different countries are not perfectly correlated. Also the differing volatility across markets means that the contribution-to-duration from a given market is not entirely comparable to that of another market. The use of volatility-adjusted duration[11] is one means of addressing this impracticality. An additional compromise would be to compare volatility-adjusted contribution-to-duration only between the highly correlated markets within each trading bloc. Thus, a portfolio could have the same modified duration as the benchmark but show a different sensitivity to global bond market moves as a result of different weightings in especially low or high volatility markets or in markets with low correlation to other markets.

The shortcomings of duration as a measure of interest rate risk internationally can be reduced by accounting for differing volatilities and correlations across markets. This requires either a manual interpolation of portfolio risk from a volatility and correlation matrix or use of a risk measure that incorporates these relationships. One example would be a market risk measure that captures the rela-

---

[11] For example, if interest rates were twice as volatile in Italy than in Germany, a factor of 2 could be applied to bond holdings in Italy when comparing them to the German bond holdings.

tive volatility of markets and yield curve sectors as well as the correlation to the "market," which could be defined as a hedged, or unhedged, global or international bond index. One approach, suggested by Goldman Sachs & Co., is to make use of beta measures similar to those found in the capital asset pricing model.[12] A portfolio with a weighted average market risk of 1.12, for example, would be 12% more sensitive to bond price changes than the international bond index. This approach could be extended to currencies as well.

Currency Exposures

Portfolio currency exposures, examined separately from the bond exposures, suffer from some of the same shortcomings as duration as an overall risk measure. A simple aggregation of currency exposures across a portfolio ignores the sometimes substantial differences in currency volatilities across markets. For example, from 1987 to 1996 a U.S dollar-based investor would have experienced three times more volatility from movements in the value of the yen than in the Canadian dollar. Thus, offsetting short or long currency positions relative to the benchmark in the yen with the opposite positions in either the dollar bloc or core Europe could lead to a misunderstanding of the portfolio's true exposure to currency risk.

Direct comparison of currency and interest rate risk measures poses another difficulty. For example, a 5% duration-weighted position in a bond market and a 5% currency exposure can represent significantly different risks to the overall portfolio. Again, measures incorporating volatility and correlation measures allow these different sources of risk to be evaluated on an equal footing. The next section discusses the virtues of a value-at-risk approach that also incorporates volatility and correlation of interest rate and currency risk.

Tracking Error and Value at Risk

Each portfolio allocation decision should be evaluated on the basis of the expected return enhancement of the trade versus its impact on portfolio volatility, both in absolute terms and relative to the benchmark. Volatility is often expressed in standard deviations of returns, i.e., movements either up or down. On the assumption that most international bond investors are concerned about limiting downside volatility (i.e., losses) more than upside volatility, the value-at-risk concept, popularized by JP Morgan, serves as a constructive framework.[13] The value-at-risk approach uses historical volatility and correlations across bond and currency markets to arrive at an estimate of the likely loss, expressed either in dollars or as a percent of the portfolio, only in the case of an extreme shift in market prices against portfolio positions. For example a value-at-risk figure calculated with a 95% confidence interval (or a 1.65 standard deviation downward move in

---

[12] Beta can be estimated by either regressing historical returns of the given market sector versus the market as a whole, or by using the following formula: Beta = Cov (R_i, R_m)/Var (R_m) where R_i and R_m represent the historical returns of the market sector and the entire market, respectively.

market prices) would estimate the magnitude of the loss that should be exceeded no more than 5% of the time.

Value-at-risk measures are especially useful for estimating the risks of assets with non-normally distributed returns, such as bond and currency options. Thus, a model that can capture the differences between the risks of a long (or purchased) option position which has a limited downside, and a short (or written) option position which has open-ended downside risk, will serve as an important risk management tool.

Exhibit 10: Tracking Error Report

Market	Portfolio Profile Summary Relative Weights		Contribution to Tracking Error (bp)		Contribution to Tracking Error (%)		Marginal Tracking Error (bp)	
	Bond (%)	Currency (%)	Bond	Currency	Bond	Currency	Bond	Currency
Austria	-1.1	-1.3	-0.2	10.8	0	7	0.0	-7.6
Australia	-1.3	-1.5	1.0	-2.4	1	-2	-1.0	1.5
Belgium	-0.2	-0.9	0.7	7.9	0	5	3.6	-7.6
Canada	6.1	0.0	27.2	0.5	17	0	7.1	2.6
Switzerland	-0.7	-0.7	0.1	6.8	0	4	0.7	-10.1
Germany	11.4	0.1	50.3	0.1	32	0	3.7	-7.6
Denmark	7.5	5.4	22.1	-43.2	14	-27	2.9	-6.9
Spain	-2.9	-3.7	-11.8	27.4	-8	17	4.2	-7.3
Finland	-0.6	-0.7	0.0	4.3	0	3	0.0	-6.2
France	-9.1	-6.4	-17.2	43.5	-11	28	2.1	-7.6
U.K.	0.0	3.8	-4.6	3.9	-3	2	3.0	1.2
Italy	-0.4	5.5	-3.4	-20.5	-2	-13	2.8	-4.1
Japan	-13.2	-5.1	6.6	28.3	4	18	-0.1	-5.8
Netherlands	-4.0	-3.2	-14.8	39.3	-9	25	-2.4	-7.8
Sweden	-0.8	-0.1	-0.4	-5.0	0	-3	2.7	-4.3
Other	0.0	0.0			0	0	2.8	0.0
Japan	-13.2	-5.1	6.6	28.3	4	18		
Dollar Bloc	4.7	-1.5	28.1	-1.9	18	-1		
Core Europe	3.7	-3.3	36.6	69.1	23	44		
Peripheral Europe	-4.7	0.9	-15.6	6.1	-10	4		
Other								
Total	-9.5	-9.0	55.7	101.5	35	65		

Total Portfolio Diversified Tracking Error	Fully Diversified	Non-Diversified
	157.3	1267

[13] The value-at-risk concept, known in prior academic papers as semi-variance or lower partial moment, is simply a transformation of the more traditionally used standard deviation measure of volatility, but expressed as a measure of downside risk only. Traditional mean-variance optimization will produce similar results when using either portfolio value-at-risk or volatility as the constraint if portfolio returns are assumed to be normally distributed. For a more detailed discussion, see JP Morgan Riskmetrics Technical Document, and W.V. Harlow, "Asset Allocation in a Downside-Risk Framework," *Financial Analysts Journal* (September-October 1991).

Although portfolio tracking error has traditionally been defined as the historical variance of portfolio returns about the benchmark, it can be extremely useful in the portfolio management process when used as an estimate of future deviation from the index, or more specifically as the relative value at risk. The total value at risk of the sample portfolio in Exhibit 16 is 590 basis points at the 95% confidence level, while tracking error equals 157 basis points. In other words, the portfolio should, at worst, lose 5.90% in value in any year, or under-perform the benchmark by 157 basis points, with 95% confidence. Which measure deserves more emphasis depends on the portfolio objectives and risk constraints. For example, an income-oriented investor with little tolerance for losses could set a portfolio constraint on value-at-risk equal to the expected income earned over a given time horizon. This could provide some assurance, with 95% confidence for example, that portfolio total return will remain positive. An investor more concerned with diversification, however, might find tracking error a more suitable risk measure as it better identifies large deviations from the benchmark which could alter the portfolio's correlation to other asset classes.

The value-at-risk framework may uncover risks to the portfolio not fully apparent in traditional measures while providing the portfolio manager a common yardstick to evaluate the risks of bond market and currency positions.

In Exhibit 16, the sample portfolio is shown to have 101.5 basis points of tracking error (65% of the total) due to currency positions away from the benchmark and 55.7 basis points (35% of the total) due to bond market positions. A manager could use these measures to ensure that the magnitude of risks taken relative to the benchmark are consistent with the level of conviction and the investment style relied upon to outperform. Presumably, this manager is comfortable taking a larger currency position than bond market position. The underweight bond and currency position in France, summarized in the left-hand column, is a net contributor to tracking error. However, the bond market position actually has the effect of reducing tracking error by 17.2 basis points. The 9.1% duration underweight in France constitutes a large allocation away from the benchmark, however, it offsets portfolio overweight in other core European bond markets; markets to which French bonds are highly correlated. The same could be said for the UK, Italy and Spain as the correlation between peripheral and core European bond markets is a high 0.76 (see Exhibit 12). As shown in the far right column of Exhibit 16, marginal tracking error (the portfolio impact from a 1% shift in assets) from a 1% shift into French government bonds results in an increase of 2.1 basis points in portfolio tracking error. Thus, the existing underweight in French bonds is a risk-reducing position and adding back French bond market exposure will increase tracking error. Almost all readings in the far right hand column are negative suggesting that adding foreign currency exposure will reduce tracking error to the benchmark. This is consistent with the estimated 65% of tracking error coming from currency positions, most of which are underweight or hedged back into U.S. dollars.

Exhibit 11: Value at Risk Report

Market	Portfolio Profile Summary		Contribution to Value at Risk (bp)		Contribution to Value at Risk (%)		Marginal Value at Risk (bp)	
	Contribution to Duration	Currency Weight (%)	Bond	Currency	Bond	Currency	Bond	Currency
Austria	—	0	0.0	0.0	0	0	0.0	8.7
Australia	—	0	0.0	0.0	0	0	0.0	3.8
Belgium	0.18	3	0.1	25.0	0	4	0.0	8.5
Canada	0.54	5	11.5	−2.7	2	0	1.4	−0.6
Switzerland	—	0	0.0	0.0	0	0	0.6	9.6
Germany	1.18	15	4.7	128.6	1	22	0.2	8.7
Denmark	0.48	8	−4.8	72.9	−1	12	−0.7	8.3
Spain	—	0	0.0	0.0	0	0	−0.5	8.2
Finland	—	0	0.0	0.0	0	0	0.0	7.0
France	0.14	5	−1.3	38.4	0	7	−0.7	7.8
U.K.	0.48	12	8.8	79.9	1	14	0.8	6.7
Italy	0.30	15	02	96.8	0	16	−0.2	6.6
Japan	1.01	24	7.9	104.0	1	18	0.0	4.3
Netherlands	0.06	2	0.0	0.0	0	0	−1.9	8.8
Sweden	0.07	3	−2.9	22.9	0	4	−1.0	6.0
Other	—	0					0.5	0.0
Japan	1.01	24	7.9	104.0	1	18		
Dollar Bloc	0.54	5	11.6	−2.7	2	0		
Core Euro	2.52	45	7.5	344.8	1	58		
Peripheral Europe	0.37	18	−2.7	119.7	0	20		
Other								
Total	4.44	91	24.2	565.8	4	96		

Total Portfolio Diversified Tracking Error	Fully Diversified	Non-Diversified
	590.0	1505

Exhibit 12: Bond Market and Currency Correlation by Currency Bloc

	Core Europe	Peripheral Europe	Japan	Dollar Bloc	Core Eur. Currency	Peripheral Currency	Japanese Yen	Dollar Bloc Currency
Core Europe	1.00							
Peripheral Europe	0.76	1.00						
Japan	0.40	0.19	1.00					
Dollar Bloc	0.65	0.44	0.43	1.00				
Core Eur. Currency	−0.39	−0.57	0.12	−0.18	1.00			
Peripheral Currency	−0.40	−0.16	−0.17	−0.28	0.51	1.00		
Japanese Yen	−0.19	−0.48	0.07	−0.14	0.64	0.24	1.00	
Dollar Bloc Currency	−0.08	0.04	0.09	0.17	−0.13	0.04	−0.26	1.00

The Value at Risk report in Exhibit 11 provides a summary of the sources of absolute risk. For example, the profile summary at left shows that the portfolio has twice as much of its market value exposed to Japanese yen as it does British pound sterling. However, after adjusting for volatility and correlation differences the contribution to portfolio value at risk from the yen position is 30% more than that for sterling, 104.0 versus 79.9 basis points. Interestingly, the bond market contributions to risk total only 4% of total risk. This results from the low volatility estimates of bond market risks and negative correlation to currency risk that are input into the model. As can be seen in the right hand column of Exhibit 11, shifting 1% of portfolio assets to either Dutch or Swedish bond markets reduces portfolio value at risk by 1.9 and 1.0 basis points respectively.

A manager looking to maximize expected excess return per unit of risk would be able to compare return expectations to the contribution to value at risk or tracking error. A certain threshold of return per unit of risk may be required to meet a portfolio target. Model outputs in this context allow managers to weigh the risks against return potential for various portfolio assets and, using the marginal value at risk and tracking error numbers, have a reasonable estimate of how potential portfolio trades will impact, portfolio risk, both relative to the benchmark and on an absolute basis. Traditional mean-variance optimization, where portfolios exhibiting the most attractive Sharpe ratios are identified on the so-called efficient frontier between expected excess return over cash and volatility, can offer some insights about portfolio risk not captured by the framework presented above. However, the flexibility and detail offered by the careful breakdown of portfolio risk above can offer significant advantages to managers seeking to better understand the sources of risk and fine-tune portfolios.

The value-at-risk approach to calculating tracking error, however, is not a perfect measure of portfolio risk. For one thing, portfolio variance measures such as value-at-risk assume that market relationships do not change, which can be misleading. For example, it has been shown that correlations tend to rise during periods of above-average volatility which suggests that value at risk models will tend to underestimate risk during periods of extreme volatility.[14] Thus, many practitioners advocate the use of worst-day or disaster scenario measures to supplement the use of value-at-risk measures. Another approach compares the diversified value-at-risk measure (the traditional portfolio variance approach) with the non-diversified measure (which assumes no correlation among assets), as the ratio of diversified to non-diversified risk can be used as a proxy for the correlation risk inherent in the diversified risk measure.

CONCLUSION: AN INTEGRATED INVESTMENT PROCESS

The objective of this chapter was to provide a broad overview of the issues facing international fixed income portfolio managers at each step of the portfolio management process. This process involves a continuous cycle of evaluating risks and returns, implementing portfolio strategy, and monitoring market movements and portfolio performance. The complexities of the international arena increase the value of a disciplined approach to investing, of which the fundamental-based approach outlined in this chapter is but one variation.

---

[14] See Bruno Solnik, Cyril Boucrelle, and Yann Le Fur, "International Market Correlation and Volatility," *Financial Analysts Journal* (Sept./Oct. 1996), pp. 17-34.

Exhibit 13: Expected Returns French/German Swap

	France	Germany	Cross Hedge
Expected Bond Market Return			
Expected Bond Return (A)	3.5%	3.0%	
c_i = Domestic Cash Rate (B)	–3.0%	–3.0%	
Bond Excess Return (C = A – B)	0.5%	0.0%	
Expected Currency Return			
$\varepsilon_{\$i}$ = Expected Currency Appreciation	2.3%	2.5%	2.5%
c_i = Domestic Cash Rate (B)	3.0%	3.0%	3.0%
Unhedged Currency Return (E = B + D)	5.3%	5.5%	5.5%
$c_\$$ = Hedged Return (F or U.S. Interest Rate)	5.5%	5.5%	
$\varepsilon_{\$i} + c_i - c_\$$ = Excess Currency Return (G = E – F)	–0.2%	0.0%	
Unhedged Expected Return (C + E)	5.8%	5.5%	
Hedged Expected Return (C + F)	6.0%	5.5%	

Exhibit 20 attempts to tie the themes of the portfolio construction and risk management sections together by showing how a portfolio manager might turn a market view into a portfolio allocation. The outlook is for the French bond market to outperform Germany's bond market, but for the French franc to provide a lower return than the German mark. The bond and currency return forecasts may have been generated by a fundamental economic approach, such as the one outlined in this chapter, or from one of the other management styles. The expected return from any allocation should be evaluated against the incremental risk it is likely to add to the portfolio.

An example comparing explicit return forecasts for 5-year duration bonds in the French and German government bond markets (i.e., duration neutral) is provided in Exhibit 19. Total returns are expressed as the sum of the excess bond market return plus the excess return due to currency, consistent with the approach explained in equations (13), (14), (15), and (16), which are restated below.

$$R_{\$i} = c_\$ + (r_i - c_i) + (\varepsilon_{\$,i} - f_{\$,i}) \qquad \text{(unhedged return)}$$

$$HR_{\$i} = c_\$ + (r_i - c_i) \qquad \text{(hedged return)}$$

$$CR_{\$i} = c_\$ + (r_i - c_i) + (\varepsilon_{\$,i} - f_{\$,i}) \qquad \text{(cross-hedged return)}$$

$$PR_{\$i} = c_\$ + (r_i - c_i) + [(\varepsilon_{\$,i} - \varepsilon_{\$,j}) - f_{j,i} \qquad \text{(proxy-hedged return)}$$

For example, the expected excess return from bonds $(r_i - c_i)$ of 0.5% in France, equal to the expected return on bonds (3.5%) less that on French cash (3.0%), is the same regardless of whether the currency is hedged, unhedged, or cross hedged. The currency hedge decision is based upon whether the expected currency appreciation is greater than the interest rate differential $\varepsilon_{\$,i} > (c_\$ - c_i)$ or less than the interest rate differential $\varepsilon_{\$,i} < (c_\$ - c_i)$ Thus, as the expected return on French francs of 2.3% is less than the interest rate differential of 2.5% over the 1-year horizon (5.5% in the U.S. − 3.0% in France), the position would offer a higher return when hedged back into U.S. dollars. Stated another way, the expected excess currency return component to a U.S. dollar-based investor from an unhedged holding of French bonds is −0.2%.

Cross hedging allows portfolio managers to create a currency exposure which can vary substantially from the underlying bond market exposure. A cross hedge replaces one foreign currency exposure with another that usually has a higher expected return. Using the currency (or far right hand) components of equations (8) and (10), a cross hedge will be attractive when $(c_j + \varepsilon_{\$,j}) > (c_i + \varepsilon_{\$,i})$; or the cash rate plus expected return in the cross currency is greater than the cash rate plus expected return in the exposure currency. Of course, if the U.S. dollar cash rate is greater than either of these two terms, a hedged, or proxy hedged, position is preferable to either foreign currency exposure. In terms of the present example, the expected excess currency return from the additional French franc exposure is a negative 20 basis points. Hence this currency exposure would probably be hedged back into the dollar. A cross hedge into German marks could also be used, however, the expected excess currency retrun from holding German marks is zero.

The next step is to estimate the incremental risk to the portfolio associated with the transaction. Exhibit 21 provides several risk measures for evaluating the proposed swap from Germany into France on overall portfolio risk. The historical volatilities of the bond and currency movements in each market can provide a rough approximation of incremental risk from the portfolio allocation (the volatility of a hedged bond market return would be approximately the same as the volatility of the local bond market return). The similar bond and currency volatilities in France and Germany,[15] and the high correlation between the markets, suggests that a shift of market exposure from one market to the other would be relatively risk neutral. However, some of the tools developed in the risk management discussion allow for a much more accurate estimation of risk. The two columns entitled marginal tracking error and marginal value at risk from Exhibits 16 and 17 provide estimates of the incremental addition to risk that would result from a 1% shift of the portfolio's market value into any individual bond market or currency. For example, on the basis of the figures from the Total column of Exhibit 21, the swap from German to French bonds reduces both value at risk and tracking error by 1.6 basis points. Risk can also be evaluated on a hedged basis, using the data in the bond market column. The risk reduction figures in this case are very similar on either a hedged or unhedged basis. However, the 50 basis points of incremental expected return from a hedged swap from Germany into France is greater than the 30 basis points of expected return on an unhedged basis.

---

[15] The variance formula treats the bond and currency components as separate assets in calculating the expected volatility for any country using the following equation: $\sigma_i^2 = \sigma_x^2 + h_y^2 \sigma_y^2 + 2 h_y \operatorname{Cov}_{xy}$, where subscript i represents a country, x represents bonds, y represents the currency and h represents the percent currency exposure (i.e., $1 - h$ = the hedge ratio), and Cov_{xy} is the covariance between the bonds and currencies.

One possible conclusion from this example is that the expected return enhancement per unit of excess tracking error is most attractive when the swap is done on a hedged basis. If the differences between value at risk and tracking error were greater, a portfolio managed more for capital preservation might place more weight upon the value at risk measure perhaps leading to a different conclusion.

As the prior example shows, the implementation of portfolio strategy can clearly be a highly involved process of evaluating the risk and reward trade-off between different portfolio investment alternatives. However, the simplified example above did not address other types of decisions confronted by international fixed income portfolio managers including ongoing management of currency hedges, yield curve strategies, and using options to take views on the direction of actual or implied volatilities. In addition to conveying the complexities presented by international fixed income investing, hopefully this chapter has been able to convey some of the excitement that comes from meeting the challenges of investing in a dynamic global market.

Exhibit 14: Risk Analysis French/German Swap

	Bond Market	Currency	Total
Volatility			
France	6.7%	13.7%	4.8%
Germany	7.4%	14.2%	5.1%
Marginal Value at Risk			
France	−0.7	7.8	7.1
Germany	0.2	8.7	8.9
Marginal Tracking Error			
France	2.1	−7.6	−5.5
Germany	3.7	−7.6	−3.9
Net Impact on Portfolio – Germany into France			
Value at Risk	−0.9	−0.9	−1.8
Tracking Error	−1.6	0.0	−1.6

Correlations			
French to German Bonds:	0.80	French Bonds to French Francs:	−0.64
Francs to German marks:	0.97	German Bonds to German marks:	−0.50

Marginal Value at Risk and Tracking Error (from Exhibits 16 and 17) are estimates of the change, in basis points, to portfolio Value at Risk and Tracking Error for a 1% addition of the relevant bond of currency exposure to the portfolio profiled in Exhibit 15.

About the Author

William R. Leach, CFA

William R. Leach is a Principal and Director of Fixed Income Strategy at Boston Partners Asset Management, L.P. Prior to the inception of Boston Partners in 1995, Mr. Leach was Senior Vice President and Director of Fixed Income Strategy at The Boston Company Asset Management, Inc. for seven years. Before that time, he was Vice President and Fixed Income Manager for Beneficial Standard Life Insurance Company since 1984. Mr. Leach is a member of the Boston Security Analysts Society and the Association for Investment Management and Research. From 1988 to 1990, he taught a fixed income course for the Chartered Financial Analysts program at the University of Southern California. His publications include "A Portfolio Manager's Perspective of Inverses and Inverse IOs" in *CMO Portfolio Management* and "The Implications of Low Interest Rates for Bond Management Styles" in *Pension World* (February 1994). He has also contributed to articles in *Forbes, The Wall Street Journal, Global Investor, Mortgage-Backed Securities Letter, Wall Street Transcript,* and *Plan Sponsor* and has spoken at numerous conferences. Mr. Leach graduated from Pomona College with a B.A. in Economics in 1977 and from Carnegie-Mellon University with a Master of Science in Industrial Administration (MSIA) degree in 1979.

Chapter 8

Using Busted Convertibles to Enhance Performance

William R. Leach, CFA
Principal
Boston Partners Asset Management, L.P.

INTRODUCTION

Active bond managers face many challenges attempting to add performance relative to broad bond market indexes. These include unpredictable interest rate changes, transactions costs, and, more recently, very narrow corporate yield spreads. One approach is to look for securities outside of benchmark indexes that have superior risk/reward characteristics. Busted convertibles fall into this category, and they are especially appropriate for active bond management styles emphasizing security selection. Furthermore, because some of the factors driving convertible performance are unique, their inclusion dampens and diversifies portfolio risk.

"Busted" describes a convertible bond when a declining stock pulls down its value. Its upside return potential is curtailed, because the equity conversion option becomes ever more out-of-the-money. However, though busted sounds unpleasant, it is not necessarily a negative, especially for fixed income investors.

Indeed, the goal of this chapter is to demonstrate the virtues of busted convertibles. It describes how fixed income managers can use them as an ongoing strategy to enhance performance. It assumes the reader is familiar with basic convertible bond terminology, investment characteristics, and valuation methods.[1]

First we distinguish busted convertibles from other types in a section that describes three convertible value regions. Then we explain how undervaluation in the busted region can be linked to differing investment orientations across the regions. We believe that equity oriented investors dominate the convertible market, and, when stocks go down, they sell to fixed income oriented investors at bargain prices. The following sections include valuation, examples of busted convertibles, and a conclusion.

---

[1] For background see Luke Knecht and Mike McCowen, "Valuing Convertible Securities," in Frank J. Fabozzi (ed.), *Advances & Innovations in the Bond and Mortgage Markets* (Chicago: Probus Publishing, 1989).

CONVERTIBLE VALUE REGIONS

Convertibles can be classified into three categories depending on their sensitivity to equity prices. If they trade at high prices, low or negative yields, low conversion premiums, and are highly sensitive to equity prices, then they are in the *equity equivalent region*.

Convertibles that trade with very little sensitivity to equity prices, large conversion premiums, relatively high yields, and low prices, are in the *busted region*. Busted convertibles are more sensitive to interest rate changes than are equity equivalent convertibles.

Convertibles trading with moderate conversion premiums, moderate sensitivity to both equity prices and interest rates, and prices near par or at-issue levels, are in the *hybrid region*. New supply is almost always sold to investors in the hybrid region. After it is issued, convertibles either stay in the hybrid region or they migrate to the equity equivalent or busted regions. Convertibles moving high enough into the equity equivalent region are frequently called, and these issuers are apt to sell another convertible in the hybrid region.

Our focus is on the busted region. This region offers the fixed income investor ongoing opportunities to buy undervalued securities.

RATIONALE FOR ATTRACTIVE OPPORTUNITIES IN BUSTED CONVERTIBLES

The rationale for persistent undervaluation in busted convertibles comes from segmentation. There are two distinct categories of investors in the convertible market.[2] One category has primarily an equity orientation while the other has primarily a fixed income orientation. In our view, the market is dominated by investors with the equity orientation.

Equity oriented investors seek equity-like returns from convertibles with less downside risk as compared to equities. These investors may also have growth and income objectives, or they may be pursuing a defensive strategy. The convertible's yield advantage versus the issuer's common stock yield helps them achieve their investment goals. These investors focus on convertibles in the hybrid region — where convertibles offer yields under comparable straight (nonconvertible) bonds yet above the common stock and modest (15% to 40%) conversion premiums.

Firms prefer to issue convertibles when their stock is strong, and it is not unusual for the stock to decline after the convertible has been sold. After significant price declines, the convertible's investment characteristics change, and it no longer offers hybrid investors significant equity-like upside return potential. At

---

[2] Another category, not discussed here, includes hedge funds who buy cheap convertibles and sell short the underlying stocks.

depressed levels and large conversion premiums, the busted convertible's stock price may move in a broad range without significantly affecting the convertible's return. During this time the busted convertible earns bond-like returns.

Accordingly, as the underlying stock price declines and the convertible becomes busted, the investor who bought it as a hybrid sells it to an investor with a fixed income orientation. We believe that the dollar demand for busted convertibles is much smaller than the potential and actual supply coming from equity oriented investors involved in the hybrid region. Consequently, selling by hybrid investors to fixed income investors cheapens convertibles *relative to fair value* as they descend to busted status.[3]

In conclusion, the supply of convertible product is designed for equity oriented investors. When convertibles become busted in secondary trading, they create attractive opportunities for the fixed income investor. The investor gets to buy the busted convertible at a discount to fair value. If the convertible subsequently moves back to hybrid status, then the investor also benefits from a diminution of the discount.

VALUATION OF BUSTED CONVERTIBLES

As described above, there is a rationale for attractive opportunities in busted convertibles based on differing investor orientations, but how do we find them? Fortunately, the search is straightforward. We look for convertibles priced at or below their value as bonds excluding the conversion option, or their bond value. This criterion limits downside risk to the downside risk of a similar straight bond. Convertibles trading below bond value are an appealing alternative to straight bonds.

The next step is to evaluate the convertible's upside potential. This analysis helps us to choose between busted convertible alternatives and to focus on those most likely to deliver superior returns. The selection process can also be guided by issuer, industry, quality, duration, yield, or other portfolio objectives.

Measuring Bond Value

Measuring a busted convertible's bond value is akin to measuring the bond value of straight corporate bonds. We analyze yields of similar bonds, credit fundamentals for the issuer, credit ratings, coupon, duration, convexity, maturity, embedded options such as puts or calls, seniority, industry considerations, scarcity value, liquidity, and so on.

A shortcut, however, is to find the trading level for a similar bond — ideally one from the same issuer with the same duration. The next best comparable is one from the same issuer with a different duration. After that we look for bonds with the same duration issued by a similar firm in the same industry. Starting with

---

[3] Interestingly, the equity oriented investor selling a busted convertible below its fair value may be pleased; although the convertible lost money, it likely lost much less than the common stock alternative.

the best comparables, we compensate for differences in seniority (convertibles are typically junior to straight debt and rated one notch lower by the rating agencies), liquidity, the credit curve, call risk, and other factors to arrive at estimated bond value. This value is generally calculated as a yield spread to the Treasury curve calibrated to the bond's duration.

Using the yield spread assumption derived above we can calculate the convertible's bond value. If this value is at or above where the convertible is offered, then the convertible is busted and worthy of further analysis. This may involve more research into the assumptions made in the bond value calculation and further investigation into market levels for comparable bonds. It could be that the convertible looks cheap relative to a comparable straight bond, but the investor would have no interest in the straight bond at its market yield. In this case, the investor may not be interested in the convertible either, or at the least he or she would demand a larger discount to bond value in order to be interested.

Measuring Upside Potential

Once a convertible is identified as busted, there are several factors important to determining its upside potential. The first is its degree of undervaluation with respect to bond value alone. The larger the discount the greater the convertible's yield advantage over the yield of a comparable straight bond. And, as these bonds approach maturity, the convertible's discount to bond value tends to shrink, further helping it outperform the straight bond alternative.

A second factor affecting potential upside is the degree of undervaluation linked to the embedded equity conversion or call option. Although, by definition, this call feature is well out-of-the-money, the fact that the conversion period may extend for several years renders it valuable. This is especially true for fast growing companies with high equity price volatility. The value of the convertible including its equity call option can be calculated via theoretical price models. These models quantitatively assess value based on assumptions about the issuer's credit spread, stock price yield and volatility, call and/or put features, the issuer's propensity to exercise call options, and maturity. They calculate a theoretical value for the convertible.[4] Since busted convertibles generally trade at a discount to theoretical value, any convergence in price to this higher value likely results in superior performance.

The third factor affecting a convertible's upside potential is the prospect for a rebound in the underlying stock. Large price gains from busted convertibles can occur when the stock rises enough to push the convertible back into the hybrid region. When this happens the convertible rises above its bond value, and it moves closer to its theoretical value (which is also moving higher as a result of the higher equity price and the fact that the convertible is closer to being in-the-

---

[4] An important factor in the valuation of busted convertibles is the long time to expiration of the conversion or equity call option. The models' primary usefulness is their ability to measure the extent to which this conversion option is implicitly mispriced by the market.

money). In some cases the convertible may rise to a level above its theoretical value. In short, a rising stock price triggers positive effects from the first two factors plus higher theoretical values.

Several factors increase the likelihood of an increase in the underlying stock price including improving fundamentals for the issuer, high growth rates, and high stock price volatility. The ideal busted convertible combines these attributes with good call protection and clear cut discounts to bond and/or theoretical values.

BUSTED CONVERTIBLE EXAMPLES

In the 1990s there have been many compelling opportunities in busted convertibles. In January 1991 the A-rated Motorola 0% due 9/7/09 were available at a yield advantage of 110 basis points over Treasuries. Also in early 1991 A-rated Browning Ferris 6.75% due 7/15/05 were offered at 220 basis points over Treasuries when longer maturity and more callable Browning debt was trading at a yield advantage of only 170 basis points. MCI Communications 0% due 12/11/04, yielding 100 basis points more than similar MCI medium-term notes, U.S. Steel 0% due 8/9/05 yielding 100 basis points more than similar U.S. Steel debt, Newscorp 0% due 3/11/13, Carnival Cruise 0% due 6/15/05, and Turner Broadcasting 0% due 2/13/07 offered attractive opportunities in 1992 to 1995. In the case of Motorola, Newscorp, and Carnival Cruise, the stock prices rose and drove the convertibles into the hybrid region, producing substantial gains. The Browning Ferris and MCI's were ultimately called, while most of the U.S. Steel issue was put. Each of these busted convertibles delivered superior returns compared to straight bond alternatives.

More recent opportunities in 1996 include National Semiconductor 6.5% due 10/1/02 yielding 8.6% or 210 basis points above Treasuries for a solid BB-rated credit and BBB-rated Ogden 5.75% due 10/20/02 at a yield spread of 118 above Treasuries, 8 basis points better than the spread offered on a 26-year maturity Ogden straight bond.

The next two examples illustrate the analysis of busted convertibles in more detail. The first example has been offered at busted levels for several years. The second example shows a recent busted convertible that, a short time later, moved up to the hybrid region.

Hollinger Inc. 0% due 10/05/13

The Hollinger zeros were issued in 1993 with a yield (or accretion rate) of 6% to three put dates (in 5, 10, and 15 years) and to maturity, a 15% premium to conversion value, and five years of call protection. Although the convertible is denominated in U.S. dollars, Hollinger equity is traded in Canadian dollars; therefore the conversion value is calculated by multiplying the Canadian price for Hollinger times the exchange rate times the conversion ratio.

Hollinger's stock price has drifted lower since 1993. As a consequence, the convertible has languished, and it currently offers a 10.3% yield to the 10/15/98 put date, 406 basis points better than comparable Treasury strips with a 44% conversion premium. This convertible is rated BB-/B2. In contrast, the Hollinger International 9.25% due 2/1/06 straight bond yields 10.0%, or 323 basis points more than comparable Treasuries and is rated BB-/B1. Hollinger International is a wholly owned subsidiary of Hollinger Inc.

Using the 100-day stock volatility of 18%, the theoretical value of the Hollinger convertible is 34. In summary, the convertible is 2% undervalued, it yields more than a similar bond after adjusting for its shorter duration, and it offers substantially more upside. Even if the equity does not move higher the investor earns a superior yield relative to both the closest alternative and the overall market after considering its duration and credit risk.

The next example begins with similar characteristics, but it shows what can happen when the equity price *does* rebound.

Solectron 6.0% due 3/1/06

The Solectron is an example of the ideal busted convertible. Its credit fundamentals are strong (more cash than debt) and improving. Its revenues and earnings per share have grown at 40% to 60% rates for the past five years and appear poised to accelerate. The stock trades with a below-market price-to-earnings ratio, and it exhibits 50% to 70% volatility, which is very high.

The Solectron convertible was issued in February 1996 with the stock at 46.625. It had an initial premium of 45%, was rated BB+/Ba3, and yielded 30 basis points less than the 10-year Treasury. The stock briefly jumped to 50 before sliding to the low 30s by late July. On August 1, 1996, the Solectron convertible was offered at a yield of 8.0%, representing an advantage of 142 basis points over the 10-year Treasury. This was also a 12 basis point advantage relative to the Solectron 7.375% due 3/1/06 straight bond rated BBB-/Ba1. With the 12 basis point difference in yield compensating for the difference in credit rating, the convertible was selling at its bond value. *Its price did not reflect the enormous value of the embedded conversion option.* This value, which is picked up in the theoretical value calculation, is heightened by Solectron's high equity price volatility, the absence of a common stock dividend, and the convertible's good call protection. It is noncallable unit March 3, 1999 and then callable at 104.2.

Assuming, conservatively, a 45% stock price volatility, the theoretical value of the convertible was 94.8. Therefore, Solectron's convertible price reflected a discount to theoretical value of nearly 9% or 900 basis points: this is an unusually steep discount. In conclusion, the Solectron opportunity offered limited downside risk and excellent upside potential relative to both its straight bond alternative and to the bond market in general.

Seven weeks later Solectron reported quarterly earnings of $.59 versus estimates of $.57, and the stock climbed to 47. The convertible rose to 100.5. For the 7-week period the convertible outperformed the 10-year Treasury and Solectron straight bond by 1,729 basis points, and it outperformed the overall bond market by 1,678 basis points. Its discount to theoretical value fell from 9% to 5%, contributing 400 basis points to its total performance.

Naturally, there are no guarantees that stocks will move up in price following a busted convertible purchase. However, the risk/reward is clearly in the investor's favor. In the worst case an attractive yield based on the convertible's merits as a bond is earned, while in the best case the convertible vastly outperforms comparable-risk alternatives. Since busted convertibles are not included in typical benchmark indexes, this strategy can be used to add substantial relative performance.[5]

CONCLUSION

Although small compared to other bond market sectors, the convertible sector offers unique opportunities for active bond managers. In particular, busted convertibles can be clearly undervalued, such that they pose little risk of underperforming straight bond alternatives, while offering substantial upside potential.

---

[5] After consulting with several dealers who maintain convertible indexes, I concluded that, due to both practical and conceptual problems, the creation of an index for busted convertibles is unlikely.

About the Author

Ronald J. Ryan, CFA

Ronald J. Ryan is the President and Founder of Ryan Labs, a quantitative money management firm with over $9 billion in assets under management and an additional $160 billion in Liability Index advisory systems. From 1977-1982, Mr. Ryan was Director of Fixed Income Research at Lehman Brothers. While at Lehman Brothers, he created and supervised the Lehman Government/Corporate index as well as over 60 custom bond indices. Since 1982, he and his staff have designed numerous index innovations, such as the Daily Bond Index, the STRIPS Index, the International Bond Index Fund, the GIC Index, the Liability Index, and the Treasury Composite Bond Index (the longest such index beginning 1949). Ryan Labs specializes in Custom Index applications to best represent client objectives. It is estimated that Ryan Labs has now designed over 1,000 custom indices for clients. Several of the indices created by Ryan Labs appear throughout the world via electronic financial networks such as Bloomberg, Reuters, Telerate, as well as financial trade journals. Mr. Ryan has an M.B.A. and B.B.A. from Loyola University of the South and is a Chartered Financial Analyst. He is a frequent speaker at seminars.

Chapter 9

Managing a Fixed Income Portfolio Versus a Liability Objective

Ronald J. Ryan, CFA
President
Ryan Labs, Inc.

INTRODUCTION

The sole objective of most institutional funds in America is to fund some type of liability schedule. Defined benefit pension funds exceed $3 trillion with the required purpose to properly fund the pension benefit payment schedule. Lotteries have grown significantly in America where now over 30 states have such a contest with the clear goal to pay a well-defined liability payment schedule. Nuclear Decommissioning Trust was created for the single objective of funding a distinct liability schedule out into the distant future. Debt service funds are built for the singular objective of funding principal and interest payments on a distinct liability payment schedule. Insurance companies sell annuities and other guaranteed interest products which become liabilities that have to be funded properly. Post-retirement medical benefits are the new liabilities of tomorrow that scare many private corporations and public plans on how to fund such a large and fast growing liability schedule. Social Security may be the mill-stone around our country's financial neck on how to finance prudently such a massive liability expense. And there are many more distinct liability objectives. In America, the liability objective growth and behavior will determine the future behavior of all the assets that are positioned to fund such liabilities.

LIABILITIES DEFINED

According to the Financial Accounting Standards Board (FASB), liabilities are to be viewed and priced as if they were high quality zero-coupon bonds whose maturities match the liability payment date and whose par values match the liability payment amount. The only high quality zero-coupon bonds in the taxable bond marketplace today are government securities. As a result, liabilities are equivalent to a government bond portfolio weighted by the liability payment schedule.

This deductive logic has been well followed through the last few decades to defease liabilities; investors have bought zero-coupon bonds that match liabilities. Moreover, dedication and immunization are other strategies that focus on the liability objective as best represented by a bond portfolio structured to match the liability payment schedule.

Unfortunately, these time tested strategies are too often disregarded and replaced with asset allocation strategies that compare asset classes versus asset classes in order to optimize the highest *absolute* returns given some level of risk. Most asset managers are given a generic market index as their benchmark which may have no similarity to the behavior pattern of liabilities. If the equity asset manager outperforms the S&P 500, does that mean these assets outperformed the liability growth rate? If a fixed income manager outperforms the Lehman Aggregate, does that mean these assets outperformed the liabilities they are funding? If any asset manager outperforms any "generic" market index does that mean those assets are funding liabilities correctly. It has become most commonplace that assets are given objectives of beating the growth rate of generic market indices instead of custom liability indices. There is little evidence that any market index behaves like any distinct and client unique set of liabilities. This sets up the obvious correlation: the wrong benchmark index produces the wrong risk/reward outcome.

Furthermore, the present value calculation or pricing of liabilities is performed differently than either the market or the Financial Accounting Standards Board (FASB) would confirm as proper. It has become common practice to price all liabilities at the same interest rate regardless of their maturity or payment date. Too often, this discount rate is much higher than the market rate, causing an underpricing of liabilities. Moreover, liabilities are analyzed annually, with the data usually available up to three months later. Given this frequency and delinquency, it is difficult, if not impossible, for the asset side to understand the liability side. Using pension liabilities as a proper proxy for all types of liabilities, one can easily see that by not focusing correctly on the true liability objective, several problems, if not crises, may develop.

THE GOAL

The goal of the liability game is to match up assets versus liabilities such that assets consistently perform and create the lowest funding cost possible. Just like a good football team, there are three steps needed to win the game:

Step 1. Understand the rules and the opponent behavior pattern (liabilities);

Step 2. Build a strategy to beat the opponent (based upon the opponent's strengths and weaknesses); and,

Step 3. Watch the scoreboard.

Let us now review these three steps in some detail to understand how to play and how to win the game. In our discussion below, we focus on the pension game — structuring assets so as to meet pension liabilities.

THE RULES

Institutional investors that manage money against liabilities face regulatory constraints. In the pension game, there are numerous regulations (FASB, Employee Retirement Income Security Act (ERISA), Internal Revenue Service (IRS), etc.). If we run down the basic rules, we may find some interesting surprises:

Teams	Assets versus liabilities
Rule book(s)	ERISA, IRS, FASB
Playing field	Present value dollars ($)
	Future value is not the consideration
	Present value = market value
Time period	Annual
	Financial statements are prepared annually
	Pension contributions are calculated annually
	Surplus is calculated annually
Opponent	Liabilities behave like a zero-coupon bond portfolio
	FAS 87 and 106 have both ruled accordingly
Scoreboard	Seldom seen
	Actuaries calculate liabilities annually
	Reports may be 3-months delinquent

The key observation here is that liabilities are to be priced as if they were a high quality zero-coupon fixed income portfolio whose par values match the liability payment amount and whose maturity dates match the liability payment dates.

THE OPPONENT

FASB does the best job of explaining how liabilities work and are to be priced. FASB regulates financial statement reporting and is quite clear on how to report and measure pension assets versus pension liabilities. FASB 87, Paragraph 44 deals with pricing of pension liabilities:

> Assumed discount rates shall reflect the rates at which the pension benefits could be effectively settled . . . In making those estimates, employers may look to rates of return on high-quality fixed-income investments currently available and expected to be available during the period to maturity of the pension benefits.[1]

---

[1] "Employers' Accounting for Pensions," *Statement of Financial Accounting Standards No. 87* (December 1985), pp.12.

Therefore, according to FASB, pension plans should use high-quality for life, noncallable for life bonds as their discount rate(s) source. Pension plans should match the maturity date(s) of these high-quality bonds to the pension benefit date(s). Since the only high-quality, non-callable bonds for life (maturity) are Treasuries, pension liabilities should be priced off the Treasury yield curve.

Furthermore, Paragraph 199 of FASB 87 says:

> Interest rates vary depending on the duration of investments; for example, Treasury bills, 7-year bonds and 30-year bonds have different interest rates . . . The disclosures required by this Statement regarding components of the pension obligation will be more representationally faithful if *individual discount rates* applicable to various benefit deferral periods are selected.[2]

Therefore, each liability should be priced individually off the Treasury yield curve with the same maturity as the liability benefit payment date.

In 1993, the SEC got involved when it questioned a registrant about the selection of discount rates under FASB 87. The SEC wrote a letter to corporations and FASB stating that the guidance provided in Paragraph 186 of FASB 106 for selecting discount rates is appropriate guidance for measuring pension obligations. Since FASB 106 was created for medical liabilities, this sounded unusual. Apparently, according to the SEC, the present value of all liabilities should be calculated the same way.

FASB 106, Paragraph 186 reads:

> The objective of selecting assumed discount rates is to measure the single amount that, if invested at the measurement date in a portfolio of high-quality debt instruments, would provide the necessary future cash flows to pay the accumulated benefits when due. Notionally, that single amount, *the accumulated post retirement benefit obligation, would equal the current value of a portfolio of high-quality zero coupon bonds whose maturity dates and amounts would be the same as the timing and amount of the expected future benefits payments.*[3]

FASB needs little or no translation here. Liabilities are to be priced as if they were zero-coupon bonds whose maturities match the liability benefit date and whose par values match the liability payment amounts. Since there are only government zero-coupon bonds in existence, it follows that pension liabilities will behave like a portfolio of Treasury zero-coupon bonds! After decades of execut-

---

[2] "Employers Accounting for Pensions," *Statement of Financial Accounting Standards No. 87* (December 1985), pp. 60.

[3] "Employers' Accounting for Postretirement Benefits Other Than Pensions," *Statement of Financial Accounting Standards No. 106* (December 1990), pp. 1310.

ing defeasance programs through the purchase of zero-coupon bonds, this should not be a surprise. By definition, to defease liabilities, the purchase bond must equal the liability. Therefore:

Liabilities (The Pension Opponent) = Treasury Zero − Coupon Bond Portfolio

Many companies appear to take great liberties with the FASB guidelines. Instead of pricing each liability uniquely, in accordance with FASB 87, Paragraph 199, most companies price liabilities at the same discount rate. Since horizontal or flat yield curves are not common, the mispricing of liabilities here seems either careless or intentional.

Moreover, companies interpret high-quality, zero-coupon bonds to be anything with a rating of AA or higher. Since zero-coupon corporate bonds do not exist, we are dealing with theoretical discount rates. The logic or strategy assumed by plan sponsors is that AA corporate bonds have higher yields which will equate to lower present values. This is true but only benefits the plan sponsor initially. Every year thereafter, given the same yield change as STRIPS, AA corporates will produce higher liability growth rates due to higher yields.

STRATEGY TO BEAT LIABILITIES

Any good strategy should be based upon the opponent's strengths and weaknesses. The liabilities opponent will behave like a portfolio of Treasury STRIPS (zero-coupon bonds). Therefore, this portfolio is extremely interest-rate sensitive, if not completely interest-rate driven, for present value calculations. Most pension plans have long durations on their liabilities, around a 15-year average, making them much more interest rate sensitive then the generic bond market indices with durations around five years.

To neutralize this interest rate risk, a prudent asset strategy would be to structure the assets identical to or similar to the term structure of liabilities. The asset allocation decision should be based on the structure of liabilities. The percent of liabilities short would support the allocation decision as to what percent is placed in short assets. The percent of liabilities intermediate would support the allocation decision as to what percent is placed in intermediate assets. Naturally, the same logic applies for long and very long asset allocation strategies. Maintaining the same term structure as the liability payment schedule produces the same interest rate risk. Since interest rate risk is by far the greatest cause of present value volatility, it should be eliminated. Due to the fact that interest rates change daily, it is critical that the term structure of assets versus liabilities be monitored frequently, if not daily, and rebalanced whenever they are out of alignment with each other.

Where the future value of liabilities are *most certain* (e.g., pension retired lives, lotteries, debt service, insurance products, etc.), then the only factor affecting the volatility of liabilities in present value dollars is interest rates. Fixed income products would be the only appropriate assets here since they are the only assets that can match the interest rate sensitivity of liabilities. That is why defeasance, dedication, and immunization only use fixed income products in their modeling procedures. Treasury STRIPS and any zero-coupon bond would be the ideal asset to match each liability payment. However, any fixed income security that will match the interest rate sensitivity of liabilities is acceptable. Corporate bonds may introduce other variables such as credit risk and event risk which could disturb and even severely violate the interest rate matching process. Mortgages have very uncertain cash flows due to uncertain principal prepayments. Therefore any uncertain cash flow asset or uncertain interest rate sensitivity asset (e.g., stocks) should be avoided.

Where the future value of liabilities are *uncertain* (e.g., pension active lives, Nuclear Decommissioning, etc.) there needs to be understood what factors affect the volatility of both the future value and present value calculations. Interest rates still play a major role in affecting the present value volatility. Inflation and factors that are unique to particular types of liabilities may cause future value volatility. If great enough, assets should be found that best hedge or match that type of volatility. Liabilities are still viewed and priced as Treasury STRIPS. Segmenting liabilities into short, intermediate, long, and very long liabilities would be a wise asset allocation foundation. Then find assets that best match each segment and allocate an amount that matches the liability amount.

If there is a surplus, this should be isolated and managed as a separate portfolio (e.g., surplus portfolio). The surplus portfolio should have its own objective with a complementary asset allocation and asset management strategy. If there is a deficit, the shorter liabilities should be matched and funded properly. The strategy should be to isolate and move the deficit to the longest area of liabilities. This buys time. Since the durations of fixed income coupon bonds peak at 12 years today, then the only fixed income investment alternatives left are zero-coupon bonds. Although zero-coupon bonds best match liabilities, they cannot be expected to outgrow liabilities significantly to recover any sizable deficits. Other assets are needed that may not match interest rate sensitivity well but are expected to outgrow long and very long liabilities significantly over time. Under a deficit strategy, a fixed income product is best suited for short and intermediate liabilities, stocks are best suited for any liabilities longer than 12 years.

LIABILITY INDICES

Treasury STRIPS were created in February 15, 1985. The next day, the Ryan team designed the first STRIP index series. In 1991, the Ryan team innovated the first Liability Index based on these STRIPS indices. In 1992, our Liability Index was trademarked. Based upon FASB and standard defeasance guidelines, STRIPS are the best proxy for pension liabilities. The reason for this is that an interest rate (discount rate) is needed that can calculate or match the correct present value for each future value liability payment. Only zero-coupon bonds have no reinvestment risk to distort the present value calculation. The only liquid and prevalent zero-coupon bonds are Treasury STRIPS. If we look at the history of risk and reward for STRIPS, we will understand the liability opponent better and strategize more effectively.

Exhibits 1 and 2 show the first 10-year history of risk and reward for STRIPS (e.g., liability proxy). Both risk and reward measurements prove STRIPS behave in a very linear pattern. As maturity or duration increases, risk and reward increase accordingly.

Analyzing the popular asset indices or generic market indices versus the STRIP curve shows a clear and separate risk/reward behavior pattern:

Cash indices	= 1-year and shorter STRIPS
Bond indices	= 4- or 5-year STRIPS
Stocks (S&P 500)	= 14- or 15-year STRIPS
International stocks (EAFE)	= 18- to 28-year STRIPS

Amazingly, STRIPS longer than 15 years consistently outperformed the S&P 500, suggesting that the present value of liabilities grew faster than pension assets. This is quite a revelation since stocks have, supposedly, always outperformed bonds over any 10-year period.

The strategy to outperform liabilities is focused on understanding the interest rate sensitivity of pension fund liabilities in present value dollars and neutralizing this risk. However, it is a rare occurrence to find any asset manager who studies STRIPS as liabilities or for any asset manager to manage assets versus STRIPS (liabilities). Obviously, *liabilities are a fixed income portfolio — a Treasury STRIPS portfolio* structured to match that unique liability schedule. So the question remains: if you beat a generic market index, do you beat liabilities? This glaring problem is due to the absence of a custom liability index (or indices) for performance measurement and asset allocation modeling.

THE SCOREBOARD

Just like an athletic team, the scoreboard dictates your asset strategy. If you are way behind in the fourth quarter, you will behave much differently than if you are way ahead. This is mainly due to the fact that asset/liability management is an annual game requiring the posting of each team's score (asset team versus liability team) at the end of the fiscal year. This will decide the pension contribution, if any, that is needed for the next year. Accordingly, it is critical that a pension scoreboard correctly and frequently displays the score (growth rate) and size of pension assets versus pension liabilities.

Exhibit 1: Risk (Standard Deviation)
(2/28/85 - 2/28/95)

Market Indices	Last 10 years	Last 7 years	Last 5 years	Last 3 years	Last 12 months
Ryan Labs STRIPS					
1 year	1.38	1.27	1.23	1.18	1.45
2 year	2.63	2.42	2.38	2.46	2.66
3 year	3.91	3.60	3.46	3.59	3.45
4 year	5.06	4.62	4.44	4.63	4.26
5 year	6.17	5.56	5.33	5.49	5.19
6 year	7.28	6.24	5.99	6.08	5.74
7 year	8.41	6.99	6.74	6.78	6.47
8 year	9.61	7.80	7.63	7.65	7.12
9 ycar	10.63	8.49	8.34	8.29	7.74
10 year	11.45	9.20	8.99	8.94	8.32
11 year	12.60	9.93	9.58	9.49	8.85
12 year	13.70	10.55	10.19	9.98	9.33
13 year	14.74	11.17	10.70	10.40	9.96
14 year	15.12	11.87	11.34	11.05	10.41
15 year	16.44	12.62	11.86	11.34	10.84
16 year	17.30	13.13	12.33	11.70	11.23
17 year	18.28	13.69	12.66	11.64	11.42
18 year	19.13	14.29	13.15	12.06	11.64
19 year	19.95	15.09	13.88	12.61	12.25
20 year	20.72	15.80	14.55	12.90	12.89
21 year	21.70	16.36	15.19	13.53	13.26
22 year	22.58	17.11	15.83	13.74	13.70
23 year	23.49	18.01	16.55	14.26	14.38
24 year	23.97	18.53	17.13	14.75	14.63
25 year	24.68	19.17	17.85	15.42	15.18
26 year	25.67	19.93	18.48	16.10	15.41
27 year	26.91	20.79	19.19	17.23	16.28
28 year	26.57	20.90	19.06	16.98	15.38
29 year	28.25	22.03	20.12	18.16	15.63
30 year	28.34	23.51	21.93	20.44	16.57
STRIPS Composite	15.70	12.30	11.44	10.45	10.01
GICs RL 3-yr. GICs	0.47	0.31	0.33	0.23	0.02
Cash RL Cash	0.80	0.76	0.72	0.54	0.65
Bonds RL Treasury	5.96	5.08	4.88	4.97	4.99
LB Govt./Corp.	5.11	4.55	4.43	4.55	4.73
ML DM	5.01	4.35	4.01	4.03	4.56
SB BIG	4.94	4.28	4.02	4.08	4.75
Stocks S&P 500	15.15	12.02	11.99	8.12	10.04
Int'l Stocks MS EAFE	19.42	18.75	19.38	15.39	10.17

Exhibit 2: Reward
(2/28/85 - 2/28/95)

Market Indices	Last 10 years	Last 7 years	Last 5 years	Last 3 years	Last 12 months
Ryan Labs STRIPS					
1 year	7.36	6.88	6.50	4.64	4.62
2 year	8.48	7.51	7.52	5.06	3.16
3 year	9.62	8.29	8.77	6.00	1.97
4 year	10.22	8.41	8.92	6.28	0.77
5 year	11.24	9.18	9.77	6.99	0.98
6 year	11.80	9.36	10.06	7.48	1.07
7 year	12.26	9.38	9.97	7.37	−0.46
8 year	12.99	9.96	10.58	8.27	−1.23
9 year	13.56	9.90	10.64	8.49	−1.17
10 year	13.80	10.40	11.33	9.28	−1.85
11 year	14.30	10.34	11.09	9.08	−2.17
12 year	14.91	10.43	11.15	9.31	−2.75
13 year	15.07	10.52	11.26	9.33	−3.41
14 year	15.30	10.49	11.23	9.41	−3.81
15 year	15.71	10.74	11.37	9.54	−4.15
16 year	16.19	10.72	11.28	9.67	−3.84
17 year	16.72	10.65	11.21	9.51	−4.20
18 year	17.07	10.83	11.54	10.00	−4.04
19 year	17.06	10.55	11.20	9.60	−4.48
20 year	17.64	10.48	11.08	9.41	−5.48
21 year	17.69	10.43	11.19	9.32	−6.30
22 year	18.12	10.40	11.09	9.20	−6.94
23 year	18.04	9.97	10.90	9.10	−7.77
24 year	17.94	9.55	10.46	8.80	−8.86
25 year	17.10	9.61	10.66	9.22	−8.85
26 year	16.11	9.27	9.46	8.30	−10.86
27 year	16.78	9.12	10.00	9.60	−9.75
28 year	15.60	8.59	9.26	9.20	−8.99
29 year	13.41	6.16	7.29	6.54	−12.34
30 year	10.13	1.07	0.83	0.87	−22.60
STRIPS Composite	14.84	9.61	10.20	8.43	−4.26
GICs RL 3-year GIC	8.53	7.67	7.36	6.53	5.64
Cash RL Cash	6.63	6.22	5.59	4.18	5.03
Bonds RL Treasury	10.06	7.85	8.27	6.18	0.53
LB Govt./Corp.	10.27	8.55	8.86	6.67	1.34
ML DM	10.43	8.62	8.89	6.54	1.87
SB BIG	10.48	8.67	8.92	6.49	1.82
Stocks S&P 500	14.14	12.48	11.35	8.77	7.34
Int'l Stocks MS EAFE	17.19	4.65	3.18	8.77	−4.19

To accomplish this requires the construction of a liability index customized to the specific pension liability schedule (e.g. any liability schedule) and broken out by term structure sectors. A custom liability index would allow short assets to understand and monitor their funding opponent — short liabilities; intermediate assets to understand and monitor their funding opponent — intermediate liabilities; and long assets to understand and monitor their funding opponent — long liabilities. Without a custom liability index, several fundamental dilemmas can develop.

FIRST DILEMMA: ASSET ALLOCATION

The goal of traditional asset allocation is to create the optimal *absolute return*. Such models use historical generic market index data. As a result, stocks have been favored consistently. However, the true objective of asset allocation should be to create the optimal *relative return* versus liabilities. Each plan sponsor has a unique liability term structure, based on the plan demographics, economic assumptions, and design. Similar to snowflakes, no two liability schedules are identical. FASB 87, Paragraph 199, recognizes this difference for pension liabilities: "A plan covering only retired employees would be expected to have significantly different discount rates from one covering a work force of 30-year-olds."[4]

Logically, therefore, the liability term structure should dictate the shape of the asset allocation. A pension plan skewed to retirees would have a shorter average life than a plan skewed to active lives. Accordingly, the discount rates would be weighted much differently producing much different present value calculations. Unfortunately, most asset allocation models have no input for a client's liability characteristics. They only analyze historical generic market indices. Without a client's liability structure, all clients could get approximately the same asset allocation. In fact, this is a national trend. According to the annual surveys of the top 1,000 defined benefit pension plans, asset allocation ratios have been quite static. It is hard to imagine that this generic allocation model fits most liability schedules, and that the asset/liability ratio (surplus/deficit) is so static that it doesn't require dynamic asset allocation shifts.

Let's take, for example company A and company B. Company A is a very young firm with no retirees. It has 82% in long liabilities suggesting an allocation of 82% in long assets, unless there is an unusual deficit situation. Company B is an old mainline firm with pension liabilities heavily skewed to retirees. It has only 28% in long liabilities suggesting an allocation of 28% to long assets, unless there is an unusual deficit situation. Indeed, the term structure of each pension liability payout schedule should become the foundation for asset allocation. Asset allocation should be tailored to each plan sponsor's unique liability situation and not based on generic models.

---

[4] "Employers Accounting for Pensions," *Statement of Financial Accounting Standards No. 87* (December 1985), pp. 60.

SECOND DILEMMA: PERFORMANCE MEASUREMENT

Historically, pension assets are given generic market indices (e.g., S&P 500) as their objective. Their performance is measured by comparing the total return of an asset class (e.g. stocks, bonds) to the generic market index for that asset class. Money managers are hired and fired based on their performance versus this generic asset index as well as their corresponding universe of fellow managers.

An important reason why this situation persists is that pension liabilities are traditionally calculated annually and reported months after the fact! More importantly, the calculation or present value pricing of liabilities is very subjective; and the asset side is unclear as to how this process is done. It is extremely difficult, if not impossible, for an asset manager to manage against an invisible opponent such as liabilities.

What is needed is a liability index system that correctly prices plan sponsor liabilities (in conformity with FASB) as a tangible, frequent (e.g., daily) system for investment management. The asset side must know frequently the liability growth rates and behavior patterns. Performance measurement can then be properly assessed as the *growth rate of assets versus the growth rate of liabilities for any sub-section of liabilities (e.g. short, intermediate, long, very long) or total liabilities.*

THIRD DILEMMA: PRICING LIABILITIES

FASB governs the financial statement reporting of pension liabilities and requires that the *market value of assets be compared to the present value of liabilities marked to current market rates.* In addition, FASB requires that the present value of liabilities be calculated (priced) using individual discount rates for each liability payment date. As noted earlier, according to FASB 106, Paragraph 186 "(the obligation) would equal the current market value of a portfolio of high-quality zero coupon bonds whose maturity dates and amounts would be the same as the timing and amounts of the expected future benefit payments."[5]

By definition, since there is no other high-quality zero-coupon yield curve, the bonds that qualify are those that make up the Treasury STRIP yield curve. However, most plan sponsors do not adhere to FASB standards. Instead, a single discount rate is used to price all liabilities. This single discount rate is normally around 100 basis points higher than the market rate. Most actuarial studies of the largest corporate pension plans found that the average discount rate for pension liabilities in 1995 was 7.35% for measurement dates as of December 31, 1995 when the average yield of the Treasury STRIP curve was 5.92%. This is a difference of 1.43%. To convert this difference to a present value difference, multiply the yield difference by the average duration of liabilities (Exhibit 3). Actually, this is rather common as the normal discount rate differential.

---

[5] "Employers' Accounting for Postretirement Benefits Other Than Pensions," *Statement of Financial Accounting Standards No. 106* (December 1990), pp. 1310.

Exhibit 3: Comparison of Average Discount Rate (Corporate) to the Average Yield on STRIP Yield Curve (at 12/31/95)

Year	Average Discount Rate (%)	Average STRIP Yield (%)	Yield Difference	Average Duration	Present Value % Difference
1995	7.35	5.92	1.43	15	21.45
1994	8.28	7.95	0.33	15	4.95
1993	7.29	6.27	1.02	15	15.30
1992	8.17	7.18	0.99	15	14.85
1991	8.33	7.24	1.09	15	16.35
1990	8.59	8.25	0.34	15	5.10

Accordingly, there is evidence to believe that liabilities, on average, are undervalued by about 15% per year. This is strictly a pricing problem of using inflated discount rates.

In Exhibit 3 for the year ending 1990, the difference was only 34 basis points or 5.1%. For years ending 1991 to 1992, however, when the STRIP rate dropped to 7.24% and 7.18% respectively, companies kept their discount rates in the 8.25% range in order to smooth out pension expenses, causing a major difference between the actual versus reported present value of liabilities (approximately 15%).

In 1993, when the average STRIP rate fell to 6.27%, the SEC alerted corporations that a discount rate significantly above 7% would be under review. Therefore, companies quickly dropped their discount rates to 7.29%. However, compared to 1990, they maintained a much higher spread (about 100 basis points).

In 1994, when rates shot up about 170 basis points (from 6.27% to 7.95%) companies raised their discount rates about 100 basis points (from 7.29% to 8.28%) thus narrowing the spread to only 33 basis points. This is an indication that corporations are either moving to more realistic market rates or that they are trying to smooth their pension expenses by averaging market rate changes. However, 1995 seemed to represent back to tradition as the average corporation set their discount rates for year-end 1995 well above market rates.

FOURTH DILEMMA: BENCHMARKS

The appropriate asset benchmark for a liability objective is a liability index that properly represents the present value growth of the plan sponsor's liability schedule. Generic indices that measure asset classes (e.g., S&P 500) are, obviously, not appropriate measurements of liability growth. *Only a liability index that matches the plan sponsor's payment schedule can properly represent the client.*

Liability indices should conform to FASB regulations. Accordingly, such an index should be priced off the Treasury STRIP yield curve. As Exhibit 4 indicates, using generic market indices for asset objectives, instead of a liability index, results in significant opportunity costs. For example, no generic market index correlated well or moved similar to the Ryan Labs Liability index. The most popular asset benchmarks (e.g. S&P 500 and Lehman Aggregate) behaved much differently then the Ryan Labs Liability index. Traditional asset indices (generic market) are a poor proxy for liabilities and should not be the objective of the assets.

SOLUTION: CUSTOM LIABILITY INDICES

It is critical that each client's objective is properly measured and supported. Until a custom liability index is tailored to accurately calculate liability present value and present value growth, the plan sponsor cannot be well served. Asset allocation (all asset classes) is dependent on the liability term structure for its proper *relative* allocation. Performance measurement is dependent on such a liability index to accurately assess asset growth versus the liability growth these assets are funding.

For asset managers to function effectively, a liability index should be calculated frequently. This index should conform to FASB pricing requirements. Asset allocation and performance measurement can best be understood once the weight and growth rate of each liability maturity sector (term structure) is calculated. Term structure precision is the critical calculation. Without accurate liability term structure definitions and measurements, plan sponsors face ambiguous asset allocations and performance measurements.

If asset managers can better understand the risk/reward behavior pattern of the liability opponent, they can better strategize on how to outperform such an opponent. If asset managers can understand the term structure of liabilities, they can build proper asset allocations for each term structure area (long assets versus long liabilities, etc.). Without accurate liability term structure measurements, clients face the greatest risk there is — mismatching assets versus liabilities by term structure.

Exhibit 4: Asset/Liability Total Return Analysis

Index	1990	1991	1992	1993	1994	1995	Cum. 12/31/89 to 12/31/95
Ryan Labs Liability	3.23	19.26	7.87	22.46	−12.60	41.16	100.65
Ryan Labs Cash	8.73	7.42	4.12	3.51	3.94	7.11	40.13
Ryan Labs 3-yr. GIC	8.71	8.61	7.77	6.58	5.66	5.82	51.61
Ryan Labs Treasury	7.87	15.27	6.31	11.35	−4.98	20.13	68.02
Lehman Govt./Corp	8.28	16.13	7.58	11.03	−3.51	19.24	72.82
Lehman Aggregate	8.96	16.00	7.40	9.75	−2.92	18.47	71.36
Salomon MTG	10.90	15.64	7.37	7.03	−1.42	16.77	69.65
S&P 500	−3.15	30.45	7.64	10.07	1.29	37.29	108.16
MS EAFE	−23.32	12.48	−11.85	32.95	8.06	11.56	21.85

About the Authors

Frank J. Jones, Ph.D.

Frank J. Jones is Chief Investment Officer and Executive Vice President of The Guardian Life Insurance Company, where he is responsible for the bond, stock, and real estate portfolios in The Guardian's general and separate accounts. He is also responsible for The Guardian's internally managed mutual funds and variable annuity funds. Among other activities, he is on the Board of Directors of Guardian Baillie Gifford Limited. Prior to joining The Guardian Life, Dr. Jones was Director of Global Fixed Income Research and Economics at Merrill Lynch Capital Markets and Managing Director of Institutional Futures and Options at Kidder Peabody & Co. He has written several articles and books on the financial markets and the economy, including *The International Government Bond Markets* with Frank J Fabozzi. He is an Adjunct Associate Professor of Finance at New York University and Lecturer in The School of Management at Yale University. Dr. Jones has a Ph.D. from Stanford University, an M.S in Nuclear Engineering from Cornell University, and B.A and B.S. degrees from the University of Notre Dame.

Leonard J. Peltzman

Leonard J. Peltzman is an analyst in the Fixed Income Securities Department at The Guardian Life Insurance Company. He is primarily responsible for managing the portfolio analytics systems. Mr. Peltzman joined The Guardian in June 1993 and holds a B.A. in Economics and an M.B.A. in Finance from New York University.

Chapter 10

Fixed Income Attribution Analysis

Frank J. Jones, Ph.D.
Chief Investment Officer
Guardian Life Insurance

Leonard J. Peltzman
Analyst, Fixed Income Securities
Guardian Life Insurance

INTRODUCTION

Attribution analysis is *ex post* portfolio rate of return (ROR) analysis. Specifically, the *ex post* total ROR on a bond portfolio is "attributed" to the various risk factors of the bond portfolio; that is, portions of the ROR are associated with each of the risk factors. Attribution analysis, however, cannot be considered in isolation, but only in a broader structure of bond portfolio benchmarks, risk factors, strategies, and a wider set of portfolio return analyses, as summarized in Exhibit 1. This chapter considers attribution analysis in this broader analytical framework and provides an empirical example. The next sections discuss the benchmarks, performance measurement, risk factors, strategies, and portfolio return analysis as the basis for considering attribution analysis.

BENCHMARKS

To answer the question, "How big is big?" a frame of reference or benchmark (often called a "bogey") must be provided. A person who is 6'0" tall will be very big in the eighth grade (where the average height may be 5'4") but very small in the National Basketball Association (where the average height may be 6'5"). Is the benchmark for assessing someone's relative height the eighth grade or the NBA? Similarly, to evaluate bond portfolio returns, a benchmark must be provided. A return of 6% on a fixed income portfolio during a year when the bond market rallied might be very good if the portfolio was cash; but inferior if the portfolio was composed of long-term bonds. Similarly a given return may be good for a Treasury portfolio but weak for a non-investment grade corporate bond portfolio.

Exhibit 1: Portfolio Analysis

Benchmarks	Investment Managers by Benchmark	Risk Factors	Strategies	Portfolio Return Analysis*
Asset Group (e.g., Lehman Aggregate)	Mutual Funds	Duration Convexity	*Passive* (Replicate all or some risk factors). • Indexation • Immunization	Ex Ante Sensitivity Analysis
Liability Driven ("Customized")	Pension Funds/ Insurance Cos.	Yield curve shape (Duration Buckets) Sector Weightings • Macro (e.g. Corporate versus MBS) • Micro (e.g. Utilities versus Industrials in Corporates). • Security (e.g. Niagara Mohawk versus Florida P&L in Utilities) Credit Rating Short-Term Dislocations • Trading.	• Dedication *Active* (Actively deviate from one or more risk factors) • Trading • Market Timing	*Ex Post* Attribution Analysis

* Returns calculated according to AIMR.

Fixed income benchmarks can be driven by either broad/aggregate fixed income asset classes or the liabilities related to the asset portfolio. Three investment banks have constructed broad and disaggregated bond indexes: Lehman Brothers, Inc. (the Lehman Aggregate); Salomon Brothers (the Salomon Broad Investment Grade (BIG)); and, Merrill Lynch (the Merrill Lynch Domestic Master). The subsets of the Lehman Aggregate are shown in Exhibit 2. A rate of return for the Aggregate and each subset can be calculated on a daily basis. Thus, from this list, portfolio managers may choose the Lehman Aggregate, the Lehman Corporate, or the Lehman Short Term (1-10 years), or High Grade (AAA/AA) Corporate Index as a benchmark, whichever is most appropriate, and compare the return on their portfolio to any of these indexes.

Most institutional investors, however, do not find a portfolio based on the composition of the broad market or a sector relevant to their needs, but instead want a portfolio which can fund their specific liabilities as a benchmark. In such cases, they develop their own "customized" benchmarks which reflect their liabilities. To develop their own benchmarks, they must determine the expected cash flows of their liabilities and specify the types of investments they wish to make (e.g. sectors, subsectors, credit ratings, etc.). They can then specify their own customized asset group and calculate the return on the benchmark from the returns on its components over a period of time.

Exhibit 2: Lehman Brothers Fixed Income Indices

January 1-31, 1997	Number Issues	Durat. ToWorst	Mod.Adj. Durat.	Coupon	Matur.	Price	Yield ToWorst	Market Value	% of Index	% of Aggregate
aggregate	5799	5.19	4.62	7.21	8.73	102.43	6.73	4710228	100.00	100.00
int. aggregate	4299	3.96	3.40	7.03	5.26	101.31	6.64	3803485		80.75
government/corporate	5085	5.35	5.06	7.13	9.51	103.34	6.50	3261687	100.00	69.25
int. gov/corp	3585	3.42	3.26	6.82	4.20	101.84	6.27	2354944	72.20	50.00
long gov/corp	1500	10.35	9.73	7.98	23.30	107.47	7.11	906743	27.80	19.25
governments	1387	4.99	4.76	6.97	8.44	103.85	6.31	2414134	74.01	51.25
int. governments	1247	3.13	2.97	6.64	3.78	101.79	6.13	1816375	55.69	38.56
long governments	140	10.61	10.20	8.04	22.58	110.72	6.87	597759	18.33	12.69
1-3 year govt.	423	1.75	1.70	6.30	1.88	100.80	5.88	913614	28.01	19.40
treasuries	170	4.94	4.79	7.05	8.27	105.14	6.26	2105810	64.56	44.71
int. treasuries	125	3.09	3.00	6.64	3.66	102.06	6.07	1579275	48.42	33.53
long treasuries	45	10.49	10.17	8.48	22.10	115.69	6.84	526535	16.14	11.18
20+ year treasuries	23	11.53	11.15	7.85	24.52	110.95	6.88	358185	10.98	7.60
agencies	1217	5.30	4.56	6.41	9.58	95.84	6.63	308324	9.45	6.55
int. agencies	1122	3.44	2.80	6.66	4.61	99.99	6.48	237100	7.27	5.03
long agencies	95	11.52	10.42	5.70	26.11	84.22	7.13	71224	2.18	1.51

January 1-31, 1997	Number Issues	Durat. ToWorst	Mod.Adj. Durat.	Coupon	Matur.	Price	Yield ToWorst	Market Value	% of Index	% of Aggregate
corporates	3698	6.39	5.91	7.57	12.57	101.91	7.05	847553	25.99	17.99
int. corporates	2338	4.40	4.24	7.40	5.61	102.01	6.74	538570	16.51	11.43
long corporates	1360	9.84	8.82	7.87	24.71	101.73	7.58	308984	9.47	6.56
industrials	1278	6.88	6.46	7.83	14.53	103.09	7.15	293681	9.00	6.23
int. industrials	706	4.38	4.23	7.64	5.67	102.77	6.78	161821	4.96	3.44
long industrials	572	9.96	9.20	8.06	25.41	103.49	7.61	131860	4.04	2.80
utilities	786	7.45	6.23	7.51	16.92	100.33	7.28	146809	4.50	3.12
int. utilities	391	4.48	4.26	7.11	5.72	100.97	6.76	68175	2.09	1.45
long utilities	395	10.02	7.93	7.85	26.62	99.78	7.73	78634	2.41	1.67
finance	1116	4.95	4.70	7.27	7.79	100.82	6.81	231461	7.10	4.91
int. finance	926	4.05	3.91	7.30	5.06	101.78	6.68	191109	5.86	4.06
long finance	190	9.22	8.44	7.14	20.73	96.53	7.43	40352	1.24	0.86
yankees	518	6.56	6.32	7.62	11.97	102.76	6.97	175603	5.38	3.73
int. yankees	315	4.97	4.80	7.42	6.36	101.98	6.77	117464	3.60	2.49
long yankees	203	9.77	9.40	8.02	23.29	104.39	7.39	58138	1.78	1.23

January 1-31, 1997	Number Issues	Durat. ToWorst	Mod.Adj. Durat.	Coupon	Matur.	Price	Yield ToWorst	Market Value	% of Index	% of Aggregate
AAA corporates	142	6.89	6.29	7.53	14.66	101.18	6.82	36824	1.13	0.78
int. AAA corporates	75	4.41	4.21	7.80	5.62	103.44	6.50	20325	0.62	0.43
long AAA corporates	67	9.95	8.86	7.21	25.79	98.54	7.21	16498	0.51	0.35
AA corporates	561	6.21	5.57	7.22	11.68	100.98	6.86	153793	4.72	3.27
int. AA corporates	365	4.42	4.25	7.00	5.64	101.27	6.59	105857	3.25	2.25
long AA corporates	196	10.17	8.50	7.71	25.01	100.33	7.47	47936	1.47	1.02
A corporates	1947	6.35	5.93	7.51	12.38	101.70	6.99	445976	13.67	9.47
int. A corporates	1251	4.33	4.18	7.39	5.46	101.98	6.70	285206	8.74	6.06
long A corporates	696	9.94	9.04	7.72	24.66	101.22	7.51	160770	4.93	3.41
BAA corporates	1048	6.50	6.05	7.98	13.26	103.18	7.32	210961	6.47	4.48
int. BAA corporates	647	4.56	4.40	7.72	5.91	102.50	6.99	127181	3.90	2.70
long BAA corporates	401	9.44	8.56	8.39	24.41	104.23	7.84	83780	2.57	1.78
asset backed	108	2.90	2.81	6.59	3.38	100.35	6.43	47342	100.00	1.01
charge/credit cards	73	3.25	3.15	6.71	3.83	100.42	6.49	37436	79.07	0.79
autos	28	1.56	1.51	6.15	1.68	100.08	6.20	9038	19.09	0.19
home equities	7	1.72	1.67	6.40	1.85	100.10	6.37	869	1.83	0.02

January 1-31, 1997	Number Issues	Durat. ToWorst	Mod.Adj. Durat.	Coupon	Matur.	Price	Yield ToWorst	Market Value	% of Index	% of Aggregate
mortgages	606	4.90	3.66	7.41	7.10	100.48	7.27	1401199	100.00	29.75
gnma	209	5.21	3.69	7.79	7.86	101.69	7.42	397521	28.37	8.44
gnma 15 yr	32	3.73	3.24	7.00	4.63	100.35	6.85	24155	1.72	0.51
gnma 30 yr	177	5.31	3.72	7.84	8.07	101.78	7.45	373366	26.65	7.93
fhlmc	208	4.70	3.63	7.22	6.69	100.02	7.20	468974	33.47	9.96
fhlmc 15 yr	47	3.75	3.20	6.82	4.64	99.66	6.88	118114	8.43	2.51
fhlmc 30 yr	112	5.32	3.97	7.46	7.89	100.18	7.40	316909	22.62	6.73
fhlmc balloon	49	2.32	2.00	6.40	2.59	99.77	6.49	33951	2.42	0.72
fnma	189	4.83	3.67	7.28	6.90	99.98	7.23	534703	38.16	11.35
fnma 15 yr	52	3.80	3.21	6.85	4.71	99.56	6.89	124513	8.89	2.64
fnma 30 yr	106	5.33	3.92	7.48	7.92	100.14	7.40	378228	26.99	8.03
fnma balloon	31	2.93	2.45	6.66	3.35	99.80	6.60	31962	2.28	0.68

TREASURY BELLWETHERS:

			Durat. ToWorst	Mod.Adj. Durat.	Coupon	Matur.	Price	Yield ToWorst	Market Value		
3 month	0.000	5/01/1997	1	0.24	0.24	0.00	0.24	98.76	5.15	44459	
6 month	0.000	7/31/1997	1	0.49	0.48	0.00	0.49	97.46	5.28	11311	
1 year	0.000	1/08/1998	1	0.93	0.91	0.00	0.93	95.04	5.51	18340	
2 year	5.875	1/31/1999	1	1.91	1.86	5.88	2.00	99.91	5.92	17491	
3 year	5.875	11/15/1999	1	2.58	2.50	5.88	2.79	99.55	6.05	18653	
5 year	6.250	1/31/2002	1	4.37	4.24	6.25	5.00	99.98	6.26	12502	
10 year	6.500	10/15/2006	1	7.21	6.98	6.50	9.70	99.92	6.51	22871	
30 year	6.500	11/15/2026	1	13.05	12.62	6.50	29.79	96.17	6.80	9757	

Typically, mutual fund managers use asset-based benchmarks since they do not know the liabilities of their investors. However, companies which manage portfolios against the liabilities of a particular pension fund (which requires an actuarial analysis of the prospective obligations to retired and working lives) or an insurance company product (e.g., a single premium deferred annuity, a book of individual life insurance, or a book of universal life insurance) develop liability-based benchmarks. Since these liabilities relate to a specific company, they are individually developed and are called "customized benchmarks." The cash flows of the specific liabilities are then translated into collections of cash flows and these cash flows and desired credit risk parameters (and other risk parameters) are converted to desired fixed income asset classes to form a benchmark portfolio. The returns on this benchmark portfolio can then be calculated from the returns on its components.

PERFORMANCE MEASUREMENT

The objective of selecting an appropriate benchmark is to compare the rate of return (ROR) on the portfolio with the ROR on its benchmark and evaluate the difference. The ROR on the benchmark, or at least its components if a customized benchmark is chosen, is usually calculated by the sponsoring agency of the benchmark (e.g. Lehman Brothers, Salomon Brothers, and Merrill Lynch). If the benchmark is constructed from scratch on a security-by-security basis, the ROR on the benchmark will have to be calculated by the portfolio manager. In most cases, the ROR on the managed portfolio is calculated by the portfolio manager.

Calculating the ROR on a fixed income portfolio is no mean feat. Until recently, there was little standardization in calculating RORs. That is, by employing different methods, different RORs for the same portfolio over the same time period using the same security prices would be calculated. To standardize ROR calculations for pension fund portfolio managers, in 1993 the AIMR (Association for Investment Management and Research) developed and propagated "AIMR Standards" for calculating RORs.[1] Currently these standards are used for pension fund portfolio management and increasingly for other types of portfolio managers (e.g. the SEC has adopted standards for mutual fund performance reporting).

Specifying the prices of the securities in the portfolio is also essential to calculating the portfolio ROR. While the prices of some standard and liquid securities are readily available, the prices of other less "on-the-run," less liquid securities are not as commonly available.

Assume the ROR for the portfolio and the benchmark over a period of time are determined. The next step is to interpret and evaluate the portfolio performance. To do so requires an understanding of the original strategy of the portfolio manager. And to be able to interpret the strategy, the "risk factors" or "risk characteristics" of the type of portfolio managed must be understood and, in fact,

---

[1] A brief discussion of the AIMR standards is provided in the appendix.

measured. The next two sections consider the risk factors of a fixed income portfolio and the portfolio strategies that can be used based on these risk factors.

RISK FACTORS

The risk factors of a bond portfolio are shown in Exhibit 3. The risk factors of a common stock portfolio would be different, including the portfolio beta, the average market capitalization, the sector composition, etc. There is, however, comparability of risk factors between stocks and bonds. For example, the duration on a bond portfolio and the beta on a stock portfolio both measure exposure to market risk. Stocks, however, do not have a risk factor which is comparable to convexity for bonds.

Any fixed income portfolio and fixed income benchmark will have a set of risk factors. Thus, changes in market behavior may affect the performance of the portfolio and the benchmark differently due to their differences in risk factors. The specification measurement of a portfolio's risk factors and the benchmark's risk factors are critical in being able to compare the performance of the portfolio and benchmark due to market changes. Exhibit 3 provides the risk factors, the measurement of the risk factors, and types of market behavior which affect these risk factors. This chapter does not discuss the individual risk factors and measurements.

Exhibit 3: Risk Factors and Portfolio Performance

Risk Factors	Risk Factor Measurement	Market Changes which Affect Risk Factors
Market Risk	Duration	Change in Yield Levels-Parallel
Yield Curve Risk	Convexity/Distribution of Key Rate Durations (Bullet, Barbell, Ladder, et. al.)	Change in Slope and Shape of Yield Curve.
Exposure to Market Volatility	Convexity • Negatively convex assets (e.g., callables)/portfolios are adversely affected by volatility • Positively convex assets (e.g., putables)/portfolios are benefited by volatility.	Market Volatility • Historical, based on past actual prices or yields. • Expected, as indicated by implied volatility of options.
Sector Allocation • Macro Sector • Micro Sector • Security Selection	Percent allocation to each macro sector, micro sector, and security and the option-adjusted spread (OAS) of each.	Change in option-adjusted spreads (OAS) of macro sectors, micro sectors, or individual securities.
Credit Risk	Average credit rating of portfolio and its sectors.	Changes in credit spreads (e.g. spread between Treasuries versus AAA corporates; or spread between AAA corporates versus BBB corporates). Also specific company rating changes.

Overall, however, two different portfolios or a portfolio and a benchmark which have different risk factors will experience different RORs due to identical market changes. The portfolio manager should calculate or measure the risk factor variable *ex ante* and either be aware of the differential response to the relevant market change or, if undesired, to change the risk factor by portfolio actions.

STRATEGIES

Having selected a benchmark, being aware of the risk factors of the portfolio, and having calculated the risk factors for the benchmark, the portfolio managers must decide whether or not they want their portfolio to replicate the risk factors of the benchmark or to deviate from them. Replicating all the risk factors is called a *passive strategy*; deviating from one or more of the risk factors is called an *active strategy*.

Of course, the portfolio manager could be passive with respect to some risk factors and active with respect to others — there is a large number of combinations given the various risk factors. Passive strategies require no forecast of future market changes — both the portfolio and benchmark respond identically to market changes. Active strategies are based on a forecast, since the portfolio and benchmark will respond differently to market changes. In an active strategy, the portfolio manager must decide in which direction and by how much the risk factor value of the portfolio will deviate from the risk factor value of the benchmark on the basis of expected market changes.

Thus, given multiple risk factors, there is a pure passive strategy. There is a pure active strategy and there are several hybrid strategies which are passive on some risk factors and active in others. Exhibit 4 summarizes some of the common passive and active strategies.

Exhibit 4: Passive and Active Strategies

Strategy	Description	Comment
Passive (in order of decreasing passivity)		
Indexation (pure passivity)	Replicate all risk factors in the "index" or benchmark.	The only certain way to accomplish this is to buy all the securities in the index in amounts equal to their weight in the index. While this can easily be done in the stock market, say for the S&P500 stock index by buying all 500 stocks in the appropriate amounts, it is difficult to do so in the fixed income market. For example, the Lehman Aggregate is based on approximately 5,694 bonds, many of them illiquid.
Dedication	Replicates the duration of the benchmark and also replicates all the cash flows (or key rate durations)	By replicating all the cash flows, the portfolio is not exposed to the risks of non-parallel shifts in the yield curve as well as parallel shifts in the yield curve. Dedication is a more expensive strategy.

Exhibit 4 (Continued)

Strategy	Description	Comment
Immunization	The duration of the portfolio is constructed to be the same as the duration of the benchmark.	There are many portfolios with the same duration which may have very different compositions of key rate durations and thus have different convexities. Immunized portfolios eliminate risk relative to the benchmark due to parallel shifts in the yield curve, but are exposed to risks due to non-parallel shifts in the yield curve. Dedicated portfolios have neither risk.
Active Strategies		
Market Timing	Deviate from duration of the benchmark.	If the portfolios has greater duration than the benchmark: • it outperforms the benchmark during market rallies; • it underperforms during market contractions; • and vice versa.
Yield Curve Trades	Replicate duration of the benchmark but vary the convexity and yield curve exposure by varying the composition of key rate durations.	Bullets outperform during yield curve steepenings; barbells outperform during yield curve flattenings.
Volatility Trades	Deviates from optionality of benchmarks: • callables are more negatively convex than bullets; • putables are more positively convex than bullets.	Volatility increases benefit putables (which are long an option) and negatively affect callables (which are short an option).
Asset Allocation/ Sector Trades: Overweights/ Underweights • Macro Sector • Micro Sector • Security	Deviate from macro sector, micro sector or security weightings of benchmark: • macro – overall sectors (Treasuries; agencies; corporates; MBS; ABS; municipals); • micro – components of a macro sector (e.g. utilities versus industrials in corporate sector); • Securities – overweight/underweight individual securities in a micro sector (e.g. Florida Power and Light versus Niagara Mohawk in corporate utility sector).	Deviations based on OAS of sectors, subsectors and securities relative to historical averages and fundamental projections. Can use break-even spreads (based on OAS) as a basis for deviations. On overweights, spread tightening produces gain; spread widening produces losses, and vice versa.
Credit Risk Allocations	Deviate from average credit rating of macro sector or micro sectors and composites thereof.	Credit spreads typically widen when economic growth is slow or negative. Credit spread widening benefits higher credit rating, and vice versa. Can use spread duration as basis for deviations.
Trading	Short-term changes in specific securities on the basis of short-term price discrepancies.	Often short-term technicals, including short-term supply/demand factors, cause temporary price discrepancies.

Exhibit 5: Spectrum of Strategies

Replicate all   Deviate from One or More but
Risk Factors   not all Risk Factors of Benchmark

Pure   Pure
Passive   Active

Indexation (Repli-	Dedication (Replicate only	Immunization (Replicate	Deviate from all risk
cate all risk factors	duration and duration buck-	only duration risk factor of	factors of benchmark
of benchmark)	ets of risk factors of bench-	benchmark; deviate from	
	mark; deviate from other risk	other risk factors)	
	factors)		

The range of passive to active strategies can be regarded as a spectrum or continuum wherein a pure passive strategy replicates all the risk factors of the benchmark. A pure active strategy replicates none of the risk factors of the benchmark. Intermediate active/passive strategies replicate some but not all of the risk factors. This spectrum is depicted in Exhibit 5.

PORTFOLIO RETURN ANALYSIS

Changes in market values affect a portfolio's return marginally via its risk factors and thereby in aggregate determine the portfolio's total ROR. A portfolio model determines a portfolio's ROR given its risk factors (RF(i)) from the market variable changes as illustrated in Exhibit 6.[2] For example, RF(A) may be the portfolio's duration and MC(A) the change (in a parallel way) in the level of the yield curve.

The same portfolio model would apply to the benchmark portfolio given its specific risk factors, which may be the same (passive strategy) or different (active strategy) as the risk factors of the portfolio. If the model is well specified, the actual market changes given the portfolio's risk factors will provide a calcu-

---

[2] The use of factor models to explain security or portfolio returns originated in the common stock literature. The concept was that common stock prices and returns could be described by an econometric model with a small number of explanatory variables. These variables are called factors (or attributes). In general, the equation would be:

$$y = a_1 + b_1 x_1 + b_2 x_2 + \dots + b_n x_n + e$$

where the x_i's are the factors and the b_i's are the sensitivities (to the factors). A model with N factors is called an "N-factor model." A "one factor model" for stocks would specify that the X is the return on the market and its sensitivity, b, is then the beta of the stock or portfolio of stocks. Additional factors might be specified as capitalization (size) and P/E (price-to-earnings ratio). The equivalent one-factor model for bonds specifies the factor as the percent change in the price of the bond market (say as measured by the Lehman Aggregate) and the b would be the (negative) relative duration of the bond or bond portfolio to that of the bond market. The Taylor series expansion of the bond price/yield equation would dictate that the second factor would be the square of the bond market price and the sensitivity of this factor would be the relative convexity of the bond or bond portfolio. Other factors could be added as discussed herein. See Frank J. Fabozzi, *Investment Management* (Englewood Cliffs, NJ: Prentice Hall, 1995), pp. 264-267 and pp. 488-503.

lated ROR which is very close to the actual portfolio ROR over the period of time. The model is "fit" or specified by relating actual market changes and RORs in the past, given the portfolio's risk factors via theoretical price/yield relationships.

Portfolio return models have been developed and are commercially available. Given a portfolio return model specified from past data, the model can then be used in two major ways — sensitivity analysis and attribution analysis.

SENSITIVITY ANALYSIS (EX ANTE)

The portfolio return model depicted in Exhibit 6 is specified (that is the risk factors are identified based on theory and practice) and fit (that is the coefficients of the variable are estimated by using historical, data). Once the model is specified and fit, it can be used for two types of simulations, one ex ante, that is "running" the model the way the arrows are shown in the exhibit — this is *sensitivity analysis*. The other type is *ex post*, that is "running" the model in the opposite direction of the arrows between ROR and the market value changes — this is called *attribution analysis.*[3]

Sensitivity analysis uses projected or assumed market changes and calculates the portfolio ROR in response to these changes. Often only one variable is changed, so the effect of that one variable, say the slope of the Treasury yield curve, on the portfolio ROR can be determined. In addition, changes in a set of market values can be assumed. Specifically, a set of correlated market variables can be jointly tested (e.g., Treasury yields increase the Treasury yield curve flattens, and corporate spreads widen). Sensitivity analysis can also be conducted on both the portfolio and the benchmark and the resulting differences in the RORs determined.

A related form of sensitivity analysis is "cash flow testing" whereas future portfolio cash flows (which may vary significantly due to prepayments) rather than portfolio RORs in response to assumed changes in market variables are analyzed. Multiple market variable changes can be assumed and statistical studies of cash flow outcomes can be studied.

Exhibit 6: Portfolio Return Model

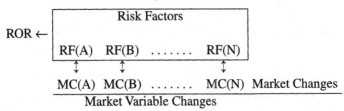

---

[3] This is similar to the way a Black-Scholes options pricing model (or any other option pricing model) can be run either forward, that is using a volatility input to calculate the option price; or can be run backward, that is using an assumed option price input to calculate the implied volatility consistent with this price.

Exhibit 7: Difference between Managed Portfolio and Benchmark

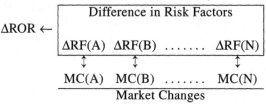

The portfolio return model depicted in Exhibit 6 can also be applied both to the managed portfolio and the benchmark portfolio, although they may have different risk factors. Of course, both portfolios will experience the same market variable changes. Applying the portfolio return model in Exhibit 6 to both the managed portfolio and the benchmark portfolio and subtracting the latter from the former provides the relationship in Exhibit 7, wherein ΔROR is the difference between the return on the managed portfolio and the benchmark, and ΔRF(I) is the difference in the Ith risk factor between the managed portfolios and the benchmark (for example, if the Ith risk factor is duration, ΔRFC(I) is the difference in their durations).

ATTRIBUTION ANALYSIS (EX POST)

Another way to utilize the portfolio return model is to run it backwards, that is to use the actual market changes (MC(I)) and the difference in the actual rates of return between the portfolio and the benchmark (ΔROR) to *attribute* this difference in returns to the differences in the various risk factors. For example, assume there are four risk factors, A, B, C, and D and the differences in these four risk factors between the managed portfolio and the benchmark are measured (ΔRF(A), ΔRF(B), ΔRF(C), and ΔRF(D)). Assume the ΔROR is known and is 200 basis points (bp), that is the managed portfolio outperforms the benchmark by 2% during this period.

Attribution analysis permits answering an important question about this analysis. Why did this outperformance occur? Was it a market bet — that is, was the duration of the managed portfolio longer than the duration of the benchmark and yields declined? This outperformance would most likely reverse itself if yields increased. Or was it due to a correct allocation to MBS versus corporates; to expert allocation between utilities versus industrials in the corporate sector; or to expert issuer selection in the utility sector? Knowing which risk factor contributed to the return outperformance is very important in portfolio management evaluation. It serves as a quality control check on the investment process of a money manager. It can also be used to identify the strengths and weaknesses of money managers so they may improve their skills.

Exhibit 8 provides an example of attribution analysis for the case described above which had four risk factors and for which the managed portfolio outperformed the benchmark portfolio by 200 bp during the period in question.

Of the 200 bp outperformance, 40 bp was due to risk factor A; 130 bp to risk factor B; 50 bp to risk factor D; and the managed portfolio underperformed the benchmark by 30 bp due to risk factor C. There was also a "residual" component of 10 bp of outperformance that could not be attributed to any risk factor.

As indicated, an attribution analysis system is simply one application of a portfolio return model. The requirements of developing an attribution analysis model include:

1. develop a general portfolio return model
   - define risk factors
   - measure risk factors
2. define a benchmark
   - measure risk factors
3. calculate the RORs on the managed portfolio and the benchmarks (according to AIMR standards)
   - requires data on portfolio composition and cash inflows and outflows for the portfolio.
4. requires data on market value changes and risk factors.

Attribution analysis packages are commercially available. The next section provides an example of one attribution analysis package.

ATTRIBUTION ANALYSIS — EXAMPLE

This example is based on a model developed by Global Advanced Technology (G.A.T.), a fixed income research, consulting, and analysis firm, that markets a return attribution model as part of its Integrative Bond System (I.B.S.), a PC-based fixed income portfolio management application.

This model, as in other commercially available models, decomposes a portfolio's return into a series of factors. These factors[4] are:

Total Return = Static Return + Interest Sensitive Returns
+ Spread Change Returns + Trading Return + Residual (error)

Exhibit 8: Attribution Analysis Example

Risk Factor	Return Outperformance Due To Risk Factor (bp)
A	40
B	130
C	-30
D	50
Residual	10
	200

These factors allow a user to identify the sources of return. The factors are defined as follows:

Static Return:	The portion of a portfolio's return that is due to "rolling down the yield curve." It calculates how much is earned assuming a static (meaning zero volatility) world, where the yield curve evolves to its implied forward curve.
Interest Sensitive Return:	The portion of a portfolio's return that is due to changes in the level, slope and shape of the entire yield curve.
Spread Change Return:	The portion of a portfolio's return that is due to changes in both bond sector spreads and individual security richness/cheapness.
Trading Return:	The portion of a portfolio's return that is due to changes in the composition of the portfolio. This identifies the value added by changing the composition of the portfolio as opposed to applying a buy-and-hold strategy.
Residual:	An error term that represents the part of the return that is not attributable to any of the above factors.

---

[4] These factors provide a more general level of detail. Each factor can be further decomposed to reveal more information. The more detailed model decomposition is as follows:

Static Return = Risk-Free Return + Accrual of OAS Return

Risk-Free Return is the return earned from rolling down the yield curve if the portfolio consisted of zero-coupon Treasuries.

Accrual of OAS Return is the return earned from being invested in assets other than zero-coupon Treasuries while rolling down the yield curve

Interest Sensitive Returns = Effective Duration Return + Convexity Return

where Effective Duration Return = Key Rate Return 1 + Key Rate Return 2 +... + Key Rate Return 11

Effective Duration Return is the return due to changes in the yield curve. It is measured by the sum of the *Key Rate Returns*. A *Key Rate Return* is the product of the *Key Rate Duration* (a measure of portfolio sensitivity to changes in one *key rate* on the yield curve) and the difference between the actual spot rate at the end of the period and the rate it would have evolved to if the yield curve evolved to its implied forward rate.

Convexity Return is the return that is due to the changes in the duration of a portfolio. As the yield curve changes its slope, shape, and level, a portfolio's duration changes as well and this has an impact on its return.

Spread Change Return = Delta OAS Return + Delta Rich/Cheap Return

Delta OAS Return is the return due to the widening and tightening of the sector OAS.

Delta Rich/Cheap Return is the return due to the widening and/or tightening of a security's specific spread.

G.A.T.'s software, as in many others, can apply the attribution model to various cross sections of a portfolio. The attribution model can be applied to a portfolio's benchmark index as well. A portfolio and its benchmark can both be "sliced and diced" according to a variety of risk factors. This makes possible an evaluation of the different bets that a portfolio manager puts on versus a benchmark. Examples of the possible segmentations that could be made are by bond type (i.e., Treasuries, corporates, mortgages, municipals, etc), by credit rating (i.e., AAA, AA, A, etc.), by effective duration (i.e., 0-2 years, 2-4 years, 4-6 years, etc.). These breakdowns answer the following questions "How and why did the portfolio outperform (underperform) its bogey?"

In the example that follows, an attribution performed on a portfolio of corporate securities during the month of September 1996 is considered as summarized in Exhibit 9. The bogey to which the portfolio is compared is the Merrill Lynch Corporate Index. During the month of September 1996, the yield curve shifted downward in almost a parallel fashion which led to a significant rally in the bond market.

Portfolio A outperformed its bogey by 23 bps during September. This makes intuitive sense since its duration is longer than its bogey and the market rallied during September. The Merrill Lynch Corporate Index returned 1.95%. The sector allocation of Portfolio A, which is what is being evaluated in Exhibit 9, is different than that of the benchmark — it is overweighted in industrials, utilities, telephones, oils, and internationals while being underweighted in agencies and Financials. This allocation reflects the portfolio manager's view of the market.

Overall, the portfolio manager did well with sector allocations. All of the sectors had positive returns. Compared to the benchmark, the bets on industrials, telephones, and internationals were successful, as they outperformed the bogey by 20, 11, and 15 bps, respectively. The bets on utilities and oil companies were not successful at all, as they underperformed the benchmark by 186 and 156 bps, respectively. The Financials outperformed the bogey's financials by 31 bps, though it was underweighted in the portfolio by 22%.

Considering the model decomposition of the total portfolio, the source of returns becomes more clear. (See Exhibit 10.) The static returns were quite good for both Portfolio A and the bogey (about 45 bps). The larger duration of the portfolio led to a higher interest sensitive return for the portfolio versus the benchmark (1.813% versus 1.433%). The spread change return was very small for the portfolio and for the benchmark, though it seems that there was evidence of some spread widening in Portfolio A (spread change return of −8 bps) compared to spread tightening in the benchmark (spread change return of +10 bps). Trading return was very small (less than 1 bp) because the portfolio's size and composition did not change very much over the month. Residuals are also very small (1 bp for Portfolio A and −3 bps for the benchmark). From looking at this data, the main story here was that the beneficial change in interest rates was the biggest source of return for Portfolio A and contributed to its outperformance relative to the benchmark.

Exhibit 9: Performance Attribution Example

Portfolio A: $3.0 billion corporate bond portfolio with an effective duration of 7.09

Merrill Corporate Index: Benchmark index with a duration of 5.76

	% of Portfolio	Total Return	Static Return	Interest Sensitive Return	Spread Change Return	Trading Return	Residual
Portfolio Totals							
Portfolio A	100.000	2.187	0.453	1.813	−0.087	−0.003	0.011
Merrill Corporate	100.000	1.954	0.452	1.433	0.098	0.000	−0.029
Difference	0.000	0.233	0.001	0.379	−0.185	−0.003	0.040
Sector Analysis*							
Agencies							
Portfolio A	0.000	0.000	0.000	0.000	0.000	0.000	0.000
Merrill Corporate	12.044	2.083	0.476	1.918	−0.118	0.000	−0.193
Difference	−12.044	−2.083	−0.476	−1.918	−0.118	0.000	0.193
Industrials							
Portfolio A	31.480	2.325	0.459	1.924	−0.026	−0.059	0.027
Merrill Corporate	26.769	2.121	0.460	1.606	0.108	0.000	−0.053
Difference	7.711	0.204	−0.001	0.318	−0.134	−0.059	0.080
Financials							
Portfolio A	15.580	2.023	0.439	1.560	0.077	-0.057	0.004
Merrill Corporate	37.363	1.707	0.444	1.210	0.060	0.000	−0.008
Difference	−21.783	0.316	−0.006	0.350	0.017	−0.057	0.012
Utilities							
Portfolio A	15.900	0.310	0.528	−0.090	0.540	0.042	−0.711
Merrill Corporate	7.385	2.167	0.469	1.564	0.185	0.000	−0.051
Difference	8.515	−1.857	0.060	−1.654	0.356	0.042	−0.660
Telephones							
Portfolio A	17.080	2.439	0.439	1.843	0.027	0.144	−0.014
Merrill Corporate	4.440	2.331	0.447	1.723	0.201	0.000	−0.040
Difference	12.640	0.108	−0.008	0.120	−0.174	0.144	0.026
Oil							
Portfolio A	4.940	0.562	0.467	2.035	−1.939	0.000	0.000
Merrill Corporate	1.670	2.123	0.462	1.513	0.194	0.000	−0.047
Difference	3.270	−1.561	0.004	0.522	−2.133	0.000	−0.047
Internationals							
Portfolio A	14.180	2.264	0.443	1.891	−0.079	0.021	−0.011
Merrill Corporate	10.022	2.118	0.446	1.597	0.095	0.000	−0.021
Difference	4.158	0.147	−0.004	0.294	−0.174	0.021	0.010
Miscellaneous							
Portfolio A	0.000	0.000	0.000	0.000	0.000	0.000	0.000
Merrill Corporate	0.308	0.796	0.416	0.384	−0.025	0.000	0.021
Difference	0.308	−0.796	−0.416	−0.384	0.025	0.000	−0.021

* In the sector analyses, we are comparing the constituents of Portfolio A that fall into a particular sector to the constituents of the benchmark that fall into the same sector. For example, the industrials from Portfolio A are being evaluated against the industrials from the Merrill Corporate Index.

Source: G.A.T. Integrative Bond System

Exhibit 10: Summary of Return Attribution Analysis

Risk Factor	Portfolio A Returns (bps)	Merrill Corporate Index Returns (bps)	Difference	% of Total Return Difference
Static Return	45.3	45.2	0.1	0.4%
Interest Sensitive Return	181.3	143.3	37.9	162.7%
Spread Change Return	−8.7	9.8	−18.5	−79.4%
Trading Return	−0.3	0.0	−0.3	−1.3%
Residual	0.1	−2.9	4.0	17.2%
Total	218.7	195.4	23.3	100%

The next step in the process is to try to understand what caused the various sectors to perform the way they did. Static returns are not significant except for utilities (a 6 bp outperformance), which could be explained by higher coupons which led to a more favorable roll down along the yield curve. The interest sensitive returns for all sectors, except for utilities (a 165 bps underperformance), show good outperformance. A possible explanation for the utilities' significant underperformance would be the presence of negative convexity associated with the call options present in many utility bonds (bond rallies make the call option on callable corporate bonds more in-the-money for the issuer and therefore, more likely to be called, which has a negative effect on callable corporate bond performance). The other sectors are less callable and longer in duration and therefore performed better in a bond rally. Spread change returns reveal a more mixed bag of results. In Portfolio A, we see evidence of spread widening in industrials, oils, and internationals and tightening in financials and utilities. Relative to the benchmark, spreads moved more favorably for the industrials, oils, and telephones in the bogey than they did in Portfolio A, while they moved more favorable for financials and utilities in Portfolio A than they did for the bogey. Trading returns do not reveal much except for telephones, where during the month, it shows that the portfolio manager added value by shifting the portfolio into the telephones sector. Note that trading return for the benchmark is zero in all cases. This is the case because during a month the benchmark constituents do not change.

This type of analysis can be extended to almost any risk factor. A portfolio can be sliced and diced according to the effective duration distribution, credit rating distribution, or its coupon distribution and then compared to its benchmark to see how much value was added and from where the added value came. Any bet that the portfolio manager can put on can be analyzed in the attribution process. This type of analysis adds to a portfolio manager's knowledge of his/her own strengths (are they good "sector pickers," or are they better at placing bets on yield curve movements?) and is designed to assist them in the investment decision making process.

OVERVIEW

Knowing only whether a portfolio outperformed its benchmark or not, and by how much, does not provide complete information for the evaluation of the portfolio manger and the portfolio management process. Was it due to having a long duration during a rally; a barbell duration bucket composition during a yield curve flattening environment; macro or micro asset allocation; expert security selection; or some other reason? Attribution analysis answers these questions and provides for a more comprehensive and detailed evaluation of portfolio management. Understanding and applying attribution analysis requires a thorough understanding of all the risk factors which affect bond pricing. All the concepts and practices in understanding bond market performance, which are discussed in other chapters in this book, come together in attribution analysis.

APPENDIX
AIMR PERFORMANCE CALCULATION METHODOLOGIES

In 1993, the Association for Investment Management and Research (AIMR) codified a set of standards for presenting performance results. AIMR's intent was to protect the users of performance data, namely, the investor community, by "keeping the investment managers honest." These standards call for full disclosure and fair representation by investment managers in reporting their investment results. They also call for uniformity in both the calculation and reporting of performance results so that investors can more directly compare among investment managers.

When an investment manager is said to be "AIMR compliant," it means the performance results he/she is providing are prepared and presented in such a way as to conform with these standards. There are different levels of compliance which reflect the degree to which the manager is complying with the standards. Some aspects are mandatory and some aspects are recommended. One should note that there is no legal statute compelling investment managers to comply with the AIMR standards. However, being in compliance provides a degree of comfort to an investor who is utilizing or seeking to utilize the services of a manager. Also, the investment management industry as a whole does not want to invite further regulation on the part of the Securities and Exchange Commission (SEC) or even worse, Congress, so these standards are a way for the industry to show that it can police itself.

Minimum Requirements
The AIMR standards stipulate that there should be some uniformity in the methodology used to calculate return. These apply to both the equity world as well as the fixed income world. Listed below are some of the more important requirements for calculating total rates of return. Total returns must:

1. Include realized and unrealized capital gains and losses plus income.
2. Include accrued interest
3. Be *time weighted* at least quarterly, then geometrically linked
4. Account for cash balances
5. Reflect *reasonable* pricing for all assets

Of these, the requirement that returns must be time weighted is important enough to warrant further attention. A time weighted return answers the question *"What happened to my first dollar of investment?"* Time weighting neutralizes the impact of cash flows not under the discretion of the portfolio manager. These "cash flows" can come in the form of a cash contribution or withdrawal or a security contribution or withdrawal. This is important because it reflects how much value was added to or subtracted from the portfolio by the actions of the portfolio manager only.

Reasonable pricing of all assets is also very important and is a bigger issue for fixed income securities portfolios than for equity portfolios. This is primarily due to the fact that the equity market is more efficient than the fixed income market. Stocks are bought and sold on an exchange where there is a great deal of liquidity which is evidenced by the very tight bid-asked spreads. Stocks are traded every day, so the last trade price provides the best estimate of a stocks' value at the close of trading. The exchange also facilitates access to the final closing prices for each and every stock.

The fixed income market, in contrast, is an over-the-counter market, where, except for U.S. Treasuries, there is no consistent liquidity among different bond types. Bid-asked spreads can vary considerably by bond type (i.e., private placements versus public corporates) and are on the whole much wider than in the equity market. Also, not every bond trades every day, which forces investment managers to rely on sophisticated pricing matrices utilized by the various pricing services to estimate the value of their bonds. All of these structural issues in the fixed income market make it very cumbersome to value a bond portfolio daily. Certainly, there are many more sources of error in the calculations of performance for bonds than for stocks.

Calculations

There are many mathematical approaches to calculating performance. However, only the three that are acceptable to AIMR will be discussed. The three approaches are ranked from best to worst in terms of the exactness of the performance results generated by them. These methods can be applied equally to both equity and fixed income portfolios. The three approaches are:

1. Daily valuation method
2. Unit valuation method
3. Modified Dietz method (linked dollar-weighted internal rate of return (IRR))

Daily Valuation Method

The *daily valuation method* is the most accurate method available. The portfolio is valued at the close of every business day and by using the formula below, the daily total rate of return can be calculated:

$$R_{Daily} = \frac{Market\ Value_{End\ of\ Day}}{Market\ Value_{Beginning\ of\ Day}} - 1$$

Income that was earned and accrued as well as any amortized principal are included in the market value of the portfolio. If there are any cash or security contributions or withdrawals these are included in the following day's beginning market value.

To get a return for a longer period of time, like a week or a month, the following formula shows the linking process:

$$R_{n\ Days} = [(1 + R_{Daily_1}) \times (1 + R_{Daily_2}) \times ... \times (1 + R_{Daily_n})] - 1$$

For example, assume that a portfolio of publicly traded fixed income securities of a life insurance company has a market value of $10 million on 12/2. On 12/3, new premiums of $1 million are paid in that the manager must invest and on 12/5, expenses of $500,000 must be paid by the portfolio. Assuming that the market value end of day (pre flow) column below reflects the daily changes in the portfolio's market value, the interest income earned, realized and unrealized capital gains, and the daily accruing of interest, the weekly return is calculated as follows:

Date	Market Value Beginning of Day ($000)	Market Value End of Day (Pre Flow) ($000)	Inflow/ Outflow ($000)	Market Value End of Day (Post Flow) ($000)	Daily Returns	
12/2	10,000	10,150	0	10,150	10,150/10,000 =	1.50%
12/3	10,150	10,100	+1,000	11,100	10,100/10,150 =	−0.49%
12/4	11,100	11,500	0	11,500	11,500/11,100 =	3.60%
12/5	11,500	11,000	−500	10,500	11,000/11,500 =	−4.35%
12/6	10,500	10,750	0	10,750	10,750/10,500 =	2.38%

Linking daily returns gives the weekly return:

$$Weekly\ Return = [(1 + 0.015) \times (1 - 0.0049) \times (1 + 0.036) \times (1 - 0.0435)$$
$$\times (1 + 0.0238)] - 1$$
$$= 1.0246 - 1 = 2.46\%$$

The daily valuation method provides the highest degree of accuracy because there is a market value for each day. Returns are computed without the influence of contributions and withdrawals from the portfolio. (Note that the market value end of day (pre flow) is used as the numerator, not the market value end of day (post flow). The portfolio manager is evaluated on how much value was added based on his/her actions for the day.

Mutual funds are required to publish their net asset values (NAV's) daily, which requires them to price their portfolios daily. However, as mentioned above, the more illiquid the security, the more difficult it is to get a daily price and hence the more difficult it is to use this method to calculate performance. This is a problem faced by insurance companies that have large portions of their portfolios allocated to illiquid private placements. For them, using this method to calculate performance is impratical.

Unit Valuation Method

The next best approach is the *unit valuation method*. This method requires the valuation of the portfolio at each significant cash flow contribution/withdrawal date, instead of every day. The returns are then calculated for the subperiods between the cash flow dates using the following formula:

$$R_{Subperiod} = \frac{Market\ Value_{Ending}}{Market\ Value_{Beginning}} - 1$$

As was the case with the daily valuation method, income that was earned and accrued as well as any amortized principal are included in the market value of the portfolio. When a cash inflow or outflow occurs, it is added to the beginning market value of the next subperiod.

To compute a return for a longer time interval such as a month or quarter, the following formula shows the linking process:

$$R_{Subperiod} = [(1 + R_{Subperiod_1}) \times (1 + R_{Subperiod_2}) \times \cdots$$
$$\times (1 + R_{Subperiod_{n-1}}) \times (1 + R_{Subperiod_n})] - 1$$

With this approach, one needs to link the subperiod returns together.

For example, assume that a portfolio of publicly traded fixed income securities of a life insurance company has a market value of $10 million on 12/2. On 12/3, new premiums of $500,000 are paid in that the manager must invest, and on 12/5 and 12/13, expenses of $250,000 and $300,000, respectively, must be paid by the portfolio. Assuming that the market value end of subperiod (pre flow) column below reflects the changes in the portfolio's market value, the interest income earned, realized and unrealized capital gains, and the accruing of interest for each subperiod, the monthly return is calculated as follows:

Period	Market Value Beginning of Subperiod ($000)	Market Value End of Subperiod (Pre Flow) ($000)	Inflow/ Outflow ($000)	Market Value End of Subperiod (Post Flow) ($000)	Subperiod Returns	
12/02-12/10	10,000	10,150	+500	10,650	10,150/10,000 =	1.50%
12/10-12/13	10,650	10,509	−250	10,259	10,509/10,650 =	−1.32%
12/13-12/25	10,259	10,488	−300	10,188	10,488/10,259 =	2.23%
12/25-12/31	10,188	10,384	0	10,384	10,384/10,188 =	1.92%

Linking the subperiod returns gives the monthly return.

Monthly Return = [(1+0.015) × (1-0.0132) × (1+0.0223) × (1+0.0192)] − 1
= 1.0436 − 1 = 4.36%

The unit valuation method is more practical than the daily valuation method because it requires less frequent pricing on the part of the investment manager. He/she only has to value the portfolio on days when there are significant cash flows. However, if there is significant cash flow activity in the portfolio, it may require frequent pricing of the portfolio which may become impractical.

Modified Dietz Method

To reduce the pricing problem significantly, the third and last method, the *modified Dietz method* was developed. This method, named after its developer, Peter Dietz, unlike the unit valuation method, does not require the valuation of the portfolio at each significant cash flow date. This approach is also called a *linked dollar-weighted internal rate of return* (IRR). It provides a return that is approximately the same as that provided by the unit valuation method. The returns are calculated for the entire period using the following formula:

$$R_{Period} = \frac{(MV_E - MV_B) - (\text{Gross Contributions}) \ \text{OR} \ + (\text{Gross Withdrawals})}{MV_B - (\text{Adjusted Contributions}) \ \text{OR} \ + (\text{Adjusted Withdrawals})} - 1$$

where MV_E and MV_B are the ending and beginning market values, respectively. The gross cash contributions (withdrawals) are added to (subtracted from) the numerator, while in the denominator an adjustment must be made for the number of days the cash flows were available to be invested.

To make the adjustment in the denominator for a contribution into the portfolio, the following formula is applied:

$$1 - \frac{\text{Number of days in the period before cash was invested in portfolio}}{\text{Total number of days in the period}}$$

This represents the percentage of the period that the cash contributed was available for investment. This number is then multiplied by the dollar amount of the contribution and subtracted in the denominator.

To make the adjustment in the denominator for a withdrawal from the portfolio, the following formula is applied:

$$1 - \frac{\text{Number of days in the period invested in portfolio}}{\text{Total number of days in the period}}$$

This represents the percentage of the period that the cash withdrawn was not available for investment. This number is then multiplied by the dollar amount of the withdrawal and added in the denominator.

The modified Dietz method is the most common method used today. It is easier to implement because the information requirements are much less demanding. Valuations of the portfolios are not needed more frequently than at the ends of months and the cash flows into and out of the portfolio are well known.

To illustrate this method, assume that a portfolio of publicly traded fixed income securities of a life insurance company has a market value of $10 million on 12/2. On 12/3, new premiums of $500,000 are paid in that the manager must invest and on 12/5 and 12/13, expenses of $250,000 and $300,000, respectively, must be paid by the portfolio. Assuming that the market values column below reflects the changes in the portfolio's market value, the interest income earned, realized and unrealized capital gains, and the accruing of interest for each subperiod, the monthly return is calculated as follows:

Date	Transaction	Market Values ($000)	# of Days in portfolio	% of Period Cash was/was not Available ($000)	Adjusted Cash Flow ($000)
12/1	Beginning MV	10,000			
12/10	Contribution	500	20	$1 - ((30 - 20)/30) = 66\%$	$0.66 \times 500 = 333$
12/13	Withdrawal	250	13	$1 - (13/30) = 56\%$	$0.56 \times 250 = 142$
12/25	Withdrawal	300	25	$1 - (25/30) = 16\%$	$0.16 \times 300 = 50$
12/31	Ending MV	10,384			

$$\text{Monthly Return} = \frac{(10{,}384 - 10{,}000 - 500 + 250 + 300)}{(10{,}000 + 333 - 142 - 50)}$$

$$= \frac{434}{10{,}141} = 4.28\%$$

Note that the difference between the results computed from both methods is only 8 bps (4.36% − 4.28%) which suggests that the modified Dietz method provides a very good approximation to the unit valuation method. However, when there are cash flows greater than 10% of the value of the portfolio, the approximation becomes worse. Clearly, the magnitude of the cash flows within the period is critical to the performance calculation. AIMR prefers the unit valuation method when there are cash flows greater than 10% into and out of the portfolio because it provides a better approximation since it utilizes more data than the modified Dietz method.

Performance By Security

The formula for calculating the return on a security, stock or bond, is similar to those formulas for calculating the return on a portfolio. However, with an individual security, the amount of income earned by the security must be included in the numerator. The formula below can be used for any time period:

$$R_{\text{Security}} = \frac{\text{Market Value}_{\text{Ending}} - \text{Market Value}_{\text{Beginning}} + \text{Income}}{\text{Market Value}_{\text{Beginning}}}$$

Summary

AIMR set out to establish standards for calculating and reporting total rates of return on portfolios. The goal was to create a level playing field for the investment management industry so that investors can feel comfortable about their comparisons of managers. This standardization addressed the reporting of performance results as well as calculating performance data.

Portfolio managers also need to see and understand their performance in order to develop strategies to keep adding value for their clients. There are three methods to calculating performance that are accepted by AIMR — the daily valuation method, the unit valuation method, and the modified Dietz method. All three methods arrive at acceptable total rate of return numbers although they differ as to the information required to get there. The daily valuation method provides the most accurate results and is the most rigorous in terms of the data required. The modified Dietz method is the least accurate of the three, but it is also the least stringent in terms of the information required. The unit valuation method lies somewhere between those two in terms of accuracy and information requirements.

About the Author

Kevin E. Grant, CFA

Kevin Grant is a portfolio manager at Fidelity Management & Research. He manages fixed income portfolios in the Fixed Income Division. Additionally, he manages the bond component of a number of Fidelity equity portfolios including the Puritan Fund. Mr. Grant specializes in quantitative approaches to managing fixed income portfolios. Prior to joining Fidelity in 1993, Mr. Grant was the Chief Mortgage Strategist for Morgan Stanley Group, Inc. He began his investment career at Aetna Life and Casualty where he developed quantitative models for securities analysis and portfolio management. He specialized in mortgage-backed securities having developed option-valuation models and total return analytics. Additionally, he developed computer models and algorithms for bond portfolio dedication, immunization, and indexing. Mr. Grant later managed portfolios for Aetna. He is a Chartered Financial Analyst, and has an MBA from The University of Hartford.

Chapter 11

Bond Convexity: Hidden Risk, Hidden Value

Kevin Edward Grant, CFA
Portfolio Manager
Fidelity Management and Research

INTRODUCTION

Consider two portfolios of U.S. Treasury securities, both constructed to have the same market risk (duration) as a Treasury Index on January 1, 1994. Portfolio manager 1 used traditional methods of risk control and return enhancement — he matched his portfolio's duration to his index and held bonds with superior rolling returns. This strategy also resulted in a portfolio with a 21.5 basis point (bp) yield advantage over the index. Portfolio manager 2 employed a far different strategy — his portfolio held bonds that did not benefit from rolling down the yield curve and his portfolio sacrificed 16.7 bp of yield versus the index. Over the ensuing six months, portfolio manager 1 was aghast at his results. His supposed 21.5 bp yield advantage resulted in below-market total returns. Indeed, his results were quite inferior to the market; Portfolio 1 underperformed the index by 54 bp, quite a sad result for a Treasury portfolio over a 6-month period. Portfolio manager 2 was quite pleased. Portfolio 2's supposed inferior yield resulted in above-market total returns. Indeed, Portfolio 2 handily outperformed the index by 65 bp, quite a significant result for a Treasury portfolio over a 6-month period of time. The results are summarized in Exhibit 1.

While the first six months of 1994 were among the nastiest in the history of the U.S. bond markets, the difference in the results of the two portfolios is striking. Portfolio 2 outperformed Portfolio 1 by 119 bp over only a 6-month investment period. Most market participants would doubt this could be possible for two Treasury-only portfolios with the same duration. Examining the composition of the two portfolios reveals important structural differences that are the heart of fixed income portfolio management.

The author wishes to thank James Gerard, Andrew Hall, and Harold Naparst for their considerable assistance in formulating the ideas in this chapter.

Exhibit 1: Realized Total Returns of Two Treasury Portfolios: January 1, 1994 through June 30, 1994

	Duration	Yield	Number of Bonds	Realized Total Return	Variance
Index	6.9	5.68%	156	−5.98%	NA
Portfolio 1	6.9	5.89%	5	−6.52%	−0.54%
Portfolio 2	6.9	5.52%	5	−5.33%	0.65%
Port 2 − Port 1	0	−0.37%			1.19%

The index is a static index of U.S. Treasury coupon-paying securities.
Portfolios 1 and 2 are static.
All returns are unannualized.

Exhibit 2: Holdings for Portfolio 1 and Portfolio 2 as of December 31, 1993, Total Returns Realized through June 30, 1994

Portfolio 1 Percent of Portfolio	Treasury Issues		Yield Index	Duration	Convexity	Realized Return
			5.68%	6.9	78.4	−5.98%
6.71%	5.625	31-Jan-98	4.97%	3.5	16.3	−2.97%
18.29%	8.250	15-May-05	5.63%	6.1	24.6	−5.92%
25.00%	11.750	15-Feb-10	6.03%	7.2	61.7	−6.93%
25.00%	13.875	15-May-11	6.04%	7.5	80.0	−6.98%
25.00%	14.000	15-Nov-11	6.07%	7.6	82.5	−7.05%
100.00%		Portfolio	5.90%	6.9	61.6	−6.52%
		vs. Index	0.21%	0.0	−16.8	−0.54%
Portfolio 2 Percent of Portfolio	Treasury Issues					
25.00%	6.125	31-Dec-96	4.48%	2.7	9.6	−1.85%
25.00%	8.000	15-Jan-97	4.61%	2.6	9.2	−1.75%
1.59%	6.250	31-Jan-97	4.61%	2.7	9.8	−1.90%
23.41%	9.125	15-May-18	6.55%	11.3	166.8	−9.04%
25.00%	9.000	15-Nov-18	6.55%	11.4	169.8	−9.13%
100.00%		Portfolio	5.51%	6.9	86.4	−5.33%
		vs. Index	−0.17%	0.0	7.9	0.66%

Notes: Portfolios and index were static and not rebalanced over the period.
Cash flows were reinvested in Treasury bills for both the index and portfolios.
All returns are unannualized.

Exhibit 2 lists the holdings of the two portfolios. Portfolio 1 is relatively bulleted, that is, it holds primarily intermediate maturity bonds. Portfolio 1's yield advantage comes from the normal bowed shaped of the yield curve. The generally bowed shape of the yield curve also promises superior rolling returns as intermediate Treasuries age down the yield curve. Portfolio 2 is much more bar-belled; it holds 3-year and 25-year bonds, no intermediates, hence its yield disadvantage. The two portfolios' durations are equal to the index. Their convexities are not. This convexity difference is the primary source of the differential results. A secondary source of the differential results stems from the precise change in the shape of the yield curve; we will address shape-change risk later in this chapter.

While most fixed income practitioners are reasonably facile in the use of duration as a risk measure, convexity generally receives far less attention. Indeed, many institutional money managers pursue market neutral strategies and attempt to enhance returns by employing relative-value analysis of market sectors and sector rotation. While this is a popular strategy, it can conceal the interest rate risk that frequently accompanies sector-rotation strategies. This chapter describes a practitioner's point of view: how does one evaluate the convexity of a portfolio and manage that convexity as the portfolio and market dynamically change through the passage of time.

CONVEXITY ILLUSTRATED

Duration, while it is generally taught as one of the early tools for immunization techniques, is really a measure of market risk, much like beta is commonly used in equity portfolios. While beta has its roots in the statistics of market price behavior, duration has its roots in the calculus of the price-yield equation of a bond. Duration is simply the first derivative of the price-yield function; that is, duration is the proportional change of a bond's value due to a change in the bond's yield. To continue the calculus, convexity, the second derivative, is the change in the bond's duration due to a change in the bond's yield. More commonly from a practitioner's perspective, however, convexity is stated as an additional change in the bond's price due to a change in its yield. The Taylor series expansion of the price-yield function should illuminate the common way of thinking about duration, convexity, and the higher order terms:

$$\Delta P/P = -D \times (\Delta i) + C/2 \times (\Delta i)^2 - \alpha/3 \times (\Delta i)^3 + \beta/4 \times (\Delta i)^4 \ldots \qquad (1)$$

A few observations about this equation (1) are in order. First, the sign on C, convexity, is positive and since Δi is squared, its sign is always positive as well. If the value of C is positive, C always helps a bond's price appreciate, regardless of the direction of interest rates; that is, when interest rates rise, C pushes the bonds price up and when rates fall, C accelerates the bond's price appreciation. Thus, when one compares two bonds of equal duration, *all else equal*, one would always choose the bond with greater convexity. That is to say, the more convex bond would appreciate more in a rally and depreciate less in a market backup.

Exhibit 3: Taylor Series Expansion for a 30-Year Bond

Parameter	Value	Parameter × 50 bp
D	−12.47	−6.2362%
C	251.23	0.6281%
α	−3,060.78	−0.0383%
β	27,365.36	0.0017%
Total Price Change		−5.6447%

Assumes a 30-year 7% semiannual bond priced at par.
Parameters were computed numerically using four interest rate shifts and solving four simultaneous equations.

The sign on α again turns negative and, since Δi is cubed, α can have either a positive or negative impact on the bond's price, just like duration, D. However, Δi^3 is a very small number when one uses common volatility assumptions and, in practice, values for α tend to be modest. If Δi is 10 basis points, the term is 0.001^3 or 0.000000001. Thus, α, β, and the later terms in the Taylor Series expansion have generally minuscule impacts on a bond's price under normal volatility assumptions. If one wishes to stress test a portfolio under high-volatility environments, say perhaps 200 bp instantaneous shifts, α and later terms begin to have meaning.

A numerical example will serve to illustrate these important points. Exhibit 3 shows the numerically derived values for D, C, α, and β for a 30-year par bond with a 7% semiannual coupon. The coefficients were derived by computing the bond's price change under four separate interest rate shifts. Equation (1) was then applied to create four equations which could then be solved simultaneously. Additionally, Exhibit 3 breaks down the price effect of a 50 basis point instantaneous rise in interest rates and the resultant price impact of the four parameters. Observe that D, duration, has the most significant effect, −624 basis points, on the bond's price. Convexity has approximately one tenth the impact, only +63 bp (note the positive sign). α impacts the bond's price by less than 4 bp and β's effect is virtually inconsequential at under one bp. While most fixed income practitioners have become comfortable applying risk management techniques using duration, convexity is less-well understood and, as shown, can have a very significant impact on the performance of fixed income portfolios. Hence, this chapter focuses on convexity.

If two portfolios have the same duration, convexity is likely to be the most meaningful measure of the portfolios' relative interest rate risk and, eventually, differences in realized total return. Convexity's impact, however, is a function of the actual change in yields over the investment period in question and the cost of owning that convexity. The greater the change in interest rates, the greater the difference in performance of the two portfolios. Thus the value of convexity is a function of realized volatility, much like an option position. If realized volatility is low, a short option position and/or a short convexity position performs well. If realized volatility is high, a long option position and/or a long convexity position performs well. A numerical approach to examining the valuation of convexity should illuminate this trade-off.

Exhibit 4: Projected Total Returns for Parallel Yield Curve Shifts

Weight	Coupon	Maturity	Mkt Index	Yield	-1.250%	-1.000%	-0.750%	-0.625%	-0.500%	-0.375%	-0.250%	-0.125%
				6.470	8.62%	7.13%	5.69%	4.99%	4.30%	3.62%	2.94%	2.28%
Portfolio 1												
15.72%	6.000	30-Nov-97	100.117	5.886	2.704%	2.483%	2.262%	2.153%	2.043%	1.933%	1.824%	1.715%
25.00%	7.625	15-Feb-07	103.617	6.807	8.821%	7.430%	6.038%	5.332%	4.631%	3.928%	3.224%	2.524%
25.00%	10.375	15-Nov-09	121.981	6.805	9.751%	8.138%	6.540%	5.749%	4.962%	4.181%	3.407%	2.635%
25.00%	8.750	15-Nov-08	110.805	6.808	9.659%	8.070%	6.494%	5.711%	4.933%	4.154%	3.376%	2.603%
9.28%	9.125	15-May-09	113.617	6.803	9.846%	8.211%	6.595%	5.796%	4.997%	4.198%	3.408%	2.621%
		Portfolio		6.662	8.40%	7.06%	5.74%	5.07%	4.42%	3.76%	3.10%	2.45%
		vs. Index		0.192	-0.22%	-0.07%	0.04%	0.09%	0.12%	0.14%	0.16%	0.17%
Portfolio 2												
19.46%	8.000	15-Jan-97	100.742	5.294	1.341%	1.331%	1.321%	1.315%	1.310%	1.305%	1.300%	1.295%
25.00%	8.500	15-Jul-97	102.156	5.645	2.133%	2.003%	1.874%	1.809%	1.745%	1.681%	1.616%	1.552%
15.16%	8.625	15-Aug-97	102.398	5.753	2.282%	2.131%	1.981%	1.906%	1.831%	1.756%	1.682%	1.607%
15.38%	7.125	15-Feb-23	100.766	7.060	18.143%	14.527%	11.080%	9.416%	7.792%	6.205%	4.654%	3.140%
25.00%	6.250	15-Aug-23	90.375	7.053	18.924%	15.112%	11.485%	9.737%	8.031%	6.367%	4.743%	3.157%
		Portfolio		6.163	8.66%	7.10%	5.60%	4.88%	4.18%	3.49%	2.81%	2.16%
		vs. Index		-0.307	0.04%	-0.04%	-0.09%	-0.11%	-0.12%	-0.13%	-0.13%	-0.13%

Exhibit 4 (Continued)

Weight	Coupon	Maturity	Mkt	0.000%	0.125%	0.250%	0.375%	0.500%	0.625%	0.750%	1.000%	1.250%
				1.63%	0.99%	0.36%	−0.26%	−0.87%	−1.47%	−2.07%	−3.23%	−4.36%
Portfolio 1												
15.72%	6.000	30-Nov-97	100.117	1.606%	1.497%	1.389%	1.281%	1.172%	1.064%	0.957%	0.742%	0.527%
25.00%	7.625	15-Feb-07	103.617	1.824%	1.114%	0.410%	−0.290%	−0.995%	−1.696%	−2.391%	−3.789%	−5.173%
25.00%	10.375	15-Nov-09	121.981	1.865%	1.102%	0.343%	−0.410%	−1.157%	−1.897%	−2.639%	−4.103%	−5.549%
25.00%	8.750	15-Nov-08	110.805	1.836%	1.070%	0.310%	−0.447%	−1.204%	−1.958%	−2.705%	−4.188%	−5.650%
9.28%	9.125	15-May-09	113.617	1.837%	1.061%	0.288%	−0.486%	−1.254%	−2.0154%	−2.773%	−4.272%	−5.757%
		Portfolio		1.80%	1.16%	0.51%	−0.13%	−0.77%	−1.41%	−2.04%	−3.30%	−4.54%
		vs. Index		0.17%	0.16%	0.15%	0.13%	0.10%	0.07%	0.03%	−0.07%	−0.18%
Portfolio 2												
19.46%	8.000	15-Jan-97	100.742	1.290%	1.285%	1.279%	1.274%	1.269%	1.264%	1.259%	1.249%	1.238%
25.00%	8.500	15-Jul-97	102.156	1.488%	1.424%	1.360%	1.296%	1.232%	1.168%	1.104%	0.977%	0.850%
15.16%	8.625	15-Aug-97	102.398	1.533%	1.458%	1.384%	1.310%	1.236%	1.162%	1.088%	0.940%	0.793%
15.38%	7.125	15-Feb-23	100.766	1.660%	0.213%	−1.200%	−2.582%	−3.932%	−5.253%	−6.544%	−9.040%	−11.428%
25.00%	6.250	15-Aug-23	90.375	1.610%	0.099%	−1.377%	−2.817%	−4.225%	−5.599%	−6.941%	−9.534%	−12.010%
		Portfolio		1.51%	0.88%	0.27%	−0.33%	−0.92%	−1.49%	−2.06%	−3.14%	−4.19%
		vs. Index		−0.12%	−0.11%	−0.09%	−0.07%	−0.05%	−0.02%	0.01%	0.09%	0.17%

We will again consider alternative portfolios having identical durations, this time, at the beginning of October 1996. These portfolios are shown in Exhibit 4. Portfolio 1 is bulleted; the duration of Portfolio 1's individual holdings are generally quite close to the index's duration. Compared to the index, this portfolio structure results in a yield advantage of 19.2 basis points and a projected total return advantage of 17 bp over a 90-day holding period under unchanged interest rates. It is short convexity, compared to the index, by 21.9 units. Exhibit 4 shows projected total returns for a variety of parallel yield curve shifts. Note that if interest rates change, the total return advantage begins to diminish. A risk averse portfolio manager can then judge his risk of underperforming his index. In this case, if interest rates fall or rise by more than 75 bp over the 90-day investment horizon, the portfolio begins to underperform the index. Armed with this information, the portfolio manager may then gauge the likelihood of a 75 bp interest rate shift over a 90-day horizon relative to historical volatility.

Portfolio 2 is a different story. Portfolio 2 is highly barbelled, owning only short- and long-duration securities. Compared to the index, Portfolio 2's structure results in a yield disadvantage of 30.7 bp and a total return disadvantage of 12 bp in the standstill interest rate environment. Portfolio 2, however, has a convexity advantage of 14.8 units. Presumably, this convexity advantage will aid the portfolio under volatile interest rate shifts. Note that the return advantage over the index of Portfolio 2 improves as the magnitude of the interest rates shift increases. If interest rates drop by more than 100 bp or rise by more than 75 bp, Portfolio 2 beats the index.

Assuming a long-term interest rate volatility of 12% (annualized), a 75 bp interest rate shift over 90 days translates into an approximately two standard deviation event. Thus, a key to judging whether convexity is expensive or cheap on any given day, one must compare the return payoff pattern of a given portfolio to the probability of an interest rate shift of sufficient magnitude to cause differential results. On some days, the shape of the yield curve may suggest a 75 bp shift is required; on other days, perhaps only a 50 bp shift may be required.

While the above analysis utilized parallel yield curve shifts to examine the impact of convexity on a portfolio's realized return, the yield curve frequently does not move in parallel.

DIGRESSION: FORWARD RATES AND PARALLEL YIELD CURVE SHIFTS

Fixed income portfolio managers often focus their portfolios on securities that "roll down" the yield curve. That is, as a 5-year bond ages and becomes a 4-year bond, its price should tend to appreciate since the yield curve is generally upwardly sloped. While this strategy is common, one should realize that this is a three-pronged active bet: (1) a bet against forward interest rates, (2) a bet on the liquidity premium, and (3) a bet against volatility. If forward rates occurred and no liquidity premium exists along the yield curve, over a 6-month investment horizon all bonds would have the same total return, otherwise arbitrage would exist. The common theories intended to explain the normal positive slope of the yield curve focus on the implied inflation term structure and the liquidity premium term structures. That is, market equilibrium for the yield of a 10-year Treasury bond forces it to offer a higher yield than a 3-month bill because the investor takes more inflation risk in a 10-year bond and the investor requires a higher expected return to be attracted to a security with greater volatility. For the purposes of this chapter, we have simplified the examples to assume that the expected future shape of the yield curve is today's shape. That is, we'll assume the shape of the yield curve is explained entirely by liquidity premia. We'll assume that the term structure of inflation is flat. This assumption rationalizes parallel yield curve shifts: a parallel shift means that the term structure of liquidity premia does not change.

This, of course, is not always the case and this assumption could lull investors into assuming that rolling bonds down the yield curve will always offer enhanced returns. One especially prickly example: when the yield curve inverts, i.e., the market expects inflation to plummet and the inflation term structure is highly inverted, portfolios that roll well end up performing miserably. The purpose of the assumption is to simplify the illustrations, not to promise a free lunch.

Additionally, one technical note must be made about the definition of "parallel yield curve shift." If one shifts the Treasury spot curve in parallel, the Treasury coupon yield curve will not necessarily shift in parallel. For the purposes of this chapter, we will simplify and assume that parallel shift means equal yield changes in actual coupon-paying Treasury securities. The spot curve, then, may not shift in parallel. Once again, this is intended to simplify the illustrations.

CONVEXITY AND NON-PARALLEL YIELD CURVE SHIFTS

So far, we've confined our discussion of convexity to its impact under parallel yield curve shifts. This approach pairs the value of convexity to volatility; we have not yet examined the impact of non-parallel yield curve shifts on portfolios that are long or short convexity. As one can surmise from the previous illustrations, convexity adjustments in a Treasury-only portfolio are nearly always accompanied by yield-curve exposures. For portfolios of non-call securities, a long convexity portfolio is nearly always barbelled, and a short-convexity portfolio is nearly always bulleted. Careful portfolio structuring necessitates examination of non-parallel yield curve shifts. The question then arises: exactly what form do non-parallel shifts take? While an exhaustive examination of yield curve shape dynamics is beyond the scope of this chapter, statistical methods may be utilized to describe historical yield curve shape changes.

Exhibit 5: Principal Component Yield Curve Changes

Maturity	Shift	Twist	Butterfly
1	0.307	−0.199	−0.297
2	0.342	−0.066	−0.195
3	0.351	0.011	−0.130
5	0.334	0.123	0.028
7	0.308	0.177	0.117
10	0.283	0.216	0.219
30	0.225	0.259	0.262

1-month normalized yield curve shape changes

One approach to the issue entails statistically measuring the historical yield curve shifts. Rudimentary regression-analysis fails to aid in this endeavor because of the high level of multicolinearity in the data. Principal component analysis solves this issue since it is designed to deal with highly correlated multi-variate datasets. Exhibit 5 shows the normalized 1-month yield curve shifts that resulted from a principal-component analysis of yield curve data. Exhibit 5 presents a subset of the output from the principal component analysis. Historically, the more common shape changes have been shift (somewhat parallel), twist, and butterfly. Higher-order shape changes may also be identified using principal component techniques but the first three shape change varieties are the most relevant.

Once reasonable yield curve shifts have been identified, various levels of volatility of shape changes may be incorporated into the scenario analysis shown in Exhibit 4. Projected returns may then be computed for each bond of interest (including all the bonds in the index). Optimization techniques may then be employed which incorporate the portfolio manager's risk tolerance and return goals. Thus, this approach requires the investor to explicitly specify how much he is willing to underperform his index in various yield-curve shifts. Exhibit 6 does precisely that.

Exhibit 6 presents projected total returns for three optimized portfolios under several yield curve shape changes. The shape scenarios are from Exhibit 5 and apply several levels of volatility to the shape changes. For example, scenario c is a −2.0 × shift shape change, that is, −2 shifts. Additionally, three portfolios are presented. Portfolio 1 was designed to perform well under an unchanged yield curve environment, scenario s; that is, the objective function was to maximize total return from bonds rolling down an unchanged yield curve. Portfolio 2 was designed to maximize the portfolio's convexity without regard to the optimal portfolio's exposure to non-parallel yield curve shifts. Portfolio 3 was designed to maximize the portfolio's convexity with one important addition to the constraint set: Portfolio 3 was constrained to underperform the index by no more than 10 bp if the yield curve changed shape.

Exhibit 6: Projected Total Returns, 90-Day Investment Horizon

					Yield Curve Shape Change Scenarios								
					a	b	c	d	e	f	g	h	i
Weight	Coupon	Maturity	Mkt	Yield	Shift -1.0×	Shift 1.0×	Shift -2.0×	Shift 2.0×	Shift 3.0×	Shift 3.0×	Twist -1.0×	Twist 1.0×	Twist -2.0×
Portfolio 1 — Maximize Roll Down Returns													
25.00%	13.750	15-Aug-04	142.723	6.680	3.255%	0.126%	4.870%	-1.391%	6.519%	-2.877%	2.591%	0.769%	3.520%
25.00%	11.750	15-Feb-10	131.266	6.790	3.277%	-0.180%	5.058%	-1.864%	6.874%	-3.515%	2.653%	0.421%	3.786%
25.00%	11.125	15-Aug-03	124.559	6.617	3.246%	0.226%	4.801%	-1.240%	6.386%	-2.679%	2.515%	0.936%	3.317%
17.06%	12.000	15-Aug-13	140.578	6.928	3.706%	-0.399%	5.839%	-2.369%	8.031%	-4.290%	3.087%	0.190%	4.574%
7.94%	10.750	15-Feb-03	121.383	6.584	3.180%	0.259%	4.682%	-1.161%	6.213%	-2.554%	2.404%	1.014%	3.109%
		Portfolio		6.726	3.33%	0.00%	5.05%	-1.62%	6.81%	-3.20%	2.66%	0.64%	3.68%
		vs. Index		0.259	0.32%	-0.30%	0.63%	-0.62%	0.94%	-0.94%	0.01%	-0.02%	-0.01%
Portfolio 2 — Maximize Convexity													
25.00%	6.250	31-Jan-97	100.285	5.319	1.313%	1.293%	1.324%	1.283%	1.334%	1.272%	1.246%	1.360%	1.189%
25.00%	6.250	15-Aug-23	90.375	7.053	4.426%	-1.086%	7.368%	-3.667%	10.444%	-6.140%	4.864%	-1.488%	8.284%
25.00%	8.000	15-Jan-97	100.742	5.294	1.294%	1.285%	1.299%	1.280%	1.304%	1.276%	1.261%	1.319%	1.232%
16.54%	7.125	15-Feb-23	100.766	7.060	4.378%	-0.947%	7.214%	-3.447%	10.174%	-5.846%	4.741%	-1.279%	7.973%
8.46%	6.750	28-Feb-97	100.594	5.255	1.351%	1.306%	1.374%	1.284%	1.397%	1.261%	1.237%	1.421%	1.145%
		Portfolio		6.029	2.60%	0.33%	3.81%	-0.74%	5.07%	-1.76%	2.73%	0.21%	4.09%
		vs. Index		-0.438	-0.41%	0.03%	-0.61%	0.26%	-0.80%	0.50%	0.09%	-0.45%	0.40%
Portfolio 3 — Maximize Convexity — Low Loss Constraint*													
25.00%	10.375	15-Nov-12	126.453	6.923	3.972%	-0.221%	6.145%	-2.239%	8.377%	-4.205	3.338%	0.383%	4.852%
25.00%	7.875	15-Jan-98	102.383	5.915	1.884%	1.286%	2.185%	0.989%	2.487%	0.693%	1.400%	1.768%	1.217%
22.00%	6.250	15-Aug-23	90.375	7.053	4.426%	-1.086%	7.368%	-3.667%	10.444%	-6.140%	4.864%	-1.488%	8.284%
20.66%	8.750	15-Oct-97	102.891	5.836	1.798%	1.373%	2.012%	1.161%	2.226%	0.950%	1.401%	1.769%	1.218%
7.15%	13.375	15-Aug-01	128.574	6.444	2.828%	0.448%	4.046%	-0.715%	5.283%	-1.860%	1.960%	1.299%	2.293%
0.18%	11.750	15-Feb-01	120.027	6.419	2.756%	0.516%	3.900%	-0.580%	5.061%	-1.660%	1.848%	1.410%	2.068%
		Portfolio		6.440	3.02%	0.34%	4.42%	-0.93%	5.86%	-2.17%	2.69%	0.67%	3.76%
		vs. Index		-0.027	0.01%	0.04%	0.00%	0.06%	-0.01%	0.09%	0.04%	0.01%	0.07%

Exhibit 6 (Continued)

					Yield Curve Shape Change Scenarios									
					j Twist 2.0×	*k* Twist -3.0×	*l* Twist 3.0×	*m* B-Fly -1.0×	*n* B-Fly 1.0×	*o* B-Fly -2.0×	*p* B-Fly 2.0×	*q* B-Fly -3.0×	*r* B-Fly 3.0×	*s* Unch. Curve
Weight	Coupon	Maturity	Mkt	Yield										
Portfolio 1 — Maximize Roll Down Returns														
25.00%	13.750	15-Aug-04	142.723	6.680	-0.125%	4.461%	-1.007%	2.328%	1.027%	2.988%	0.386%	3.655%	-0.248%	1.674%
25.00%	11.750	15-Feb-10	131.266	6.790	-0.684%	4.927%	-1.778%	2.454%	0.609%	3.381%	-0.312%	4.304%	-1.230%	1.530%
25.00%	11.125	15-Aug-03	124.559	6.617	0.158%	4.128%	-0.611%	2.188%	1.258%	2.657%	0.798%	3.129%	0.340%	1.721%
17.06%	12.000	15-Aug-13	140.573	6.928	-1.221%	6.088%	-2.609%	2.943%	0.333%	4.286%	-0.937%	5.655%	-2.185%	1.627%
7.94%	10.750	15-Feb-03	121.383	6.584	0.329%	3.819%	-0.351%	2.055%	1.359%	2.406%	1.012%	2.758%	0.668%	1.706%
Portfolio				6.726	-0.34%	4.72%	-1.32%	2.41%	0.89%	3.18%	0.14%	3.96%	-0.60%	1.64%
vs. Index				0.259	-0.07%	-0.06%	-0.14%	-0.06%	0.06%	-0.16%	0.08%	-0.30%	0.08%	0.01%
Portfolio 2 — Maximize Convexity														
25.00%	6.250	31-Jan-97	100.285	5.319	1.417%	1.132%	1.475%	1.364%	1.242%	1.425%	1.182%	1.485%	1.121%	1.303%
25.00%	6.250	15-Aug-23	90.375	7.053	-4.438%	11.880%	-7.249%	4.854%	-1.480%	8.262%	-4.423%	11.844%	-7.229%	1.610%
25.00%	8.000	15-Jan-97	100.742	5.294	1.348%	1.203%	1.377%	1.323%	1.257%	1.355%	1.224%	1.388%	1.191%	1.290%
16.54%	7.125	15-Feb-23	100.766	7.060	-4.083%	11.365%	-6.760%	4.706%	-1.248%	7.901%	-4.023%	11.251%	-6.674%	1.660%
8.46%	6.750	28-Feb-97	100.594	5.255	1.513%	1.053%	1.606%	1.402%	1.256%	1.475%	1.183%	1.549%	1.110%	1.329%
Portfolio				6.029	-0.97%	5.52%	-2.08%	2.78%	0.15%	4.19%	-1.07%	5.67%	-2.24%	1.44%
vs. Index				-0.438	-0.69%	0.74%	-0.90%	0.31%	-0.68%	0.85%	-1.13%	1.42%	-1.56%	-0.20%
Portfolio 3 — Maximize Convexity — Low Loss Constraint														
25.00%	10.375	15-Nov-12	126.453	6.923	-1.056%	6.393%	-2.472%	3.194%	0.527%	4.564%	-0.769%	5.961%	-2.044%	1.848%
25.00%	7.875	15-Jan-98	102.383	5.915	1.953%	1.034%	2.139%	1.291%	1.878%	1.000%	2.173%	0.710%	2.470%	1.584%
22.00%	6.250	15-Aug-23	90.375	7.053	-4.438%	11.880%	-7.249%	4.854%	-1.480%	8.262%	-4.423%	11.844%	-7.229%	1.610%
20.66%	8.750	15-Oct-97	102.891	5.836	1.953%	1.036%	2.138%	1.360%	1.811%	1.136%	2.037%	0.912%	2.264%	1.585%
7.15%	13.375	15-Aug-01	128.574	6.444	0.971%	2.628%	0.644%	1.593%	1.665%	1.557%	1.701%	1.522%	1.737%	1.629%
0.18%	11.750	15-Feb-01	120.027	6.419	1.191%	2.289%	0.974%	1.468%	1.789%	1.307%	1.951%	1.147%	2.112%	1.628%
Portfolio				6.440	-0.28%	4.88%	-1.19%	2.59%	0.77%	3.56%	-0.08%	4.57%	-0.89%	1.66%
vs. Index				-0.027	0.00%	0.10%	-0.01%	0.12%	-0.06%	0.21%	-0.14%	0.32%	-0.21%	0.03%

Some important observations are in order. Both Portfolio 1 and Portfolio 2 have significant yield curve exposures. Portfolio 1 performs especially well under the negative shift scenarios; its bullet structure benefits when the intermediate portion of the yield curve rallies more than the long and short portions. Portfolio 2 benefits in the opposite scenarios; it benefits most in the positive shift scenarios, that is, when the long and/or short portion of the yield curve rally more than the intermediate portion. Note the magnitude of the variance in total return from the index. Portfolio 1 in scenario *b*, for example, underperforms the index by 30 bp, quite a significant variance for only a 3-month horizon. Portfolio 2 in scenario *a* underperforms the index by 41 bp. These variances represent significant yield curve risk exposures not captured by duration and convexity alone.

Portfolio 3 in Exhibit 6 is a more risk controlled portfolio. While all three portfolios are duration matched to the index, the goal in Portfolio 3 is to find a portfolio with minimal shape change exposure. Here, the optimizer found the highest convexity portfolio with six additional constraints: the optimal portfolio was not allowed to underperform the index by more than 10 bp in any of the shift or twist changes specified. Returns under butterfly shape changes were not constrained. Note the structure of Portfolio 3: it is barbelled but not so severely as Portfolio 2. It also does not have the convexity advantage of Portfolio 2. It does not benefit or suffer from the return variance relative to the index as Portfolio 1 or 2. Thus, the approach of Exhibit 6 may be utilized to control yield curve risk or, for active managers, structure portfolios to benefit from anticipated shape changes.

CONVEXITY AND CONTINGENT CASH FLOWS

Thus far, this chapter has focused on the convexity properties of portfolios of bonds with stable structures. Of course, many modern fixed income securities contain contingent claims of one sort or another. The simplest example is a callable bond. Here, the timing of the cash flows of the individual bond are contingent on the level of interest rates through the life of the security. Once again, we can use a numerical method to estimate the convexity, and higher-order terms, of a callable bond. Exhibit 7 shows the duration, convexity, and higher order terms for a 2-year callable bond. A 2-year U.S. Treasury note is shown for comparison.

Note the convexity of the callable FNMA. It is negative. This means that as interest rates change, in either direction, the negative convexity always causes its price to suffer. As interest rates fall, the bond appreciates by less than its duration alone would suggest. As interest rates rise, its price falls by more than its duration alone suggests. Compared to a non-call security, the 2-year U.S. Treasury for example, this inferior price behavior is further illuminated. The far right column of Exhibit 7 shows the price performance of the callable FNMA relative to the U.S. Treasury. Note that as interest rates change, the price movement of the callable FNMA will always underperform the 2-year U.S. Treasury. Exhibit 7 does not address the valuation of callable securities; market forces should cause the valuation of the callable FNMA to produce total returns competitive with the U.S. Treasury. This, of course, is highly dependent on realized volatility.

Exhibit 7: Taylor Series Expansion for a 2-Year Currently Callable Corporate and a 2-Year U.S. Treasury

Parameter	FNMA 4.875% 10-15-98, Currently Callable		2-Year U.S. Treasury		FNMA – UST
	Value	Parameter × 50 bp	Value	Parameter × 50 bp	
D	−1.85	−0.9250%	−1.85	−0.9250%	0.0000%
C	−3.29	−0.0082%	4.32	0.0108%	−0.0190%
α	104.87	0.0013%	−51.30	−0.0006%	0.0020%
β	−153,806.22	−0.0096%	41,038.37	0.0026%	−0.0122%
Total Price Change		−0.9415%		−0.9123%	−0.0292%

Pricing as of September October 30, 1996.
Parameters were computed numerically using four interest rate shifts and solving four simultaneous equations.

The yield curve shape exposures of a callable bond are complex. As interest rates change, a callable bond's expected cash flows move from its maturity to call dates, or back. Thus, not only is a callable bond's price performance inferior under parallel yield curve shifts, but, additionally, its shape change exposures add a level of complexity to the investment decision process. A numerical approach, such as illustrated in Exhibit 6, is a useful approach. By examining the total return behavior of callable securities, one can identify and control shape change risk in addition to convexity and duration.

CONCLUSION

The convexity of a fixed income security can have a meaningful impact on its total return relative to alternative investments. Convexity alone, however, masks risk exposures to yield curve shape changes. A total return framework allows portfolio managers to identify and control these exposures explicitly. This becomes especially important when securities with contingent claims are considered.

About the Author

Robert I. Gerber, Ph.D.

Robert I. Gerber is a Senior Portfolio Manager and Head of the Mortgage Securities Group at Sanford C. Bernstein & Co., Inc. Prior to joining Bernstein, he spent more than four years at the First Boston Corporation, most recently as Vice President of Fixed Income Research. Before 1987, Mr. Gerber taught economics at Columbia University, the State University of New York at Albany, and Vassar College. He earned a B.A. from Union College in 1976 and a Ph.D. in Economics from Columbia in 1983.

Chapter 12

A User's Guide to Buy-Side Bond Trading

Robert I. Gerber, Ph.D.
Senior Portfolio Manager
Sanford C. Bernstein & Co., Inc.

INTRODUCTION

The mythic trader, living by his wits and betting vast sums on market fluctuations, does not work for an investment management firm (buy-side).[1] Although he may flourish at a broker-dealer (sell-side), the odds are stacked against him on the buy-side.[2] On the sell-side he is a market-maker, earning, rather than paying, the bid-ask spread on each transaction. Moreover, greater (limited) access to information about investor preferences creates opportunities (barriers) for the sell-side (buy-side) trader to exploit short-term market technicals.

The natural question is, what is buy-side trading? There is no simple answer, because traders do different things at different firms, and the distinction between research, portfolio management, trading, risk management, and compliance is often blurred. A common thread, however, does exist — traders gather and interpret market information, and execute transactions.

Upon learning this, a sell-side trader once commented to me, "Oh, you mean they're *just* order takers." To which I responded, "Yes, in the same sense that a golfer *just* hits the ball in the cup." Both are highly specialized and highly skilled, and both face complex challenges not easily understood by laymen.

The main purpose of this chapter is to discuss some of the complexities of buy-side trading.[3] What are the relative advantages of an instantaneous auction, a bid list and a sale order? Does market liquidity or volatility matter? What

---

[1] The terms "buy-side trader" and "investor" are used interchangeably, as are the terms "sell-side trader" and "broker-dealer."

[2] Certainly, buy-side traders also have some advantages, such as partial access to dealer inventories. A detailed comparison, however, of the relative advantages of buy- and sell-side traders is beyond the scope of these discussions.

[3] In the language of a strategic game, how should you construct the game, what are the optimal strategies of the players, and what is the game's solution?

I would like to thank Fred Cohen, Sloane Lamb, Elaine Mintzer, Walter Prahl, and Frank Trainer for their insightful comments on an earlier draft. This chapter is dedicated to the memory of William S. Vickrey — a gentleman and a scholar whose ideas inspired generations of his students.

should you expect from sell-side traders? What is your optimal strategy? How much can you hope to gain from a job well done?

MARKET CONDITIONS

Selecting the best buy-side trading strategy is very difficult. It depends on numerous factors, many of which are intangible. Although there is no adequate substitute for an experienced trader, one axiom certainly applies — market conditions matter a great deal, and often in a predictable way. In this context, it is useful to consider two market extremes: liquid and illiquid.

Although liquidity is somewhat in the eye of the beholder, a liquid market can generally be defined by *small bid-ask spreads which do not materially increase* for large transactions. These conditions make liquidity the financial-market equivalent of perfect competition in the goods economy. In a perfectly competitive market, consumers and producers have no individual influence on price. Likewise, the sell-side trader's influence over price declines with financial-market liquidity. Nonetheless, complications — such as imperfect information and real-time execution — make trading skills valuable even in a very liquid market. A good buy-side trader might add a couple of basis points in return by choosing the optimal bidding process and closing the transaction.[4]

Illiquid markets pose somewhat different challenges. Acquiring reliable information becomes much more difficult because securities are typically less homogeneous and are infrequently traded. Moreover, the cost of ignorance can be great, as the notion of a market clearing price is not well defined. Executing a transaction might take days, rather than seconds, and can resemble the mating ritual of a praying mantis. Under some circumstances, enhanced information and negotiating skill can add a few percentage points to a transaction.

Exhibit 1 provides indicators of market liquidity for a cross-section of the fixed-income universe. Bid-ask spreads are estimated for typical and distressed conditions, because the liquidity of a particular market can fluctuate. For example, the bid-ask spreads on Fannie Mae Trust Interest-Only Strips (IOs) have ranged from less than 0.5% to more than 5%. In light of this variability, identifying the determinants of liquidity becomes important.

FACTORS INFLUENCING LIQUIDITY

Market liquidity is defined in terms of bid-ask spreads. The exact meaning of "bid-ask spread," however, is open to interpretation. For the sake of exposition,

---

[4] A couple of basis points per trade can add up; if annual turnover were high on liquid investments (say, 2½ times), this would translate into 5 basis points in performance. Although this figure seems small, it is significant in light of the fact that a bond manager need outperform the market by only about 75 basis points a year in order to be ranked in the top quartile.

suppose that on November 27, 1996, four broker-dealers simultaneously bid (to buy) and offer (to sell) $100 million Freddie Mac 7.0% Gold PCs for delivery on December 11, 1996 (Exhibit 2).

Prices are quoted in terms of points ($ per bond with $100 face value) and 32nds of a point (called ticks), where + denotes one-half of one 32nd. Dealer 1 is willing to buy the bonds at a price of 99 points and $4/32$, and sell them for a price of 99-06. The dealer might view this two-tick difference in his bid-to-offer price as the bid-ask spread. From a market perspective, however, the bid-ask spread is one tick: the difference between the highest bid (99-05, by Dealer 4) and the lowest offer (99-06, by Dealers 1 and 3).[5] In this example — one from a very liquid market — the two measures of bid-ask spread arrive at almost the same value. For an illiquid market, the result can be quite different.

Exhibit 1: Indicators of Market Liquidity

	Market Size ($ billions)	Bid-Ask Spreads (% price)	
		Typical	Distressed
Mortgage-Backed Securities (MBS)			
Fixed-Rate Generic	1,500	0.06	0.25
ARM	150	0.13	0.38
Companion CMO	260	0.50	1.50
IO Strip	70	0.63	5.00
Treasuries			
Bills	760	0.002	0.005
On-the-Run Notes and Bonds	70	0.03	0.06
Off-the-Run Notes and Bonds	2,760	0.06	0.09
Corporates (Intermediate)			
A Finance	130	0.12	0.50
B Industrials	80	0.50	5.00
Municipals (Long)			
Aa/Aaa	1,300	0.25	0.75

Source: Salomon Brothers, Lehman Brothers, and Sanford C. Bernstein estimates

Exhibit 2: Identifying Bid-Ask Spreads

Price	Dealer 1	Dealer 2	Dealer 3	Dealer 4
Bid	99-04	99-04+	99-04+	99-05
Offer	99-06	99-06+	99-06	99-07+

---

[5] Although the market bid-ask spread is theoretically well defined (best bid minus best offer), in practice it can be somewhat ambiguous. As discussed later, it may be desirable to limit the number of potential counterparties in a transaction. Absolute certainty that the best bidder or offerer has been included is therefore not possible.

Dealer competition is a requisite for a liquid market. Without it, dealers can usually widen their bid-to-offer price in the natural pursuit of profits.[6] The lure of stable trading profits — large markets, modest entry costs, and low security volatility (good hedging vehicles) — serves as a magnet for dealer competition. Markets for complex, heterogeneous securities tend to violate all three conditions. These securities are often volatile and difficult to hedge and therefore have very high research and distribution costs. Some mortgage derivatives — such as IOs and inverse floaters — fall into this category. Researchers, elaborate databases, computer systems, and a knowledgeable sales force are all necessary to success-fully compete in this arena. Not all derivatives, however, are illiquid. For example, many interest rate derivatives, such as futures, swaps and caps, are much easier to hedge[7] and require neither a significant research commitment nor a large scale distribution network. In fact, although some interest rate derivatives appear to be complex, they can often be reduced to a bundle of simpler instruments.

Markets for heterogeneous, complex securities tend to be illiquid for another reason as well. By their very nature, these markets cannot have a single price to signal aggregate investor preferences. Information is therefore much more diffuse and must be imprecisely inferred via recent trades of similar securities and conversa-tions with potential investors. As a result of this uncertainty, rational sell-side traders will widen their bid-to-offer spread in order to avoid the "winner's curse."[8]

The "winner's curse" describes the tendency for a competitive auction — a public sale of any security to the highest bidder[9] — to produce sale prices in excess of an asset's value. Understanding an auction's impact on the behavior of sell-side traders is the first step in selecting optimal buy-side trading strategies.

WINNERS, COVERS, AND BID-ASK SPREADS

Traders try to avoid the winner's curse. Suppose five sell-side traders are bidding on a bond worth 95-00, but because their information is imperfect they don't know its true value. They do know, however, that winning the auction is tantamount to ten-dering the highest bid. Moreover, because professional traders' expectations are unbiased (over many auctions, they average close to the true value),[10] the winners' subjective valuation will tend to exceed the true value. Sell-side traders therefore know that they must shave (raise) their bid (offer) or risk overpaying (underselling)

---

[6] As illustrated in Exhibit 2, increased dealer participation (certainly in excess of one) also tends to reduce bid-ask spreads by increasing the chance that the best bid or offer will improve.

[7] Interest rate volatility, which is relatively easy to quantify and hedge, is the dominant source of risk.

[8] For a detailed discussion of the winner's curse, see Richard H. Thaler (ed.), *The Winner's Curse: Para-doxes and Anomalies of Economic Life* (Princeton, NJ: Princeton University Press, 1992).

[9] Due to its importance to the fixed-income markets, the Treasury Auction — the sale of newly issued gov-ernment securities — is sometimes referred to as "The Auction." In all the following discussions, the more general usage is intended.

[10] Otherwise, they would go out of business, because they would consistently lose money by overpaying for securities or miss trades by underbidding.

for the security. The larger the number of participants and the greater the uncertainty surrounding the true value, the more hazardous the auction.[11]

Exhibit 3 provides the results from a series of simulations in which security valuations are drawn from a normal distribution centered around the true value (95-00). Each entry — based on 1,000 simulations — differs only by the number of participants in the auction and the standard deviation perceived by the traders. For example, the entry in the first row and column states that, in two-participant auctions in which trader opinions have a standard deviation of 0.25 points, the average high valuation is 0.14 points above the true value.

The marginal impact of additional participants is at first large, but diminishes rapidly. For example, the probability of the tenth participant's valuation exceeding the first nine is much lower than that of the third participant's exceeding the first two. However, the marginal impact of market uncertainty — as we move from left to right — does not taper off. Intuitively, the probability of a high valuation (expressed in terms of standard deviations) is constant. As a result, high valuations (expressed as absolute increases over the true value) increase proportionally with uncertainty. For example, the entries in the fourth column — 1 point standard deviation — are about four times the magnitude of those in the first column — ¼ point standard deviation.

The rational sell-side trader will cheapen (richen) his bid (offer) by at least the expected difference between the mean high (low) valuation and true value.[12] Otherwise, he can expect to lose money trading. For instance, in a three-person auction where the perceived standard deviation is 0.25 points, the high valuation tends to exceed the true value by 0.21 points. Trader rationality therefore requires bid reduction by at least this amount. The larger the auction, therefore, the more traders will tend to cut their bids. In this regard, increasing competition may seem to have no impact on sale price, because each time the number of bidders grows, the individual bids are further reduced to neutralize the heightened danger of the winner's curse.[13]

Exhibit 3: The Winner's Curse

Participants (#)	Standard Deviation (points)				
	0.25	0.50	0.75	1.00	1.50
2	0.14	0.28	0.42	0.56	0.85
3	0.21	0.42	0.63	0.84	1.26
4	0.26	0.53	0.76	1.03	1.56
5	0.30	0.58	0.85	1.15	1.72
6	0.31	0.63	0.95	1.25	1.89
8	0.36	0.71	1.07	1.41	2.11
10	0.38	0.80	1.13	1.55	2.31
15	0.44	0.86	1.34	1.74	2.62

[11] In fact, sell-side traders routinely ask the buy-side trader to reveal the number of participants in the auction.
[12] In statistical terms we can think of the winning bid as the highest order statistic of independent draws of a random variable. The expected value of the highest (winner) and second highest (cover) order statistic and the random variable (true value) refers to the values being discussed.
[13] Unless, of course, bidders are consistently and successfully deceived about the number of other participants — an unlikely possibility.

Exhibit 4: Uncertainty, Auction Size, and Anticipated Cover

Participants (#)	Standard Deviation (points)				
	0.25	0.50	0.75	1.00	1.50
2	0.28	0.56	0.84	1.12	1.70
3	0.21	0.42	0.63	0.84	1.26
4	0.17	0.37	0.56	0.73	1.10
5	0.17	0.33	0.48	0.67	1.00
6	0.15	0.31	0.46	0.60	0.94
8	0.14	0.27	0.43	0.58	0.90
10	0.13	0.29	0.40	0.56	0.79
15	0.12	0.24	0.38	0.49	0.78

Competition, however, can systematically raise bids because it reduces the bargaining leverage of individual broker-dealers. "Bargaining leverage" refers to the amount by which the winner *believes* he can lower his bid (after compensating for the winner's curse) and still win the auction. After the auction has taken place, the *realized* difference between the winner and the second highest bidder is called the "cover." Bargaining leverage is the a priori analog of the (ex post) cover and is, therefore, sometimes referred to as "anticipated cover."

The anticipated cover is shown in Exhibit 4 to be decreasing with the number of participants and increasing with the asset's perceived volatility. Intuitively, the greater the number of participants with similar opinions, the less likely that the winner's valuation will significantly exceed the second most aggressive bidder. A profit-maximizing trader trying to just outbid the second highest bid will lower his bids as his bargaining leverage increases. Taking into account rational sell-side trader behavior, the process by which auction size and uncertainty determine market liquidity (bid-ask spread) is illustrated in Exhibit 5.

Step 1 of Exhibit 5 provides a distribution of valuations for two environments. Column A describes a very liquid market — many participants with similar opinions (represented by dots along the line). Column B depicts an illiquid market. In Step 2 all the valuations are adjusted downward (translated to the left) by the amount by which traders expect the average high valuation to exceed the true valuation, over many identical auctions. Note that in both auctions (Columns A and B) the true value and high adjusted valuation are equal to 95-00. Although this result will certainly not occur in all circumstances, it should hold *on average* as traders alter their valuations to the auction's characteristics. As illustrated in Step 3, bids will be reduced below the adjusted valuations, in relation to the trader's bargaining leverage — the greater the anticipated cover, the lower the ultimate bid. The expected difference between the true value and the winning offer price in a purchase auction can likewise be derived. In Step 4, the equilibrium bid-ask spread results from combining the expected winning bids and offers.

Exhibit 5: Equilibrium Bid-Ask Spreads

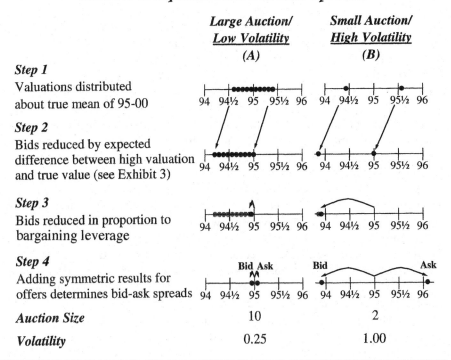

	Large Auction/ Low Volatility (A)	Small Auction/ High Volatility (B)
Step 1 Valuations distributed about true mean of 95-00		
Step 2 Bids reduced by expected difference between high valuation and true value (see Exhibit 3)		
Step 3 Bids reduced in proportion to bargaining leverage		
Step 4 Adding symmetric results for offers determines bid-ask spreads		
Auction Size	10	2
Volatility	0.25	1.00

The missing piece in determining equilibrium bid-ask spreads is the amount of the surplus (due to bargaining leverage) that sell-side traders will systematically attempt to extract.[14] In theory, traders might try to extract anywhere from a small fraction to a multiple of the surplus. Traders would limit their attempts to extract the surplus if they believed that these attempts significantly increased the odds of losing the trade. Alternatively, traders would attempt to extract a large multiple of the surplus if they believed that all other traders were doing likewise and that, therefore, the bid necessary to win the trade was actually much lower than rational valuations would indicate. Absent other compelling reasons (such as the need to cover a short position), neither of these are frequent occurrences. From the trader's vantage point, there is little to lose in attempting to extract some surplus, because it is not (yet) a profitable trade. As the trader extracts greater amounts of the surplus, the trade becomes increasingly profitable, and further attempts are increasingly risky. In practice, it seems as though traders often attempt to extract the entire surplus, but not much more. [15]

[14] In the common vernacular, they will attempt to leave as little money on the table as possible.

[15] For a further discussion, see the appendix to Robert I. Gerber, "A User's Guide to Buy-side Bond Trading," Chapter 16 in Frank J. Fabozzi (ed.), Managing Fixed Income Portfolios (New Hope, PA: Frank J. Fabozzi Associates, 1997).

AUCTION DESIGN FOR A LIQUID MARKET

The results of the preceding section argue that increasing the auction size improves buy-side execution by reducing the temptation for the broker-dealer to shave his bid. Although there is no disputing this conclusion, the potential benefit from increasing the auction beyond a handful of participants is often quite small. For instance, consider a generic par-priced mortgage passthrough (with a standard deviation of about 0.25 points). As shown in Exhibit 4, adding the third bidder reduces the anticipated cover by 0.07 points to 0.21 points. Adding the next 5 bidders reduces the anticipated cover by an additional 0.07 points. Moreover, even for a liquid security there are rarely more than a half dozen or so contending counterparties. It is the job of the buy-side trader to know their identity.

Large auctions do have their disadvantages. As the number of competitors increases, the time required to gather the bids (or offers) increases; in turn, this raises exposure to market volatility, which introduces uncertainty about best price. Transactions are not final until a bid is accepted and confirmed. The greater the time between bid and acceptance, the less certain the confirmation. There are a variety of potential solutions to this problem (e.g., multiple traders, spread trades versus a reference Treasury benchmark, hedging), but these solutions have associated costs that must be weighed against the benefits.

Our experience suggests that the optimal auction for a liquid security is usually three to five participants. It provides a good balance between timely execution and a small cover. Real time execution, however, creates another opportunity for the highest bidder to lower his price: trade confirmation.

Once bids have been tendered, the buy-side trader identifies and accepts the highest price. It is then up to the bidder to confirm the price. Even in the absence of any market movements, the bidder has an immediate incentive to lower his bid, because he knows that it must have been the highest. If real time frictions were not an issue, and if bonds traded in infinitely small price units, there would be only a small incentive for the sell-side trader to lower his bid price, because he has already selected his optimal bid and lowering the price further would increase the probability that the trade would fall through. These complications, however, provide the would-be winner an opportunity to lower his bid by the minimum amount in which the particular bonds trade. For instance, mortgage passthroughs trade in units of a + ($\frac{1}{64}$). As a result, the winner has the incentive to lower his bid by that amount. Theoretically, although this type of behavior (opportunistic re-bidding) doesn't necessarily affect execution,[16] it can in practice.

---

[16] If traders raise their initial bid by a +, realizing that they will lower their bid by a + at confirmation, there is no net effect. Due to the conventions of trade confirmation, however, this type of behavior is somewhat unlikely. If the last bid to arrive is the best, the buy-side trader can immediately accept it, with confirmation essentially guaranteed. Sell-side traders are reluctant to admit to opportunistic re-bidding, and it is difficult to attribute a bid change to external factors when acceptance is immediate.

Only a minority of sell-side traders seem to display this sort of behavior. It complicates the trade and jeopardizes its completion, all for a modest and uncertain gain — on the order of a + for mortgage passthroughs ($15,625 on a $100 million transaction). Moreover, buy-side traders can discourage re-bidding by reducing its profit potential. For example, bids can be sequentially requested with habitual re-bidders put last in the queue, thereby increasing the odds of an instantaneous acceptance (confirmation virtually assured) when the best price is tendered. In addition, buy-side traders can declare that ties will not be awarded to opportunistic re-bidders. Nonetheless, opportunistic re-bidding cannot be completely eliminated.

AUCTION DESIGN FOR AN ILLIQUID MARKET

The main goal of the buy-side trader is to achieve best execution. With liquid (homogeneous) securities, this amounts to encouraging competition without unduly increasing transaction time. There is no fundamental difference between a purchase and a sale. Bids or offers are tendered for essentially identical securities. Illiquid[17] securities, however, are often heterogeneous and, although this does not affect sale mechanics (you can still request competitive bids for the particular security), it does affect purchases because only one dealer will typically be able to offer any particular security. Although the basic conclusion about the desirability of competition still holds, other considerations are also important, and sales and purchases must be separately examined.

Sales can be conducted, much like those for liquid securities, as an instantaneous auction. A much larger standard deviation of the true asset value, say on the order of 1.5 points, would suggest a very large auction size. As shown in Exhibit 4, bargaining leverage doesn't really level off until the auction reaches a size of about 10 bidders — a seemingly unwieldy number. The benefits and costs of a large auction, however, are not as great as is indicated by a liquid market.

Competition does not increase commensurately with auction size because, in most cases, there are only a few genuine competitors in these markets. As a result, the level of competition in an instantaneous auction is limited. Sell-side traders understand market conditions and act accordingly — they attempt to exploit their bargaining leverage.

Although an experienced buy-side trader will have a good notion of the best competitors' identities, a larger auction sometimes produces a surprising winner due to a special interest in a particular bond.[18] Fortunately, the problems associated with a large auction do not usually increase much with illiquid securities — as long as they are hedged. Transaction time may increase and execution might erode somewhat with uncertainties concerning best price. The possible loss

---

[17] "Illiquid" refers to the entire continuum of bonds that are not classified as liquid.

[18] In the municipal market, it is not always possible to identify the best competitors in advance, and so it is often desirable to cast a wide net.

of a couple of 32nds, however, is dominated by the possible gain from a surprise winner — sometimes on the order of a half point or more. Of course, common sense argues for avoiding times of heightened market volatility, such as the release of economic news.

The greatest expected gain in an illiquid transaction may be achieved not by increasing auction size, but by decreasing trader risk (asset value uncertainty). As shown in Exhibit 4, lowering risk reduces bargaining leverage by concentrating security valuations. Moreover, risk reduction also lowers the return requirements (raises the bids) of traders. These are not material considerations for liquid markets in which traders have timely and accurate information and a very short holding period — risk is already close to a minimum. Quite the opposite is true for an illiquid market.

Allowing bidders the opportunity to broker the bonds can essentially eliminate their risk. There are two common ways of brokering bonds — a sale order and a bid list. A *sale order* is an exclusive agreement in which the investor will sell a bond to the dealer at or above some reservation (minimally acceptable) level. A *bid list* is a delayed (rather than instantaneous) auction. Both provide dealers the opportunity to collect bids from potential investors, and thereby shift risk to the ultimate purchaser. The beneficiary of the risk transfer, however, differs by method.

There are two advantages of a bid list — risk reduction and competition. Bid-ask spreads can, at times, be reduced to those of a liquid market. A sale order, however, lacks the advantage of direct competition; as a result, transaction prices rarely exceed the reservation level, because brokers extract the surplus. In order to achieve a good execution level, the buy-side trader must have exceptionally accurate information when setting the reservation level and selecting the broker. Heroic information requirements, together with broker incentives to extract some surplus, make sale orders a much less effective sale mechanism than bid lists for most MBS and municipal bond sales.

Why would a sale order ever be the preferred course of action? It can be argued that in some instances the inclusion of several brokers, as in a bid list, can erode execution. Dealers will approach their clients, the ultimate investors, with suggested bid levels based upon their (possibly unique) read of the market. Most institutional investors will be contacted by several dealers. Some investors will select the dealer (and the bid) with a low suggested bid level, even though they might be willing to pay more for the security — a practice that can reduce transaction price — in order to avoid the winner's curse. Including only well informed participants on the bid list is one way to limit this sort of price erosion. For these reasons, as well as for the fact that they comprise a much less diverse universe (information is more readily available), making it easier to ascertain the level at which they should trade, a sale order is often the preferred course for corporate bonds. In general, however, it is probably better to err on the side of including too many than too few participants.[19]

---

[19] Hybrid strategies such as bid lists with a reservation level can be used to mitigate the potential hazards of a bid list.

One exception to the "more is better" rule about bid lists versus sale orders does exist. Very complicated securities sometimes require a significant amount of time and effort to sell. A sale order might be necessary to attract the appropriate effort from a broker. In these circumstances market knowledge and negotiating skill determine execution price.

The perception of competition is also valuable when *buying* illiquid securities. Because the available supply of similar securities is often limited, dealers need not necessarily offer the best price to sell their bonds. It is therefore usually not in the buyer's best interest to shatter the illusion of competition by revealing a large demand. As with a very illiquid sale, purchase price may be most sensitive to negotiating skill and the quality of information.

Benefiting from the reduction in dealer risk is much less likely when buying illiquid bonds. Once the dealer owns the bonds, he has already placed his capital at risk and is therefore reluctant to sell them at razor thin margins. Moreover, when buying off a bid list, you are much more likely to suffer from the winner's curse than benefit from the lower bid-ask spreads. The optimal strategy, in that case, mirrors that described for the rational trader of a liquid product.

THE LONG-TERM RELATIONSHIP

Individual transactions are part of a long-term relationship. Trades must therefore be viewed in a broader context. As with any other relationship, people get to know some of each other's behavior patterns pretty well. For competitive auctions, the import of this knowledge is limited. With negotiations, however, long-term credibility becomes important. Tactics such as bluffs and threats must be used prudently and with the understanding that misuse may have consequences for future transactions and the relationship at large.

A satisfactory relationship serves both dealer and investor. The investor can benefit from a combination of liquidity, research, and other information (e.g., security pricing). Incremental competition is particularly valuable for trading illiquid securities. Dealers profit by making bid-ask spreads, which increase with their participation in transactions. As a general guideline, dealers have a strong incentive to encourage the relationship, especially because the marginal cost of providing research and other information is usually very low.

Incentives to the contrary, conflict can arise because each trade is a zero-sum game. Moreover, dealers are populated by many specialists — trading different securities — who are focused on their individual profitability. Some specialists at the same dealer may be much less interested in sustaining the long-term relationship than their colleagues. As a result, dealers provide investors a firm-wide representative (salesperson) who serves as the intermediary between the buy-side and sell-side traders.

The goal of the salesperson is to maximize dealer long-term profits by increasing participation in transactions, making terms more favorable to them (e.g., sale orders), and minimizing disputes. It should be realized that the salesperson represents the dealer, not the investor. Although the two parties' interests sometimes coincide, trade execution may not be the place.

SUMMARY

Competition holds the promise of enhanced buy-side trade execution, especially for volatile securities. In order for that promise to be fulfilled, the competition must be genuine. Unfortunately, increasing the number of broker-dealers in an auction does not necessarily elevate the level of competition — incremental benefits diminish with increased auction size, and not all broker-dealers have equally informed traders.

Excessive auction size can have deleterious effects, such as execution delays and adverse price selection by the ultimate investors. Adverse selection occurs when several broker-dealers solicit interest from the same client, and that client chooses to tender the lower price. On the other hand, allowing broker-dealers to shift risk to their clients can enhance execution, because the broker-dealers are not placing their firms' capital at risk, and therefore they require lower expected profits from the trade. The objective of the buy-side trader is to balance these considerations. In practice, the optimal trade-off differs by market.

Questions

Chapter 1 — Measuring and Managing Interest-Rate Risk

1. Is duration a good measure of the sensitivity of a bond portfolio's value to interest rate changes? Explain.

2. Under what circumstances is duration a good measure of the sensitivity of a bond portfolio's value to interest rate changes?

3. What is meant by a "yield curve shift" and a "yield curve twist"?

4. Empirically, what is the relative importance of yield curve shifts and yield curve twists in terms of accounting for the systematic variation in monthly yields?

5. What is the "interest rate sensitivity" measure used by Scott Richard and Benjamin Gord of Miller, Anderson & Sherrerd?

Chapter 2 — Active Bond Portfolio Management: An Expected Return Approach

1. A popular approach to managing bond portfolios is to identify the sector allocation, maturity distribution, and duration target that are consistent with the manager's overall outlook for the economy and interest rates.
   a. What are the limitations of this approach?
   b. What alternative approach is espoused by Francis Trainer?
   c. How would the tracking error of the performance associated with these two strategies differ?

2. Do you think the default experience of the past several decades is useful for adjusting the yield on corporate bonds?

3. Is event risk a relic of the 1980s, or should portfolio managers continue to factor this into their analysis?

4. Why does the valuation of options embedded in corporate bonds depend on the volatility assumed?

5. Why is scenario analysis helpful in mortgage analysis but not necessarily in corporate bond analysis?

6. What have the studies at Sanford C. Bernstein & Co. found regarding the evidence between the state of the economy and corporate spreads?

7. If the bond market is efficient, could the strategies outlined in the chapter still produce excess returns?

8. Why might the slope and curvature of the yield curve be different across countries at any point in time, or, on average, over time?

Chapter 3 — Managing Indexed and Enhanced Indexed Bond Portfolios

1. What distinguishes bond index management (pure and enhanced) from active bond management?

2. What are the advantages of bond indexing?

3. When would an investor use the "income risk" framework versus the "market value risk" framework in picking an appropriate bond index portfolio?

4. What are the primary bond indexing risk factors?

5. Why is matching the duration of the index not sufficient for matching the interest rate risk of the index?

6. What additional value comes from matching the cash flow structure of the index?

7. Why is matching the percent in each sector not adequate risk control?

8. What return enhancements do bond indexers use?

9. What is the theoretical yield curve and how is it used in issue selection?

10. a. What are the two measurements that prove successful in enhanced bond index management?
    b. Why is success in only one of the measurements not adequate?

Chapter 4 — Global Corporate Bond Portfolio Management

1. a. Describe the main task of corporate bond portfolio managers.
   b. Define corporate relative value analysis.

2. If you were a total return manager of corporate bonds, what horizon period would you use to maximize total return?

3. What are the methodologies used to evaluate the relative value of the corporate bond asset class?

4. a. What are the main rationales for trading by investors and dealers?

   b. How do trading rationales vary during the course of the global credit cycle?

5. Detail the typical constraints for not executing trades.

6. If you were a portfolio consultant to a corporate pension fund, would you rather recommend a portfolio manager who undertrades or overtrades?

7. a. What are some of the limitations of spread, structure, and credit analyses?

   b. Which factor is the most important for successful portfolio management?

Chapter 5 — Managing Municipal Bond Portfolios

1. What are some of the reasons for yield spreads between various municipal bonds?

2. When would a pension fund portfolio manager consider acquiring municipal bonds?

3. How can changes in the tax code on either the federal or state level effect the performance of a municipal bond portfolio?

4. a. Give some reasons why the valuation of municipal bonds relative to Treasury securities can change.

   b. What are the implications for a municipal bond portfolio's total return when such valuation does change?

5. Discuss some total return strategies a portfolio manager implements by using ' bonds subject to the market discount taxation rules. (Be sure to include the concepts of duration, convexity, yield curve positioning, sector rotations, and individual security selection.)

6. What are some counter arguments to the reasons why individuals find little value in bonds priced above par?

Chapter 6 — Management of a High-Yield Bond Portfolio

1. What is meant by a "high-yield bond"?

2. How may high-yield bonds be used in a portfolio?

3. What are some of the critical areas that a high-yield analyst should focus on with regard to an issuer?

4. What is the objective in market analysis of an issuer?

5. Why is the investment banker critically important in the creation of a successful high-yield issue?

6. What are the major causes of deteriorating credit?

Chapter 7 — International Bond Portfolio Management

1. In discussing the components of return in the chapter, the hedged and unhedged returns in equations (9) and (10) differ from those in equations (13) and (14) which separate out the risk-free rate.
   a. Which equations would be most appropriate for a portfolio manager whose guidelines do not allow for taking currency exposures independently of bond market exposures?
   b. Which equations would be most appropriate for a portfolio manager who uses leverage?

2. a. In what two ways could an international bond portfolio manager shift interest rate risk exposure from one market to another without altering aggregate portfolio duration?
   b. Why is duration less accurate as a measure of aggregate portfolio sensitivity to interest rate changes for international portfolios than for domestic portfolios?

3. a. What is the difference between tracking error and value at risk?
   b. Why does currency risk account for 96% of value at risk in Exhibit 11 of the chapter and only 65% of tracking error risk in Exhibit 10?
   c. Which measure would be most appropriate for a portfolio managed close to a benchmark index?

4. Unhedged international bonds had the highest return over the 12-year period from 1985 through 1996.
   a. Using the data in Exhibit 1 of the chapter, explain why an investor might choose either unhedged international bonds, hedged international bonds, or U.S. only bonds.
   b. Assuming a portfolio of 70% domestic bonds and 30% international bonds as in Exhibit 2, which hedging policy would be followed by an investor who is (i) total return oriented, (ii) risk adverse, and (iii) seeking the best risk-adjusted returns?

5. Assume the following: (i) a foreign currency is expected to depreciate by 5% over the next year, (ii) the U.S. 1-year interest rate is 6%, and (iii) the foreign 1-year interest rate is 10%.
   a. Should the currency be hedged or unhedged?
   b. Would your answer be different if the U.S. 1-year interest rate is 4% instead of 6%?

Chapter 8 — Using Busted Convertibles to Enhance Performance

1. Describe three concepts that can be used to categorize the investment characteristics of convertible bonds.

2. Why do busted convertibles tend to sell at a discount using quantitative valuation measures?

3. What structural features and investment characteristics of a convertible bond provide downside protection to an investor with a fixed income perspective?

4. What structural features and investment characteristics may enhance a convertible's upside potential?

5. Formulate an investment strategy that uses convertible bonds to add value relative to a fixed income benchmark.

Chapter 9 — Managing a Fixed Income Portfolio Versus a Liability Objective

1. How are liabilities defined according to the Financial Accounting Standards Board?

2. What is the common practice in pricing (valuing) liabilities?

3. How does Ronald Ryan suggest that the value of liabilities be calculated?

4. Ronald Ryan suggests that to neutralize interest rate risk, a prudent asset strategy should be to structure the assets identical to or similar to the term structure of liabilities. Why?

5. What is a liability index and what is its role?

6. Why does Ronald Ryan argue that generic market indices are inappropriate benchmarks by which to evaluate the performance of a portfolio manager?

Chapter 10 — Fixed Income Attribution Analysis

1. List some of the AIMR requirements for calculating total rates of return.

2. a. Why is reasonable pricing of assets important in performance measurement and evaluation?
   b. Why is it more difficult to calculate a total rate of return on a privately placed security?

3. Identify and discuss the main AIMR accepted approaches to calculating a total rate of return.

4. Using the modified Dietz methodology, calculate the AIMR compliant total rate of return for the portfolio that had the following cash flow and market value information (assume April has 30 days):

3/31	Beginning Market Value	=	$3,500,000
4/10	Contribution	=	240,000
4/15	Contribution	=	100,000
4/25	Withdrawal	=	450,000
4/30	Ending Market Value	=	$3,782,000

5. Define the four major factors that comprise the GAT Return Attribution model.

6. Provided below is some sample attribution data calculated for a managed portfolio and its benchmark.

	Total Return	Static Return	Interest Sensitive	Spread Change	Trading Return	Residual Return
Portfolio A	3.775	1.424	2.503	−0.133	0.008	0.045
Benchmark	3.447	1.349	1.994	0.117	0.000	−0.014
Difference	0.328	0.075	0.509	−0.250	0.008	0.059

a. Evaluate the performance of the manager.
b. Where does his (or her) strengths and weaknesses seem to be?

7. Discuss the role of identifying and measuring the risk factors of a bond portfolio in conducting a sensitivity analysis.

Chapter 11 — Bond Convexity: Hidden Risk, Hidden Value

Refer to the following parametrics for three securities to answer the following questions:

	Duration	Convexity	Expected 3-Month Return (%)[*]
Security A	3.7	−201	2.04
Security B	3.7	17	1.73
Security C	3.7	130	1.80

[*] The expected 3-month total return is computed assuming an unchanged yield curve and unchanged option-adjusted spreads.

1. By how much would interest rates have to fall for the total return of Security A to equal the total return of Security B? (Assume parallel yield curve shifts and unchanged option-adjusted spreads.)

2. By how much would interest rates have to rise for the returns to be equal for Security A and Security B?

3. a. Security A is a mortgage-backed security and Security C is a putable corporate bond. Assuming parallel yield curve shifts and constant yield spreads and option-adjusted spreads, which security has a higher total return if interest rates move 10 basis points?
   b. What would your to part (a) be if they move 50 basis points?
   c. What would your to part (a) be if they move 100 basis points?

4. An investor owns Security C, the putable corporate bond, but is concerned about a recession. He believes the Treasury market will rally 100 basis points over the coming three months and the yield spreads on corporate bonds will widen. By how much will the yield spread on Security C have to widen before it has the same total return as Security B (the U.S. Treasury) if interest rates fall 100 basis points over the next 3 months?

Chapter 12 — A User's Guide to Buy-Side Bond Trading

1. a. What is meant by a "liquid market"?
   b. What challenges do illiquid markets pose?

2. Why is the meaning of a bid-ask spread subject to interpretation?

3. What is the "winner's curse" and why do traders try to avoid it?

4. In an auction, what is meant by the "cover"?

5. What are the disadvantages of large auctions?

6. a. What is a bid list?
   b. What are two advantages of a bid list?